The Founding of Poricy Park

From its founding in 1969
to the end of major development of the park in 1985.

A personal memoir
by
Paul T. ("Pete") Brady

Front cover: The Gebhardt Farm and the Poricy Brook Basin and Pond, looking
southeast toward Red Bank. Photo taken in 1969 by Dorn's of Red Bank.
Back cover: Photo taken by Pete Brady, October 4, 1969, of his first view of the
Gebhardt Farm.

A Personal Account

   This book is my personal account of events that transpired 20 or more years ago and
was written entirely from my own perspective. The events occurred primarily in
Monmouth County, New Jersey. (A map faces page 1.) I am no longer associated with
Poricy Park, and therefore this book does not necessarily represent the current park and
its policies. PTB

Copyright © 2005 by Paul T. Brady

ISBN 0-7414-2736-2

Published by:

INFINITY
PUBLISHING.COM

1094 New DeHaven Street, Suite 100
West Conshohocken, PA 19428-2713
Info@buybooksontheweb.com
www.buybooksontheweb.com
Toll-free (877) BUY BOOK
Local Phone (610) 941-9999
Fax (610) 941-9959

Printed in the United States of America
Printed on Recycled Paper
Published August 2005

maíreann an crann ar an bhfál,
    ach ní mhaíreann an lámh a chuír.

The tree in the field survives, but the hand that planted it is forgotten.

Irish proverb

Photo: The Poricy Park Nature Center in autumn 1978, the year it opened.

Dedication

This book is dedicated to the children of the founders of Poricy Park.

In June 1990, my wife Cathy and I attended a conference of the Association for Living History, Farm and Agricultural Museums (ALHFAM) held at Brown University in Providence, Rhode Island. Most of the meals were served in the refectory, a standard college cafeteria in its food and service, but a handsome room with a high ceiling.

On the upper part of the walls were large murals, at least 4×8 feet each, of black-and-white photographs of athletic teams from around the 1920s. For the first few days of the conference, I paid only slight attention to them.

But at breakfast on the last day, while waiting in line to enter the serving area, I looked more carefully at one, not so much to study it, but because I had nothing else to do while I was waiting. It showed a football team at the scrimmage line, all hunched down in front, and all posing for the camera. And, I was looking directly into the face of my father, who had attended Brown.

I knew my father played baseball, but had no idea he was on the football team. There were, and still are, many things I don't know about him. He, like many other parents, never wrote down the story of his life. I have only clouded memories of stories he told.

With this book, I am making sure that our children will know what their parents did, and that other children will know what *their* parents did, for at least a part of our lives. I will not attempt to name all these people here in this dedication. But, scattered through this book are names and photographs of (I hope) nearly all of the principal players, and I intend that the knowledge of what they did will be passed down through at least a few generations.

I think I may be allowed to single out two families in particular, since they played such significant roles in founding and developing Poricy Park. Therefore, I make a special dedication to our own three children, namely, David, Stephen, and Jeremy and also to *their* children; and to the children of Marcia and Lou Rissland, namely, Louis Jr. and Laura and to *their* children.

In Memoriam

Lou Rissland died in March 2003.
Marcia Rissland died in August 2004.
Their daughter Marion Lee Rissland died in August 1980.

My fond memories of them have been an inspiration to me in writing this account.

Table of Contents

Acknowledgments

My wife, Cathy, reviewed the first draft of this book. She had once been a magazine editor, and she also was in a good position to observe and, on many occasions, participate in the events described in the time period covered here. As you will learn in reading the book, Diane Lehder was a major player during our formative years, and she edited the second draft. Karen Eastin is the training officer of the Monmouth County Park System. I asked Karen also to review the second draft precisely because she was <u>not</u> a participant in the founding, and she could take an "outsider's" point of view. All three of the above worked carefully and enthusiastically. I am most grateful to them, and the finished product is certainly an improvement from my initial effort. (However, I take sole responsibility for any factual errors, or for any passages that the reader finds uninteresting.) Finally, I thank Randy Gabrielan, the executive director of the Monmouth County Historical Commission (a county government agency), who helped with my research in several ways, especially in looking up deed transfers and obtaining the proper dates and land purchase amounts.

Renewing Old Acquaintances

I was very pleased to be able to contact many participants in the events described herein, and to renew old acquaintances, even for a brief phone conversation. I have listed these people here, in no special order.

<u>Township government and employees</u>: Former committeemen Allan MacDonald and Peter Carton; former director of Public Works John McGowan; former director of Parks and Recreation John Campbell; former township administrator Herbert ("Bud") Bradshaw and his wife Pearl; and New Jersey Assemblyman Joseph Azzolina. All still live in Monmouth County except John Campbell, who lives in Virginia.

<u>Former members of the PPCC, volunteers, park staff, and others</u> (in addition to Diane Lehder and my wife Cathy, who helped edit this book): Dwight Richardson, Hank Flanagan, Frank and Lethe Lescinsky, Kathy Whitney Gahn, Denise King Stovall, Diane Walton Wood, Carolyn Hickson, Bernie Finan, Lou Grover, Cathy Johnston, Virginia Carmichael, Jean Markowitz, Lynn Kough, Marlene Harper, Becky and Ken Albrecht, Olga Margus, Peter Brooks, and Gail and Don Abrams.

Some Misperceptions and a Few Key Paragraphs

I had discussed this book with people that were not aware of the events in our initial years, and who had some misperceptions about how we all got started. In the text of the book these issues are addressed, but I have also copied a few key paragraphs here to help set the stage for what follows.

Our Initial Motivations

When we all began our project in 1969, we never intended that we would become personally involved in the operation of a park. We thought we could write some letters, show up at a few public meetings, and then the Township would acquire the land and take charge of the park. But this turned out not at all to be what happened. (See page 61.)

The Unknown Farmhouse and Barn

The preservation of the Murray Farmhouse and Barn was <u>not</u> one of our principal reasons for preserving the parkland. We initially had no idea of the real value of the farmhouse and barn. In our flyer of November 11, 1969, we vaguely stated "Houses of historical value exist on both the Gebhardt and Morris Tracts," and then dropped the matter for <u>five years</u>! (See page 112.)

Introduction

After more than 25 years of intense involvement in Poricy Park, both Marcia Rissland and I left at about the same time, in early 1997. The reasons we left were slightly different from each other's, and have nothing to do with the story of founding the park. But, at the time we left, Marcia and I each had a collection of files we had saved over the years. And these collections just sat in boxes or in folders in file cabinets while we pursued other interests.

Around the year 2000, I met Maureen Leach, a part-time teacher at Historic Walnford, a Monmouth County Park System site where I am a volunteer. She was also a part-time teacher at Poricy Park, and she found that I had once been involved there and had some old files related to the history of the park. She began to get on my case to do something with them and tell the story of how the park came about.

But I did nothing about it. My wife Cathy and I remained close to Marcia and her husband Lou, and often ended up at one or the other's home having drinks at night, telling the same Poricy Park stories to each other, over and over again. One does that when you are approaching or even past age 70.

Just before Marcia died in August 2004, she moved her files into my house, where they continued to sit, unexamined. I realized that I was the only person that could properly understand much of the material contained therein. More important, I understood that if I'm going to write this story, I had better begin right away.

So, I started to glance through the files, and found them overwhelming. Combined, Marcia's and my files included many photographs and hundreds of pages of text, much in the form of handwritten diaries, but also in copies of flyers we had circulated, newspaper articles, and letters we had sent to friends or sent to and received from agencies, government officials, and the like.

I built a computer database and in effect created a set of 4×6 index cards which could hold lots of facts, and began to read through every page of text in the files, and look at every photo to determine which of them could be included in the book I would write. The computer file eventually grew to more than 1,150 items. This took several months, during which time I also began to write, and the whole process took more than five months to first draft.

I also had my memory of many events, and I was astonished at how inaccurate it was on some items. There were a few events I attended that I didn't remember at all. That was also true for perhaps ten people I interviewed that were also involved at the time. But, despite lapses of memory, there is a tremendous advantage to having lived through it, because I was able to identify people in pictures and determine for many people their significance in the park development. Both their identities and significance would elude a nonparticipant, especially one that tried to do this years later.

You'll meet Dwight Richardson in the book. In going through the history, I was trying to nail down the approximate dates of a few key meetings Dwight had with some people, for which I had only fragmentary evidence in a few letters and notes. I corresponded with Dwight and finally was able to deduce the dates from odd facts buried in paragraphs in two letters. He wrote back: *"It is no wonder how much history of what really happened on any subject at any time is lost in less than a generation."*

I have now developed a great admiration for professional historians who try to reconstruct the stories of events for which there are no living participants and for which there are no photographs.

I have chosen to limit this account to the period from the inception of the idea of the park in 1969 until 1985. In 1985, the main founding efforts were finished, except for a few miscellaneous items which I do cover at the end of the story.

Pete Brady, July, 2005

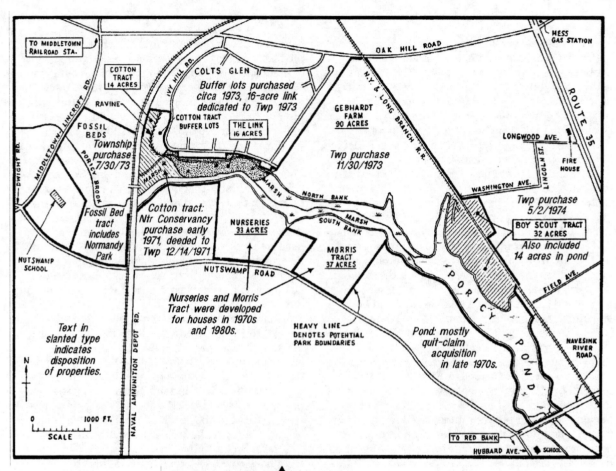

TO MIDDLETOWN
RAILROAD STA.

COTTON
TRACT
14 ACRES

RAVINE

MIDDLETOWN LINCROFT RD.

IVY HILL RD.

COLTS GLEN

*Buffer lots purchased
circa 1973, 16-acre link
dedicated to Twp 1973*

COTTON TRACT
BUFFER LOTS

THE LINK
16 ACRES

OAK HILL ROAD

HESS
GAS STATION

N.Y. & LONG BRANCH R.R.

GEBHARDT
FARM
90 ACRES

*Twp purchase
11/30/1973*

ROUTE 35

LONGWOOD AVE.

LINCOLN ST.

FIRE
HOUSE

FOSSIL
BEDS
*Township
purchase
7/30/73*

DWIGHT RD.

PORICY BROOK

MARSH

MARSH

NORTH BANK

SOUTH MARSH
SOUTH BANK

WASHINGTON AVE.

*Twp purchase
5/2/1974*

BOY SCOUT TRACT
32 ACRES
*Also included
14 acres in pond*

*Fossil Bed
tract
includes
Normandy
Park*

*Cotton tract:
Ntr Conservancy
purchase early
1971, deeded to
Twp 12/14/1971*

NURSERIES
33 ACRES

MORRIS
TRACT
37 ACRES

PORICY POND

NUTSWAMP
SCHOOL

NUTSWAMP ROAD

NAVAL AMMUNITION DEPOT RD.

*Nurseries and Morris
Tract were developed
for houses in 1970s
and 1980s.*

HEAVY LINE
DENOTES POTENTIAL
PARK BOUNDARIES

*Pond: mostly
quit-claim
acquisition
in late 1970s.*

FIELD AVE.

NAVESINK
RIVER
ROAD

*Text in
slanted type
indicates
disposition
of properties.*

N

0   1000 FT.
SCALE

TO RED BANK

HUBBARD AVE.

SCHOOL

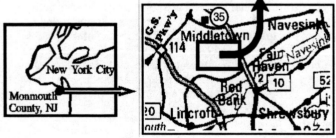

New York City

Monmouth
County, NJ

G.S. Pkwy

35

Middletown

114

Navesink

Navesink

Fair
Haven

2

10

52

Red
Bank

20

Lincroft

Shrewsbury

The Poricy Park Area of
Middletown Township

This map is based on a map drawn in 1969
and circulated by the Poricy Park Citizens
Committee.

The Sewer Line

Hank's Letter

It was Sunday evening, September 21, 1969. We had just returned from a weekend at Wildwood Crest, on the South Jersey coast. It was, for Cathy and me, our first trip away from home with our 3-month-old son and his two older brothers. After we settled in our house, I went out to pick up the weekend mail and found a letter, stuffed into the mailbox, written by someone I did not know: Henry Flanagan. That letter was perhaps the major turning point in my life. And in the lives of several others.

I was 32 years old. I had grown up in the Hudson River Valley, and then lived in and around Boston for four years. I did a lot of hiking in the White Mountains in New Hampshire, walking on trails cleared by other people on land saved by other people. After moving to New Jersey in 1961, I had dabbled at a few conservation efforts, mainly by writing some letters for causes to save land, such as the Great Swamp in northern New Jersey.

The *Daily Register*, Red Bank, NJ Thurs. 8/21/1969

Eye Poricy Sewer Line's Effect on Recreation Plan

MIDDLETOWN: The Conservation Commission will ask the Township Committee and the Sewerage Authority to delay plans to run sewer lines through the Poricy Brook meadowland pending study of public desire for recreation and conservation areas there.

The decision came at a commission meeting last night after a presentation by Henry J. Flanagan of 10 Denise Drive. Mr. Flanagan told the commission that "once that sewer line goes in there, you can forget about anything else."...

Denise Drive, Middletown
September 3, 1969

To: Citizens of Middletown

I have been asked to address you in order to shed more light on the subject of the attached Red Bank Register article dated August 21, 1969.

The area under discussion, Poricy Brook and Poricy Pond, is a relatively untouched area two miles in length... The area behind the Nut Swamp School contains Middletown's famous fossil beds, and an application has been made by the Township for funds for purchase of this tract. The area from the Naval Ammunition Road east to Navesink River Road is of great worth from a conservation and recreational standpoint.

Here, in a natural setting, we have the opportunity to create a strip park with a central feature – a large lake. Activities could include paths and trails, nature study areas, picnic areas, courts and active sports areas, swimming, boating, fishing, outdoor winter sports, and possibly camping.

... After completing its investigation, the Conservation Commission feels, "The sewer plans, as currently formulated, will permanently remove this entire area from any future use either for recreation or conservation." They recommend a study be made rerouting the line.

... The people of Middletown are spending about $40 million in addressing their pollution problem. It would be ironic if the sewer system, which finally releases Poricy's potential, would become the instrument by which it was rendered useless for all time.

... You are urged to indicate your interest and support both by letter and in person at the next public meeting in Town Hall of the Conservation Commission (Sept. 17, 7:30 pm) and the Recreation Commission (Sept. 22, 8:00 pm).

Thank you. (Signed) Henry J. Flanagan

I decided it was time for me to repay the debt I owed all those other people who had saved land I had enjoyed.

Well, I had missed the Conservation Commission meeting, so I decided to go to the Recreation Commission meeting the next evening.[1]

Right. Where was Town Hall?

We had moved to Middletown in 1966 with the rest of many hundreds of Bell Labs people that had been transferred to Holmdel. We bought a house on Marcshire Drive on a standard housing tract which was once a corn field or pasture, I guess, and, although I was told we were living in a place called Middletown, we were served by the Red Bank post office (which is still the case for many Middletown residents). I had no sense at all of our community, except that David, our eldest son, had just entered Nut Swamp School, less than a mile away.

I don't remember much about the Recreation Commission meeting itself. The real action occurred after the meeting ended, as I learned was often the case for meetings in Town Hall. Hank (Henry Flanagan) had made some kind of statement during the meeting, so I knew which person he was. At meeting's end, he was the nucleus of a group of ten or so people that wanted to get more involved.

I still remember the feeling of awe I had when I finally spoke with Hank that evening. Perhaps this sounds corny, but he was a true hero in my eyes: he was the major force behind a local, grass-roots conservation movement. Hank, then 45 years old, was a pilot for Eastern Air Lines, and his job had irregular hours, which (thank heavens) allowed him occasional time during the week to make the necessary local contacts to work on this project. He lived with his wife Chrys (Maxine) and four children

on Denise Drive, directly on the south bank of Poricy Brook, and, yes, directly in the path of the sewer line. So, in the words of his critics, he was just trying to save his back yard. But, in my eyes, he was trying to do a lot more than that.

I don't recall just who else was at Town Hall that evening, but two people stand out in my memory. One was Frank Lescinsky, also from Bell Labs, whom I had briefly met in 1961 when we were on a canoe trip together. His wife Lethe[2] was also on the canoe trip and may have been at Town Hall that night. The other person I remember at the meeting was Dwight Richardson.

Dwight was in his late 30s, and also worked at Bell Labs. He was to become one of my closest friends and allies in this cause. He, his wife Gayle, and their two children lived on Kingfisher Drive in Oak Hill, and although their property was not affected by the sewer construction, they backed onto the upstream reaches of Poricy Brook. Over the next two years, several of us were to spend a lot of time in Dwight's house. And in my house. And in Hank's house. And in the homes of many other people.

Skating on Poricy Pond, December 1972

[1] Now called the Environmental Commission and the Recreation Advisory Committee. Several organizations and people have changed their names in the intervening years, and a list of name changes is provided in Appendix C.

[2] Appendix C is a guide to pronunciation of names.

October 1969: Our first public hike through the area. Front row (children): Maxine Flanagan, Elke Wirth, David and Gordon Lescinsky, David Brady, Leo Flanagan, Hal Lescinsky, Louise Flanagan. Rear: Lethe Lescinsky, Gisela Wirth, Theresa Maloney, Hank Flanagan, Frank Lescinsky, Edwin Flanagan, unidentified, Mrs. Leistner, Heinz Wirth, two unidentified, Chrys Flanagan, and Pat Maloney. In the next few years there would be many more hikes. One in April 1970 was attended by 73 people. (Photo: Pete Brady)

The Lay of the Land

Poricy Brook drains about three square miles of Middletown Township, New Jersey, and then meanders through a mile-long bathtub-shaped marsh about 100 yards wide. After passing through a 20-acre pond, it enters the Navesink River which then flows into the ocean. From vantage points in Middletown you can see New York City, whose Manhattan skyscrapers are about 22 miles away.

In 1969 most people had no idea this area existed except for the two end points of the brook. At the west were the Fossil Beds, fairly well-known among fossil collectors, and at the southeast end was Poricy Pond, known to skaters and people who fished. Poricy Pond was artificial, made many years back, and was called "Foo Lake" by some of the locals. Who knows – the subsequent park might have been "Foo Park" instead of "Poricy Park."

I never did learn the origin of the name "Poricy." It appears in colonial records spelled in several ways. Perhaps it is from the Native American Indians.

The Nut Swamp Association

In May, 1969, The newly-formed Middletown Sewerage Authority went to some 25 residents on the southwest side of Poricy brook, along its length from the Navy Road to Navesink River Road, and asked the residents to sign easements that would allow sewer line construction in the land from the top of the bank out into the marsh. That is, they could do anything they wanted to the steep bank, including taking out all the trees. Many of the residents would not sign the easements, and instead, on June 11, 1969, they formed the Nut Swamp Association to learn more about the sewer line and if possible, to get the line rerouted. Hank Flanagan became the president of the association.

One of the association members knew of Adolph Margus and introduced Hank to Adolph. At that time, Adolph and Olga Margus lived on Poricy Lane, near the outlet of Poricy Pond. (On the area map facing page 1, Poricy Lane is in between the railroad and the word "POND" on the pond.)

There once was a bridge on the Navesink River Road crossing the outlet of Poricy Brook. Many years before the creation of the Sewerage Authority in 1969, the bridge was removed and replaced with a berm (embankment) that carried the road and had pipes for the water to pass through. In time, the pond became polluted and clogged with overgrowth. The road was raised and a larger pipe was installed, but this did not solve the problem.

The Marguses were very active in trying to get the township and the state to do something about the pond, and in so doing, they became well acquainted with various state agencies that dealt with water and pollution. They had a thick file of correspondence with the state and township and news clippings about the problem. Their contacts with the state were later essential in getting the sewer line rerouted.

Charlie Nelson (left) and Adolph Margus in April 1971. Charlie was an early member of our committee, and then became chair of the Middletown Shade Tree Commission, a position he held for many years. Adolph died in a drowning accident on July 22, 1972. This was a major loss to our cause, and the only such tragic loss during our formative years.

Hank believed that it was necessary to get public opinion behind rerouting the sewer line, and that people from throughout the township would not join forces just to save his own backyard. He realized that he would have to find a more compelling argument to get people to support his cause. Then, with widespread public pressure, Hank hoped that the Sewerage Authority might give in to reason and logical arguments and change the route.

Hank was wrong. Edward Schumann was the chairman of the Sewerage Authority, but he was more than that. He *was* the authority, and he subsequently demonstrated many times that public opinion didn't mean a thing to him.

As it turned out, the line was rerouted, and public opinion had almost nothing to do with the rerouting. But that came later. In the meantime, Hank set out to muster township support to save the area as a public park, a park that would be lost if the Sewerage Authority (ie, Ed Schumann) had its way.

So, in summer 1969, Hank examined the zoning maps and asked a lot of questions about the land in the area. What lands were undeveloped? Who owned them? Were they for sale? As a result, he and his associates put together a collection of parcels of undeveloped land totaling about 300 acres, as shown on the map at the beginning of this book.

But Hank went beyond this, and created what turned out to be a contentious diversion. He proposed raising the level of Poricy Pond to create a lake of 25 or more acres, which would form the centerpiece of a large park. A lake is often the focal point of a park, and an enlarged Poricy Pond would serve this purpose. And, Hank reasoned, with the lake there, a sewer line would not be possible.

He was wrong and he was right. He was wrong because the Authority would point out many times that you can easily have a sewer line routed along-side a lake. (The sewer line that was ultimately built was in fact routed next to the pond.) People feared that a pipe break would dump sewage into the lake, but the Authority pointed out that because the sewer line was at atmospheric pressure and was below the level of the lake, a leak would cause lake water to flow *into* the pipe rather than the other way around.

But Hank was right in that if the sewer line were built first, prior to the lake (a certainty, given the urgency of the sewer system), it would be prohibitively expensive later to raise the berm (road) carrying the sewer line to put the manholes high enough to clear the raised lake level. So, with the sewer installed, that would be the end of the lake.

Mary Morford, a talented artist who lived in the Nut Swamp area, painted a scene of a large lake that would be the center of a new park. This painting was a major display that Hank took with him when he addressed public meetings to push for his cause.

The Position in September 1969

When I read the letter from my mailbox, I knew nothing of the above events. I just saw a chance to help save some land for open space and prevent an area from environmental damage. So, I showed up at Town Hall and met the rest of our band of Don Quixotes. That was on Monday, September 22.

Where to begin? Hank offered to take me on a personal tour of the area as soon as possible, which turned out to be on Saturday October 4, 1969. In Hank's own words written in February 2005:

> "I do recall taking you on a tour of the area. The thing that impressed me was your ability to assess the area, immediately determine its merits, and decide that it should be acquired and preserved with no hesitation whatsoever on your part."

But, what I remember best from that tour was the view of the farm. I had driven by the entrance to the farm numerous times and saw "Whistling Hill Farm" on the mailbox, right next to the railroad crossing on Oak Hill Road. You can't see the farm itself from the road, you have to drive in a short distance up a slight grade. The nature center of course was not there, but the ranch house, still standing, was at the crest of the hill, and we parked next to the house and got out. That is when I took the picture on the back of this book. I was then determined to save the farm and whatever else we could do to protect the area. I had no idea of how high the odds would initially be against us.

The Next Month: Sept. 22 to Oct. 22.

Up to mid-September, most of the effort to save the land and move the sewer line centered around the members of the Nut Swamp Association. But it was after mid-September, with the addition of new volunteers and greater publicity, that support became more widespread.

During the month following the Recreation Commission meeting of September 22, those of us that did not belong to the Nut Swamp Association continued to work independently. We were not members of any committee, but our paths did cross several times.

The Conservation Commission Position

One of the first things I did was to recruit Diane Lehder to the cause. I still am surprised when I am occasionally reminded that she was only 23 years old! Diane worked with me at Bell Labs in the Human Factors Department, and she had a degree in psychology from Mt. Holyoke College. Not exactly perfect qualifications for analyzing a sewer system.

But Diane had a special gift for organizing people, writing letters, and mustering public opinion. One of the agencies she wrote to was the Middletown Township Committee, who forwarded her letter to the Conservation Commission. She received in reply a letter from the Commission's vice-chair (later to become the chair), Dr. Lynden Kibler, whose contents are excerpted here.

> Dear Mr. And Mrs. Lehder:
> …We have investigated the sewer line in the Poricy Brook area with the engineering firm who has done the design, and who will supervise the work. We feel that alternate routes are not feasible, either from a technical or economic position. As you may know, the State law establishing our Commission requires that we be responsible not only for natural preservation, but also for pollution. In the Poricy Brook area, we have a pollution problem that will only increase with time.
>
> We have been working on acquiring lands adjacent to Poricy Brook since the Commission was established on Jan. 1, 1969. We are not committed on the use of such an area, and feel that the construction of a lake may not provide the best use.
>
> We feel that the present sewer line will not seriously disrupt the natural area. To help insure this, the Commission has been granted permission by the Sewerage Authority to be a party to inspection of the sewer line installation, and to halt the work should unforeseen ecological problems arise.

Lyn Kibler became one of our allies a few months after he wrote this letter. His commission's initial position was based on a meeting their own members had on September 24 with representatives of the Sewerage Authority, namely Ed Schumann, chairman, and Dr. John (Jack) Buzzi, who was the engineer in charge and worked for Kupper Associates, the engineering firm for the project. As a result of this meeting, Conservation Commission Chairman Richard Cole wrote a letter to the Township Committee dated Sept. 26 in which he stated the same points made in Lyn's letter to Diane.

The Middletown Sewerage Authority's Position

I am not surprised that the Conservation Commission took their position. In the following nine months, Hank and I spent a lot of time with Ed Schumann and Jack Buzzi.

- Schumann and Buzzi were very persuasive people. They repeatedly told everyone that the sewer line would be "tucked into the toe of the bank" and do minimal damage. They insisted that the fact they were trying to acquire rights to use the entire bank was a mere formality to give the contractor some leeway in special situations.
- They repeatedly played their main trump card, namely, the urgent need for a sewer system. They could not take the lengthy time to redesign the whole system just to satisfy some people who were trying to save their back yards. (Later, in January 1970, Ed Schumann was quoted as saying that "Even if we thought we were wrong, things have gone so far that there's no turning back."[3])
- They just asserted that there was no alternate route, and knew that others, who lacked the qualifications to design an alternate plan, would have to accept their word for this.
- And then there was the right to be given to the Conservation Commission to stop the work. This right was never granted, as stated by Lyn Kibler at a public forum on November 19, which forum will be described presently.

---

[3] Middletown *Courier*, January 15, 1970.

Schumann's most remarkable statement came later, in August 1970, when several groups expressed outrage at the Authority's plan to dump 5 million gallons of effluent (left over from 2-stage treatment) daily into Sandy Hook Bay. Schumann's response was "Maybe the Bay is too important a resource to use just for ecological purposes."

It's worth taking a moment to see what the citizens were up against. I quote from a May 21, 1970 review of this project by the National Park Service (NPS): "The Middletown Sewerage Authority is an entirely autonomous body with a single goal [building sewers] and no charge to work through any body with a comprehensive overview of the Township." In fact, the NPS was unaware of the value of the Poricy area until the Poricy Park Citizens Committee became vocal in late 1969. At that time, 15 local and state agencies had already approved the Authority's Poricy Brook plans. Each such agency had considered only its own domain. For example, the Department of Health saw no threat to sanitary standards and thus gave approval.

The concept of *autonomous authority* means that the Authority is formed virtually as a separate governing body, not responsible to any other local body, including the Township Committee (or local government) that originally created the Authority. The only control the Township Committee has of the 5-member authority is that it appoints a member each year for a 5-year term. The Authority has power of eminent domain and has its own funding. It is a virtually unassailable force.

Mustering Public Opinion

In this story, I'm still in early October 1969. On October 8, I typed a one-page letter on my old portable typewriter (which I subsequently wore out on this project) and somehow had it reproduced so I could hand-carry it around the neighborhood, urging people to write letters to the Township. I did not re-present any organization; this was a personal appeal.

My letter produced no results at all. People said they would write, but they didn't. On November 11, I wrote a second letter to my neighbors lamenting their lack of response to my first letter, and this did yield some responses. But years later, the thing that catches my eye about my second letter is that it was mimeographed.

In those days, reproducing letters was neither an easy task nor was it cheap. So, I took a very important step. For $80 I bought a used mimeo-graph machine.

The bank alongside Poricy Marsh. The Sewerage Authority easements would have allowed them to do whatever they wanted with the entire bank, top to bottom, and would have resulted in cutting thousands of trees and gouging the bank along a 1¼-mile length of the marsh and pond. (Photo taken behind the Morris Tract, February 1, 1970.)

The Poricy Park Citizens Committee

During 2004, The Poricy Park web page contained this statement: "Since its inception, Poricy Park has been a nonprofit organization governed by a Board of Trustees."

That's a nice thought and even a compliment to the organizational skills of the founders. But it's not exactly the way it happened.

Who were the founders?

In graduate school at New York University, a fellow student was doing a thesis that involved *fuzzy sets*, which are groups for which the inclusion rules are vague. His favorite example of a fuzzy set was "the set of all numbers much greater than ten."

Poricy Park's founders constitute a fuzzy set. In my files I found several lists of people that had some kind of involvement in the first few years, and it seemed arbitrary to try to judge which of these people should be considered "founders." Instead, I have chosen to give accounts of the people that were most directly involved, and where possible, include photographs of them. And, I will consider *founders* to be all those that consider themselves to be founders, by the definitions of their choice.

Our Organizational Meeting

During summer 1969, Hank had made a major effort to recruit people from many sections of the Township, especially people many miles away. For example, Hank contacted people in Lincroft, on the southern border of Middletown, and got Ollie (Olive) Stearns to join the effort. From Belford, many miles north, he recruited Ruth and Jim Davis.[4] Those three people remained involved for many years. And, there were several people that lived closer and were not directly in the path of the sewer line.

Up through October 1969, I don't think we had a serious thought about forming another organization.

---

[4] Middletown Township, with 40 square miles, is comprised of many communities and zip codes.

The Nut Swamp Association had officers, was putting out newsletters, had legal representation, and was giving public talks. But it did occur to us to have a forum so we could discuss what actions we could take. Hank and I called a meeting at my home on Marcshire Drive on October 22, 1969.

At that meeting, we decided that it would be beneficial to form an organization separate from the people that lived in the route of the sewer construction. This would demonstrate broad-based support for a large park. We did pick officers at the meeting, as required to open a bank account, and so we could list them on our stationery: President, Hank Flanagan (the obvious choice); Secretary, Pete Brady; Publicity, Diane Lehder; and Treasurer, Gayle Richardson.

The name of the organization was more of a problem. Many suggestions were made, some even silly, and we finally settled on "Citizens for Conserving Poricy Brook Park." That name lasted less than 12 hours. The next day, Hank called me and said, "As secretary of our organization, please write this down. Our name will be the Poricy Park Citizens Committee." Some decisions are best left to one person rather than a committee.

For a while, "membership" consisted merely of those that happened to show up for a meeting. But we gradually got more formal. Our certificate of incorporation is dated July 22, 1970, and lists a Board of Trustees, which to us was a formality required just to fill in the blanks on the incorporation form. By January 1972 we had a real Board of Directors, as announced in the papers. Our tax-exempt 501(c)(3) letter from the IRS is dated October 17, 1973.

Jim Truncer

An invitee to our October 1969 meeting was Jim Truncer, then director of the Monmouth County Park System. (He still is, and has compiled a remarkable record of land acquisition and park development.) We discussed the possibility of the county's acquisition of the lands along the brook. But at that time, they had their hands full. They had only 1,419 acres (in 2004, 13,000) and a budget of $671,000 (in 2004, $30 million), and were trying to develop several tracts. They couldn't take this on. We also asked for help in protecting the stream bank, and the park system came through handsomely with that.[5]

Our Case Becomes Stronger

Legal Counsel

Catherine Dwyer and Barbara Ronan knew each other in the late 1950s as students at Trinity College in Washington, D.C. After they graduated they drifted apart, but their lives would come together a decade later in an interesting turn of fate.

Cathy married Pete Brady, and Barbara married Daniel J. O'Hern. During the summer of 1969, Hank had recruited Dan as an attorney to represent him and others in the Nut Swamp Association. Dan was a Democrat, and also happened to be the Mayor of Red Bank and was recommended especially for his analytical mind and his close attention to points of law. He proved to be a good choice.

We didn't take anyone to court!

It was generally believed at the time, and even reported in the newspapers, that the PPCC, or else the homeowners, had "taken the Sewerage Authority to court," or had "sued the Authority."

Dan pointed out that there was no need to do this, and it could even blow up in our faces. Rather, just don't sign the easements and then wait until the Authority starts condemnation proceedings. This way, we could not be held responsible for taking an action that delayed the sewer system installation with the risk of a counter suit. So, members of the PPCC joined with the homeowners as defendants against taking of the easements.

---

[5] I am indebted to Laura Kirkpatrick of the Monmouth County Park System for the land area and budget figures quoted here.

The heading on this poster read, "Poricy Brook: 360 Acre Park or Open Sewer Pipe Ditch?" It announced the public meeting to be held October 30, 1969, at the Unitarian Church on West Front Street. The accompanying text listed the guest speaker as "Henry Flanagan, chairman of the Citizens to Save Poricy Brook." It also invited people to a tour of the area on Sunday, Nov. 2.

The Unitarian Church Meeting

On Thursday, October 30, 1969 we participated in a difficult public meeting which went unexpectedly somewhat against our cause. It was sponsored by the "Bio Time Bomb Discussion Group," which was one of many "save the earth" environmental groups springing up at the time. (The first Earth Day was the following April 22.)

There may have been 50 people present, among whom were Lyn Kibler (Conservation Commission vice-chair), and Jack Buzzi (project engineer). These two were incensed over the "open sewer pipe" statement (figure caption, prior page). They were still buddies (a relationship that would soon end), and believed that this whole fuss was the result of some guy trying to save his back yard. They had a wonderful time at this meeting.

People entering the meeting were greeted by Mary Morford's painting of the proposed lake, mounted on an easel. Hank began his talk by describing the damage that would be done by the sewer construction, but he then focused on the benefits of the lake, believing that since the room was full of environmentalists, they would all be in favor of creating such a nice eco-friendly facility.

Among other things, the lake could be used for fishing, and that night it yielded its first catch: a giant red herring. Many questions were asked: "Will motor boats be allowed?" (No.) "Can people go swimming?" (Depends on what the Recreation Commission decides to do.) "Where will the public access be?" And so on.

Finally a man stood up and declared that he had lived in the area, was very familiar with it, and was a prominent member of a local conservation society. Thus, he had *qualifications*. He began with this statement: "First, I will say that I think the sewer line is badly designed and will wreak great damage, and I hope an alternate plan can be devised.

"But, I feel even stronger about the lake. I cannot imagine a more destructive move than to flood this area. The area now is a valuable marsh, which supports wildlife of many kinds, and contains an abundant collection of a wide variety of plants. You will destroy an asset of great beauty just to satisfy the recreation interests of a few."

Several others agreed with his position.

It was now time for the Sewerage Authority to chime in. Jack Buzzi stated that "The sewer line plans are completely drawn and the contracts are about to go out for bid. We have to get this project moving. As it is now, this marshland is being choked with effluent from ground saturation from hundreds of septic tanks."

"Oh," said our environmentalist, "You mean that we have all been wasting our time tonight even discussing this? Are you telling us that this project is a *fait accompli*?"

At this point I got into the act and shot back at him, "It would be nice if you had an interest in saving the environment as great as your love for French." Oh, we had a great time that night.

An Alternate Plan

It was clear to us that we needed a real alternate plan for the sewer line. Hank had obtained a complete set of plans for the Poricy Brook section of the sewer line. I was a trained engineer, although not in this branch of engineering. I started making phone calls and going to libraries to see how sewer lines were constructed. Hank and I, and probably others had occasional meetings to try to come up

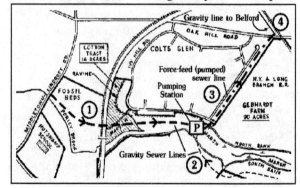

Our alternate plan. The Authority's plan would follow route (1) through the marsh to a new pumping station (P) which we proposed. The sewage would then be forced up to Oak Hill road on the new route (3) where, at point (4), it would join the originally planned gravity line to the treatment plant in Belford. Houses in Colts Glen would also be served by the pumping station as would houses on the south side of the marsh, using the route designated as (2).

with something workable. And, we were successful in this venture, although the Sewerage Authority treated our efforts with scorn.

Our next challenge was to find out what our alternate plan would cost, since it did involve adding a pumping station to the six the Authority had already proposed for their system. We were working with figures totaling in the neighborhood of around $100,000. Offsetting the pumping station cost would be the savings of not acquiring easements from many homeowners along Poricy Pond, and also the saving of not requiring construction in the difficult steep bank area along the pond. I still have some of these cost figures, and my eyes now glaze over when I read them. The bottom line is that our plan was, in cost, essentially equivalent to theirs.

Of course, the Authority claimed that our plan was unworkable. But, as our attorney explained, we needed to have this plan, not to gain the Authority's acceptance (a lost cause), but rather, to show that a viable alternative existed, if we came before a review board or a court. Put another way, without an alternate plan, we stood no chance of getting the sewer line moved.

Our November 11 Brochure

Armed with an alternate plan and a mimeograph machine, on November 11 we distributed 3000 copies of a 7-page brochure that made a general case for saving the area for parkland, and also included the outline of the alternate plan shown in the illustration on the previous page.

I think that by this time the Conservation Commission was beginning to have doubts:

- They realized that, given the scope of the easements, the contractor really could tear apart up to 1¼ miles of fragile streambank.
- It had become apparent that this was not just a few people trying to save their backyards. Many others in the Township were joining them. This was evidenced especially by the several dozen letters they had received, and by the size of the effort of our now Township-wide committee.
- There did appear to be a workable alternative.

Perhaps for these or other reasons, the Conservation Commission scheduled a public hearing in Town Hall for Wednesday November 19.

The Setup: What's the Real Reason?

Someone, perhaps Lyn Kibler, invited Hank to an informal meeting that the Conservation Commission and the Authority were having on Friday evening November 14 to discuss where we all stood, and to set the format of the November 19 meeting.

Hank couldn't go; he was working that night. So he sent me.

It was a setup. I wish I took notes, even to make a list of those present, but I do recall perhaps eight people. They certainly included Ed Schumann and Jack Buzzi. After we all settled around the conference table in the conference room that was then part of Town Hall, they turned toward me and said, "Okay, Pete, make your presentation."

Well, after stating that I was not told to prepare a formal presentation, I went over what was by now a well-plowed field. I brought up their plan and said how it would be destructive, and they countered by saying, "No, it wouldn't." Great comeback. Then I brought up our alternate plan, which they actually did seem to take seriously, but expressed many doubts, especially about the cost.

After maybe two hours of charges and counter-charges they declared the meeting to be over, and they would adjourn to the Cobblestones and have a beer. Would I like to join them?

I was a mystery to some of them. They understood why Hank wanted the sewer line out of his backyard, but why was Pete Brady putting so much effort into this? Maybe they'd find out at the bar.

So, off we went. The Cobblestones was a nice restaurant southbound on Route 35 past the Oak Hill Road intersection. (It is now a real estate agency.) It had a bar, which I guess was a watering hole for the Republican Party regulars. I sat down at the bar next to Ed Schumann, who bought me a beer.

About halfway into the beer, Ed turned to me and said, "Okay, Pete, what's the <u>real</u> reason you want the sewer line moved?"

My answer must have been all about ecology and birds and flowers and saving the earth. But what is instructive in this story is that Ed asked me that question. He just couldn't imagine that someone would become so involved just because he cared about the environment.

Just Before The Main Event

On Monday, November 17 we delivered our alternate plan to the Sewerage Authority, complete with cost estimates. By this time, as the "designated engineer" of the PPCC, I had called several engineers of sewer systems in New Jersey and had developed some sense of what things cost and how they were designed. I had made a cost comparison of our alternate plan with the Authority's and had concluded that they were roughly equal in cost.

At dinnertime Wednesday, two hours prior to the big meeting, the Authority returned our plans stating that our plan cost $148,000 more than theirs. This was going to be a kingpin of their case.

The Big Show: November 19, 1969

I have always regarded our Town Hall meeting on November 19, 1969 as the formal "coming out" of the PPCC, our first public appearance under our new name and organization.

The hall was filled with perhaps 150 people. This time, they weren't a group of anti-lake environmentalists, and this time we didn't even discuss the lake. The issue was the destruction to be caused by the sewer line. These were mainly people from the Township who had great concerns not just about what the sewer line would do to Poricy Brook, but also what it would do to <u>them</u> and their properties. The newspapers also were represented.

Dick Cole, Chair of the Conservation Commission, sat in the center of the dais in the front of the hall. He was the "neutral" moderator. [6] To Cole's left were Jack Buzzi and Ed Schumann. I don't recall if Lyn Kibler was at the dais; he probably was. To Cole's right was myself, and then Hank.

Dick began by introducing the Sewerage Authority people. Then, turning to Hank and me, he introduced us as representing the "Poricy Pond Concerned Citizens."

The Authority spoke first. There were no surprises. The Authority said they would take great care with their installation and then hammered away at our alternate plan and its excessive cost.

Now it was my turn. Each "side" (Authority, PPCC) had ten minutes for an opening statement, and Hank wanted <u>me</u> to make it, because I would be an engineer arguing against Jack Buzzi, another engineer. (Buzzi recognized that, and during the meeting remarked that, "It is interesting for me to sit here and listen to Pete Brady sharing his new-found knowledge with us.")

I began, "I want to begin with a brief statement that I don't want counted against my time. I want to make it clear who we are. We are not the "Poricy Pond Concerned Citizens." That's not what PPCC stands for. We are the <u>Poricy Park Citizens Committee</u>. We are a township-wide organization that's trying to do something right, and save open space for future generations. And I want everyone, especially the newspapers, to get our name right. Now you can start the clock."[7]

---

[6] The Conservation Commission was formed in 1969, and this was a tough first case for them. To their credit, they soon shifted away from being "neutral" about the environment and subsequently took strong stands in its favor. You'll see this here with the sewer line, and especially in the Colts Glen battle.

[7] In our first few years, some township officials had difficulty using the term "Poricy Park." Some felt it gave unwanted legitimacy to our organization, and others felt it should be <u>their</u> privilege to name the park.

I can't begin to reconstruct the whole meeting. I remember one man who came up to the microphone and declared that even if the PPCC plan cost an extra $148,000, it was worth it to save the area. (Applause.) Margaret Lopez, a fifth-grade teacher with a reputation of being outspoken and feisty (our son Stephen, then age 3, later had her as his teacher), delivered a diatribe against Ed Schumann and the way they were going to treat the environment. Lots of people spoke. It was a long meeting.

And of course, nothing was resolved, because as I have stated already, public opinion meant nothing to the Sewerage Authority, and they could say whatever they wanted. They were not giving sworn testimony and could not be held accountable.

Reliability of a Pumping Station

The other kingpin of the Authority's case was their claim that pumping stations were unreliable.

Ah, but they weren't unreliable, and I had the statistics to prove it. I showed them to Hank and I planned to include them in my opening 10-minute statement. "No," said Hank, "Just make a flat statement that pumping stations are extremely reliable. I've got several people asking planted questions, and that will be one of them, and you can then rattle off the statistics without eating into the time for your opening statement." Smart man, that Hank!

He was perhaps the third person to come to the microphone. A man, unknown to me, said, "Mr. Brady, in your statement you said that sewer pumping stations were very reliable. Just how reliable is a pumping station? Do you have statistics?"

Heh, heh, heh.

"Well, the Authority stated that our pumping station could be expected to fail four times every five years and dump raw sewage into the brook. Our proposed station, about the size of a two-car garage, could handle about one million gallons of sewage a day. It would have two pumps and motors, either of which could handle the entire load by itself should the other fail. There would be a backup diesel generator. I have called four northern New Jersey communities that have a total of 13 pumping stations, and none have failed in their histories, which for one community has been 45 years. Besides, if pumping stations were so unreliable, why has the Authority planned six of their own?"

As I said, smart man, that Hank!

A few more questions were asked, and then, about 20 minutes into the questioning, a man was called on and he came down toward the microphone. "Oh, no," said Hank, "Oh Pete, I'm sorry." "Why? What's the problem?" "You'll see."

The man began: "Mr. Brady, you stated earlier that pumping stations were very reliable. Just how reliable is a sewer pumping station?"

(Hank, in a whisper): "Pete, that's my plant. The first question was real."

I don't remember what I answered, and I don't want to be told. But I love that story.

Another meeting.

Toward the end of the meeting, a member of the audience spoke up: "We now realize that this is a complex issue and isn't going to be resolved tonight. I suggest that the concerned parties meet among themselves so they can try to resolve this, and then report their results back to the public."

There was a general sign of approval among the audience and maybe even applause for this fine suggestion. This was truly a splendid idea.

Ed Schumann and the others, including ourselves, agreed that this would be very productive and that we would arrange something.

Yeah, sure. And the big meeting ended and most people went home. But that's not where I went. I went to Dwight's bar.

Dwight's Bar

We now take a break in our story of the sewer line and indulge in one of my favorite memories.

Dwight and Gayle Richardson lived on Kingfisher Drive with their children, Scott and Kim. They had two bars in their cellar, perhaps built by Dwight and Gayle, but the Polynesian bar became Dwight's domain.

The other bar, which we almost never used, was done in Wild West décor, in the style of a saloon. The reason we never used it was that Wu would make a frantic screeching racket if we were in an adjacent room, rather than his.

Wu was a mynah bird, and he resided in the Polynesian bar. He had a repertoire:

"Hi there, Dwight."

"Martinis – Whoopee!"

"Oye, vay!"

Plus many others, the one I best remember being "Sweet Adeline," sung to the familiar tune except that the last note was wretchedly flat.

Dwight stood behind the bar and served drinks. He served me a French brandy called "Duval," which I've not seen anywhere else. It tasted as if it came from a refinery rather than a distillery.

For the two-plus years he was with us, Dwight was the soul of the organization. His optimism and belief in the good motives of others was infectious, as opposed to the cynicism of many of us. No matter what blows we endured, he was always there to push onward. And, as you will see later, he was the master at getting people over to our side.

The Sewer Battle: Its Formal Phase

We never did hold that promised meeting with the Sewerage Authority. On the following Sunday evening, Ed Schumann personally telephoned area homeowners, threatening court action if they did not sign the easements. On November 26 the Authority authorized court action to begin. I recall that the actual papers were served on only one owner: Hank Flanagan.

Also on that same Sunday (November 23), several of us met at Hank's house to discuss the possibility of a restraining order from construction.

Soon after that, Dan O'Hern reviewed the steps to be taken to restrain the Authority from (a) taking easements, (b) awarding contracts, and (c) actual construction. But he advised against any of this because it would change our status from defending ourselves from the Authority to taking a positive action to block construction, leaving ourselves open to a countersuit.

The NJ Water Policy Division

In their contacts with state agencies, Adolph and Olga Margus had found that the Sewerage Authority had applied for, and received, permits from the New Jersey Water Policy and Supply Division for five minor stream crossings in the Poricy Brook area. As a result, the Authority had stated as part of its contract bids that all necessary permits had been obtained.

But they hadn't applied for permits for the 1¼-mile continuous encroachment of the stream bank.

The Water Policy Division routinely reviewed such permits and, if the project seemed well designed, the permits were issued as a matter of course. But if problems arose, the permits were referred to the semi-judicial body, the Water Policy and Supply Council, for a hearing. The council can only judge, not raise objections themselves.

Someone else had to bring the objections to them. And that is what we did.

So, the Authority claimed they had the necessary permits and we claimed they didn't. What do we do next?

We did write the Water Policy and Supply Division requesting a hearing, but that might not be enough. We were also told about Ken Creveling, a personal friend of a friend of mine, who might help here. Ken knew several people in state government. Some of us went to see him, and he agreed to contact some people in the Division.

Ken got back to us in January. He thought that hearings might be scheduled, but he also advised us to get the required injunctions to stop immediate construction. We were in a tight spot.

But the state did act. On January 16, 1970, George Shanklin, Director of the Division of Water Policy and Supply, called me to tell me there would be a hearing, and three days later, they set the date for February 5. It turned out there would be five hearings, and we'll return to them shortly.

"A Crisis in Conservation"

While the stage was being set for a hearing, we prepared another brochure, "Poricy Park: A Crisis in Conservation." This had professionally-printed covers with photographs and ten pages of mimeographed text. It covered the sewer line problem, and also made a strong case for saving the open space in the area. We printed 5000 copies, and distributed them mainly by stuffing mailboxes. (Yes, it's unlawful to do this, but I think the statute of limitations has run out on this one.) The mimeo and stapling party was set for Saturday January 10, 1970 at my house starting at 10 am.

It was at my front door that morning that I met one of the most important persons to come onto the project, and a person who would be one of Cathy and my closest friends until her death 34 years later.

Marcia Rissland, photo taken May 18, 1974.

Marcia

Diane Lehder was our first contact with Marcia Rissland. Diane had met her at an Oak Hill Civic Association meeting, perhaps in December, and Marcia seemed interested in our cause. Diane asked me if it would be all right to invite Marcia to our brochure work party. Of course I said "Yes."

Marcia showed up at around 11:30. By this time, we were looking toward lunch, and we needed someone to go to Lincroft to get subs (two miles away). My first words to Marcia were to ask her, even before she entered our house, if she would mind running this errand.

I still remember the look of shock on her face, and I thank the Lord that she didn't just turn around and go home. Instead, she was a good gopher, brought back the sandwiches and joined the party.

Marcia had, up to this point in her life, been a housewife raising three children. Her summers were spent at the beach. She was a Jersey girl, having grown up in South Orange. She married Lou Rissland in 1952 (they both attended Columbia High School) and for a while was an Army wife. In 1962 they settled down in their home on Bamm Hollow Road, near the future Poricy Park. She had no training in ecology or public relations or politics, and certainly no training in sewer lines. She looked at this project as a chance to do something significant.

That's the reason most of us got involved. There was virtually nobody on our committee that was involved in politics, or that had much wealth. We were not connected socially. Only one or two were members of nature or environmental groups. (I was not, but I think the Marguses and Lescinskys were in either the Audubon Society or Sierra Club.) We were pretty much all completely inexperienced in this kind of movement.

Marcia did have a keen interest in history and in the structure and maintenance of houses. These skills may have seemed irrelevant at the time, but in years to come they were to prove a Godsend. We'll cover Marcia's major role in later chapters.

Lou Timolat

The stuffing party was on Saturday, and the distribution was the next day. On Monday evening, January 12, my phone rang.

"Is this the Mr. Brady that is associated with the pamphlet that I found in my mailbox today?"

"Yes. I hope you didn't mind receiving it."

"This is Lou Timolat. I've read through the entire document, and I want to say that you people are doing the right thing. It's about time that some group took our government to task about the way they've been messing up this Township."

"Well, thank you. We've taken on a difficult task."

"Yes, you have, and I want to help out. I'm going to send you a check for $1,000. Whom do I make it out to and where do I send it?"

I've already said that I wasn't used to this kind of project. $1,000 was a <u>fortune</u> to me (this was 1970) and we thus far had worked with only a few hundred dollars. Incredibly, I asked him if he really wanted to send that much, and he replied that he knew we would need that and even more. I got his phone number and said I'd get back to him. D-U-M-B.

I called Hank. He practically shouted into the phone, "Call him back and take the money. Of course we're going to need it."

So, we were now into four figures.

I didn't know who Lou Timolat was. I learned later that he was a prominent figure in the local Republican Party and lived on the Navesink River Road. At one point he had donated a strip of land to the Township to preserve the rustic character of the road (it's on your left as you drive east, shortly before you get to the Navesink Country Club).

Although I spoke with Lou Timolat a few more times, I never met him. He died a few months later. But his widow, Marie Timolat, was very generous to our cause in our early years, carrying on with her husband's legacy. You'll meet her again in this story.

Charlie Capen

In rerouting the sewer line, we had two big breaks. One, already mentioned, was the Authority's failure to get Water Policy permits. The other was our learning about Charlie Capen.

During fall 1969 I called several newspapers to get publicity for our cause, and I reached Peter Bridge of the Newark Evening News. After hearing my story, Bridge recommended we contact Charles Capen, who was consultant to Newark Municipal Utilities Authority. I called Capen on December 12 and sent him some material. He called back on December 30 to tell me he saw no problem in our alternative plan; a pumping station is cheap.

This was <u>incredible</u>. We actually found a licensed engineer that would represent us in our case against another licensed engineer. But in this case, Capen had opposed Kupper (the Authority's engineer) in one of their other projects.

Hank was very pleased. We scheduled a visit with Capen on Thursday, January 22, 1970 when Hank, Will Lehder, and I drove up to Green Pond on a cold evening and talked about the project.

The little things one remembers! Hank and I and our families again visited Capen on a beautiful Saturday, May 30, and the children played on the boat dock while we met indoors. Green Pond is an idyllic setting, a tightly-knit group of homes on a pretty, small lake in the New Jersey highlands. But the thing I remember best is that Charlie had a small notebook consisting of 6-place logarithm tables, *all hand written*. There were thousands of numbers in that table, laboriously written with steel-nibbed pen which you dip into an inkwell!

Charlie was an experienced engineer and I guess that he was in his 60s. He thought our alternate plan was fine, and would testify for us at the Water Policy hearings. But he first wanted to see the site.

He came to see the area on Sunday, January 25, when we also had Dan O'Hern with us. Shortly into the walk, Dan turned to me and said, "You guys have gotten serious. Capen is the real thing. I think we have a solid case now."

Measuring Trees

There remained one more bit of homework for us prior to the Water Policy hearing on February 5.

Lee Rissland, age 13, measuring trees, February 1, 1970.

Frank Lescinsky and I set out to estimate the damage the sewer construction would cause. We staked out the eastern 600 feet of the Morris Tract, and on Sunday, February 1 we assembled a group of volunteers to measure the circumference of every tree in the staked area. We also took measurements of the bank slope and height.

Never mind that because I botched the instructions to the volunteers, some of us had to go back the next day and repeat some of the measurements. (I could fill volumes with reports of the wasted efforts in this project over the years.) Here were the main results. In our 600-foot section:

- Slope of bank: 32° min, 48° max, 40.5° avg.
- Average height on the vertical: 27 feet.
- Distance on slant, toe to top, 50' to 55'.
- Number of trees 2" diameter or greater: 81.

We concluded that in the entire 6300 feet of sewer line construction, more than 2000 trees would be uprooted, leaving a surface area of 125,000 sq. ft. of highly erodable bank dirt exposed.

We were now ready for the Trenton hearing.

The Feb. 5 Hearing: A Bust

But the Sewerage Authority was not ready. Schumann and Buzzi showed up, but they didn't bring an attorney, and the council said that their rules clearly stated that each party must be represented by an attorney. They immediately cancelled the hearing and rescheduled for March 4, 1970.

Well, we _did_ have an attorney (for whom we paid), we _did_ have Charlie Capen with us (for whom we paid), and we _did_ have a reporter from the Newark Evening News show up after I had pleaded with the newspaper to send one.

And we also had that nice drive across the state on Route 33. These were the days prior to I-195.

The Hearings Continue

On March 4, the Authority did have their attorney present, William J. O'Hagan. Others on "their side" included Jack Buzzi plus another engineer from Kupper, Ed Schumann, and Middletown Mayor Bud Foulks.

On "our side" we had: A. Bruce Pyle of N.J. Fish and Game Division; John Dowling, a science teacher in Middletown who would discuss the value of the area; Charlie Capen, our engineer; our attorney Dan O'Hern; and Hank and myself.

The Red Bank Register and Newark Evening News were also there.

The Water Policy and Supply Council had five people hearing the case.

The hearing started at 11:30 am. The basic strategy of the Authority was to concentrate on the five minor stream crossings they had already obtained permits for, and to stress the great care they would take in implementing these crossings. The encroachment of the 6300 feet of main sewer line construction was brought up several times, and the Authority repeated their position that only the five minor crossings were at issue. This was going nowhere.

Finally, at 3:55 pm, their attorney said, "It is getting late. We have brought the Mayor of Middletown with us, and we don't want to have to ask him to come back. Would you permit him to make a short statement?" This request was granted.

Now, it was later stated by some that "The Mayor testified against the citizens." Not quite true. Here is the gist of what he said:

> "I have lived in Middletown as it has grown from 5,000 to 50,000 people. We started a sewer program years ago. First it would cost $9 million, then 13, 20, 30, and now we're up to $40 million. Please come up with a decision before this delay goes any further."

Then there was more wrangling among the lawyers and finally the hearing was adjourned. The next hearing was eventually scheduled for April 8.

Contracts Awarded

On Tuesday, April 7, 1970, the day before the hearing, the parties scheduled a meeting at Town Hall. Both attorneys were present. The Authority's attorney, William O'Hagan, told us that the Authority had awarded the contracts for the Poricy sewer line construction. Whatever came out of the Trenton hearings would be fixed with change orders.

So, the Authority awarded the contracts without having all the necessary permits.

SEWER SWATH – Mrs. Joseph Giger, with umbrella, and Mrs. John F. Sauter inspect the 30-foot swath cut by Middletown Sewerage Authority contractor through woods behind their homes. Eight-inch sewer trunk line sections awaiting installation are at the edge of the swath.

Sewer Line Job Spurs Middletown Protests

Reprinted from the *Daily Register*, April 3, 1970:

Sewerage Authority contractor's activities stirred concern yesterday as residents saw a 30-foot swath cut through the woods behind Iler Drive.

Mrs. Joseph T. Giger and Mrs. John F. Sauter were among those protesting that in order to install an eight-inch sewer trunk line, the contractor is virtually removing the woods from the rear of their homes.

A call to Edward Schumann, Sewerage Authority chairman, elicited the information that the Authority has purchased a 30-foot easement ... The equipment, Mr. Schumann explained, is working within the easement.

[The article then quoted me: "The Iler Woods are flat, and they need 30 feet to install an 8-inch pipe, but what will happen to the oaks and beeches in the Poricy bank? Indeed, what will happen to the bank?"]

Sewer Swath

Once in a while, adrenaline took control of the project.

In mid-morning Thursday, April 2, 1970, I received a call from Inge Giger who lived near the ongoing sewer construction, who said that the contractors were destroying the woods behind their homes. I rushed from work, got my camera from home, and drove over to the site, where I met the women shown in the photo. This was during noon hour. In those days, I had a Kodak "Tourist" roll-film bellows camera I had received as a Christmas present in 1948 and was shooting 620 black-and-white film with large negatives.

I then drove to Dorn's in Red Bank and asked them to develop the film and make a proof sheet by the end of the afternoon, when I would pick it up.

I had also called Bob Bramley of the *Daily Register*, and arranged to deliver the proof sheet to him in late afternoon. There were eight photos. He took a scissors and cut out the photo shown here and included this article in the next day's edition.

All this time Hank was off on a trip. I was a little reluctant to do all this on my own, but you don't just get a chance like this every day!

He returned the next day and saw the article in the paper. He called me. "Pete, that was beautiful. Really fine. For that, you should get a – a – *flower*."

This article was entered as evidence at the May Water Policy hearing.

Three More Hearings

I will spare you all the details of the many hours of testimony during the next *three* hearings: April 8, May 14, and June 3. But the April hearing was critical to our case, and I'll include some of the details of that hearing here.

First, there were the usual lawyer arguments about where they were in the hearing. Was Jack Buzzi still on direct examination? They concluded that Buzzi's testimony was finished. In that case, the

Authority's attorney stated five minutes into the hearing, their stream crossing case was finished.

"No," said Council member Robert Hardman, "We have categorically included the entire floodplain [in the area for which you need permits]. The edges of the pond define the natural and ordinary high water mark." My translation: "You need a permit for the Poricy 6300 foot sewer line construction. Your five stream crossing permits are not sufficient."

We were no longer in the Unitarian Church, where the Authority could tell the public how careful they would be and that easements on the "entire bank" would just be a formality and that restoration would leave the area in beautiful condition. This time they were under oath, and being examined by people who were skilled and experienced in water-related construction.

Here is an excerpt from the official stenographer's transcript, starting on page 209(!):

[Mrs. Hermia Lechner of the Council is addressing questions to Authority engineer, Jack Buzzi:]

Q: Your right-of-way that you have acquired, the easement is 40 feet, right?

A: That is correct.

Q: Roughly?

A: Yes.

Q: And you, then the contractor has the right to work within that 40 foot easement, this is the amount he needs?

A: That is correct.

Q: Therefore, the building of a berm ten feet wide, does not restrict him to using only the berm if he needs more distance; is that right?

A: That is correct.

Q: So, if he finds he needs – if the berm is 10 feet and he needs 20 feet more, he may, and should be able to go into the easement for that additional distance, whether or not it disturbs the natural bank, in order to accomplish the work that he has to accomplish?

A: That is correct, within the confines of restoring.

Q: But, he may rip that bank out if he finds he needs to get his equipment in and take the trees out, or whatever he needs with that 40 foot easement, to the extent that he needs?

A: That is correct.

Q: And, if he should rip down that natural bank, and acquire suitable fill, he may also add that to his berm if he needs to? In other words, there are no restrictions within that 40 foot easement, except to restore it?

A: By restore, we mean he can't put back the 24 inch oak that went, but the grading of the embankment, let's say he went and removed the whole thing, it must go back.

This kind of thing went on almost the whole day. Several other witnesses were called, some ours, who, in summary finally nailed down what we had been saying for months: The Authority could do whatever they pleased in the *entire easement*.

Agencies That Participated

Over the course of the hearings, testimony or written statements were furnished by the following people and agencies:

- U.S. Dept. of the Interior, Federal Water Quality Administration, who based their position on a National Park Service Report that was written after an on-site inspection. "Installation of the sewer line as presently proposed will do serious damage to a natural environmental resource ..."
- U.S. Dept. of Agriculture, Soil Conservation Service. They wrote a cautiously worded report that supported construction if done properly. But the author of the report, Neal Munch, was called by us as a witness and it soon became clear that the Sewerage Authority would likely not follow all of his recommendations.
- N.J. Div. Fish and Game, report by A. Bruce Pyle, recommended using our alternate route.
- Tom Kellers, Chief Naturalist, Monmouth County Park System, testified at the May hearing of the immense difficulties of restoration and gave several examples where it failed.
- Ronald Tindall, landscape architect for Monmouth County, testified at the May hearing and gave further examples of difficulty of restoration.
- Lynden Kibler, Chair, Middletown Conservation Commission (see below).

- Joseph Truncer, Director, N.J. Division of Parks, Forestry, and Recreation (see below).
- Charles Capen, professional engineer, who testified that our alternative plan was workable.
- Pete Brady, who gave statistics from our tree measurement report.
- U.S. Senators Harrison Williams and Clifford Case had each urged rerouting the sewer line.
- Pat Maloney, from Nut Swamp Association, described other local damage to the streambank.

That's quite a list. Lyn Kibler replaced Dick Cole as chair of the Conservation Commission January 1970. Lyn remained in that post and performed yeoman service for many years. At the May Water Policy hearing he spoke of damage from sewer construction that had already occurred. One statement from his testimony stands out: "Middletown still needs sewers. But we may end up with sewers and nothing else. If our natural resources are destroyed beyond restoration, we'll have only sewers."

I think Joseph Truncer (Jim Truncer's father) gave a clear overview of the potential problems with the sewer installation, and his written statement is quoted in a side bar included here. The last paragraph is particularly noteworthy.

The Settlement

By June, the Council had heard it all. Looking back, and probably influenced by the discussions Hank and I had with Dan O'Hern in that nice, long, repeated drive back and forth across New Jersey, I have concluded that the Council didn't *want* to make a decision. If they said "No," this would block or seriously delay construction of a major, badly needed project. If they said "Yes," they would be going straight in the face of a battery of experts at county, state, and federal levels with established credentials. What they wanted us to do was *settle*.

But, even without issuing a judgment, the Council provided the essential element to resolve this impasse: *delay*. The contracts had been awarded and time was running out.

Statement Before Water Policy & Supply Council
Re: Issuance of Permit for Construction of a Sewer
Line along Poricy Brook, Middletown, NJ

My name is Joseph Truncer, Director of the Division of Parks, Forestry, and Recreation ... I am a licensed land surveyor, and during the past 39 years have occupied various positions related to parks and forests...

I have reviewed the proposal for construction of the sewer line along Poricy Brook and make the following recommendation: That at least 6,000 feet of the sewer trunk line be relocated outside of the flood plain and the adjoining steep slopes. [He then compares this with installation of a sewer line along Shark River where severe erosion occurred.]

There is no question about the need of sewers. However, the time has arrived when the total environment must be considered, and sewers, highways, and other necessary improvements must be designed in a manner that will do the least possible damage to the environment even if extra cost is involved. Any project that fails to take into consideration the total effect on the environment is outmoded and unsatisfactory in light of our present knowledge concerning the preservation of our environment.
(Signed) Joseph J. Truncer, Director

The Authority still needed easements to go ahead with their original plan with or without Water Policy permits, and there were still some 16 homeowners that had not signed them. So, the Authority instituted court proceedings to get them. By this action, it appeared to us that they were going ahead with the sewer line, with or without permits.

During June, Hank and other members of the Nut Swamp Association worked on a compromise plan with the Sewerage Authority that would allow the line to be constructed basically on its original route, but out in the marsh and pond, not touching the bank. Imported fill would be used to build a berm to support the line. This proposal was put into the form of a consent order, and this proposal was cause for the court to adjourn the condemnation proceedings until July 24. We had bought yet another month of delay.

A *consent order* means that the parties have agreed to a proposal that will now be filed in court, such that a violation of the terms can give grounds for a lawsuit. It does not mean that a judge or court has ruled on the matter, but it does mean that a judge can enforce the terms of the order.

The problem was, the Authority wouldn't sign it. They made statements about the difficulty of getting change orders implemented. Or whatever.

Then, Hank proposed a daring move which Dan tried to talk him out of. Hank had Dan send a notice to the Authority, which said in part:

To: [Attorneys representing the Authority]
Please take notice that on Friday, July 24, 1970 ... the undersigned attorneys for Henry J. Flanagan [and PPCC and others named] will apply to the Honorable Francis X. Crahay, Acting Assignment Judge of the Superior Court, for interlocutory injunction pending final adjudication of the case restraining the Middletown Township Sewerage Authority from:
1. Doing or permitting to be done any construction in the area of the Poricy Brook and Poricy Pond Basin between the Middletown Lincroft Road and the Navesink River Road.
2. Doing or permitting to be done any work on the collector system on Poricy Lane or Pine Street.
3. Doing or permitting to be done any work in connection trunk lines and/or pumping station on streets or other properties so closely connected with the subject area that construction thereon will materially affect the availability of alternate plans for sewer constructed as may be recommended by the Federal Water Quality Agency or other state or federal agencies.

Put simply, all construction in a wide region of Middletown must cease on July 24 until the court rules on whether the Authority must adopt an alternate plan. And this could have been a full-blown court case, with hearings and witnesses similar to what we just went through in Trenton. Needless to say, it could have taken months.

The reason Dan tried to talk us out of this is that for the first time, we have moved from a passive position to <u>active intervention</u> to prevent sewer construction, and we could be liable for a countersuit. Nevertheless, Hank was insistent on this, and I believe that this was Hank's finest move. I am convinced that had he not done this, the Poricy Brook basin would have been destroyed.

The Consent Order

The Authority signed the consent order.

The order is dated July 24, 1970. It stipulates that "The Authority or its contractors shall not make cuts in the southerly bank or Poricy Brook and Pond, or remove trees in said bank, except where necessary to provide lateral feeders to users." It also goes on to require that certain easements are to be moved and that a berm be installed to carry the trunk line. The order is signed by attorneys representing the Authority, our own attorney, Daniel J. O'Hern, and four people named directly in the action, namely, Henry and Maxine Flanagan, Paul T. Brady, and Stanley Morford. There follow 35 signatures of property owners that were not named in the original actions.

I don't remember how I felt at the time. As you will see, we were pretty busy trying to acquire land. But I think the position of many people can be summed up in the editorial published in the Middletown *Courier* on the next page.

And, the Cost to the PPCC

We estimated that this effort cost the PPCC $3,000, covered by contributions. It was worth it.

Editorial in the Middletown *Courier*, July 30, 1970

They fought city hall

It was a six-page court order, full of technical and legal jargon, and resplendent with referrals to a number of sewer lines designated by letter and number. But it represented a victory for a persistent group of concerned citizens who had been told "you can't fight city hall."

The court order upheld the Poricy Park Citizens Committee's opinion that Middletown Sewerage Authority lines would ruin the natural area and should be rerouted.

We consider this a large victory for those people who want to preserve some of our nicer things in life.

This victory by the people should also put the Sewerage Authority on notice that it may face the same fate in the dumping in Compton's Creek question and the stately trees along Kings Highway situation. The fight would be particularly strenuous when it comes to Compton's Creek ... not only do the people want to preserve it for its natural assets, but these same men also make their living from it.

The people's determination in proving their point, and the court's decision they were right, should be a vivid warning signal to the Authority, and any agency that attempts to "progress" through raping the land, that this town and the country as a whole is not going to hold still for such actions with a "the public and the future be damned" attitude.

Senators Case and Williams should be commended for their getting behind the citizens and having their wishes be heard. Judge Crahay should be commended for a fine and practical decision.

The PPCC should be commended for their stalwart attitude, their undying efforts, and their persistent fortitude in fighting what they knew was wrong. May they have equal success with their plans to develop the area as a park.

Time Passes On – 35 Years

The sewer line turned out to be a project nearly independent of acquiring the land and establishing the nature center. So, we can leave it and go on to other things. Before we do, there are a few loose ends to tie up in a kind of epilogue to this section.

Building the Sewer Line

The Poricy Brook sewer line went in without too much trouble, but there were a few incidents involving cutting trees and cutting the bank. In September 1971 six large trees were cut, but the contractor stopped when property owners complained; it was admitted as improper. A more difficult problem occurred in late 1971 when the fill that was imported to build the berm along the pond caused bottom muck to be pushed toward the center of the pond and surface. The Division of Water Policy got involved with this one, and a drag line was subsequently used to remove the muck. Except for these incidents, installation went well.

John Buzzi, Environmental Advocate

Jack Buzzi died September 2, 2004. He had a long and productive career in civil engineering. Quoting just a fraction of his impressive obituary which appeared in the Asbury Park Press:

"He was the owner and president of Kupper Associates, one of the largest independently owned civil engineering firms in the State, from 1976 until his retirement in 1997. He was an advocate on public policy issues related to infrastructure in the NJ, NY, and PA areas and was a leader in engineering education. Many key projects involving wastewater facilities, water supply, flood control, solid waste management, and urban redevelopment benefited from his technical expertise of soils and foundation engineering.... The fight to keep the port of NJ and NY viable and competitive in a world-wide economy was one of his special interests ..."

Edward Schumann, Educator

Ed is still around. He stayed on the Sewerage Authority through 1971, and when his term expired, he was replaced by Jake Lamb.

When in April 1971 the Township Committee announced their intent to purchase the Gebhardt Farm, Schumann termed it "The ultimate triumph of public relations over reason." (*Register*, 4/16/71)

After many years out of the public spotlight, Ed, at age 77, ran for Board of Education in the April 2002 election. There were five candidates for three seats. Ed finished fourth.

Several people have observed that had Ed Schumann simply moved the sewer line away from the bank without fuss, this whole controversy would not have occurred and the public would never have learned of the potential of the area for parkland. The Gebhardt Farm would be a housing development today. I believe they are correct.

Similarly, perhaps Ed's election to the Board of Education might have resulted in great advances in our school system. I recognized that possibility, but I did not vote for him.

Dan O'Hern

Dan continued to practice law in Red Bank, but in April 1978, at age 48, he became New Jersey Commissioner of Environmental Protection under Governor Brendan Byrne. (No doubt his stellar performance in the Poricy Brook controversy was a major factor in his selection.) In the May 1978 issue of *New Jersey Magazine* (not to be confused with *New Jersey Monthly Magazine*), Brian O'Reilly wrote a comprehensive article about Dan, and in it quoted from a telephone interview the author had with me. I won't quote from the article, but I will tell you about Dan's extraordinary job offer to me.

A short time after Dan took the DEP position in 1978, the phone rang on my desk at Bell Laboratories in Holmdel. It was Dan. After the usual courtesy exchanges, he got to the point:

"Pete, as you know, I am now the New Jersey Commissioner of Environmental Protection."

"Yes. Congratulations."

"I would like you to come to work for me as my special assistant. I will offer you $5,000 a year more than whatever you are making now. The problem is, the job would last only as long as Brendan Byrne stays in office. But perhaps you could get a leave of absence from Bell Labs. If not, you would be out on the street at the end of your term, but I assure you that with the connections you would make in this job, you could get a handsome job of your choice in industry or government at a fine salary."

"I don't get it. Why are you making this offer? I don't have the qualifications to work in government. I'm not a lawyer. I'm an engineer."

"That's why I want you. We've got enough lawyers in Trenton. I want someone who can do what you did with the sewer line, namely, cut through all the fog that other people generate and ask the right questions and analyze the situation. Once you've done that, we can take over."

"Well, I don't know. Can I get back to you tomorrow?"

"Fine. Call me."

I had 17 years service at Bell Labs, in a secure job (this was prior to Bell System divestiture in 1984). We were about to open the new Nature Center and I was frantically busy. I would have to give all that up. Further, I saw myself on the stage of some high school in south Jersey until 12:30 am listening to a dreary hearing and then having to report for work in Trenton at 8 am the next morning. Also, I found that the Labs would not grant a leave of absence for this. I'd have to quit my job.

So, I turned him down. I have not regretted my decision, but I do regret having disappointed Dan.

Dan soon went on to bigger things. He became Counsel to the Governor, and then an Associate Justice of the Supreme Court of the State of New Jersey. He is retired now, but still active in civic affairs.

From Gutenberg to Boustrophedon

PRESERVE PORICY PARK

I never learned their names. They were two wonderful old men that ran a printing shop in Red Bank. I had seen it many times, because when you drove west to the end of Chestnut Street, it was on Shrewsbury Avenue directly in front of you. The sign said "Van Brunt Printers." But neither of them was a Van Brunt; I did learn that much. Van Brunt had gone away years ago.

When, in 1969, we needed stationery, I thought about that shop and visited it. The place was in chaos then, and always. The men loved to talk, and it was difficult to get away when you visited them.

Their work was beautiful. They did exclusively letterpress. A box was composed with metal slugs with raised letters, and jet-black ink was rolled over the letters and then paper was pressed against them. The letters in the box were hand-set, or sometimes were in slugs from their linotype machine. I can't begin to describe a linotype machine. Once common for about a century, they now are extremely rare, perhaps only in museums. Anyone having the slightest interest in things mechanical should find a working linotype machine and see it in action.[8]

We used Van Brunt into the 1980s. In doing the research for this book, I visited the site, which is now a furniture store. The owner remembers the men,

but not their names. I asked in a few other nearby stores, Same story: yes, the men, no, their names.

Bumper Stickers

An example of their work was our bumper sticker, shown here. Each letter was attached to a wooden block and set in a box, and then inked, and then the bright-green blank sticker impressed on the letters. We printed thousands of them beginning in early 1970. Hundreds of them made it onto cars. A few years later, somebody in the township government told Dwight that this was by far the most successful bumper sticker campaign that he had ever seen in this area.

So, our stationery and bumper stickers were done with the same movable-type process invented circa 1436 by Johann Gutenberg.

We could not find a photo of a bumper sticker from the days they were in use, so we did a creative thing. Patricia and Larry Lagan display a Poricy Park bumper sticker on their vintage '70s VW.

---

[8] In 2005 there are still just a few newspapers in the U.S.A. that use linotypes, one of which is in Garfield, NJ (*Asbury Park Press*, Mar. 28, 2005, p. C6).

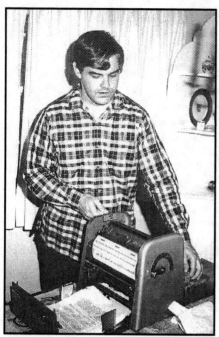

The Roneo Mimeograph

Letterpress was fine for stationery and bumper stickers, but for fast, cheap reproduction of flyers it was far too expensive and slow. We needed something we could operate ourselves.

Mimeograph is a type of *silk screening* in which a very fine mesh of silk or other material has on it a thin coating of wax. For a typewriter, there is a thin sheet of plastic covering the screen. You type directly onto the plastic sheet without a ribbon. The typeface images cut into the wax

and expose the base sheet. Then, you wrap the sheet on an oil-filled drum and crank away. As the sheets of paper fly through the machine (up to 3 per second), the oil oozes through the openings cut by the typewriter. It also oozes onto your hands and clothing. The same process is used to print on fine clothing, such as scarves, and also on the souvenir towels sold in gift shops. Silk screening is not obsolete.

In later years, we had a computer and with it, a daisy-wheel impact typewriter that could type on mimeo stencils. Later came ink-jet printers and laser printers, but these were not useful for production runs. In later years, the Middletown High School South print shop had an offset press which we used to print our calendars.

For addressing envelopes, at first we had a mailing list of only a hundred or so names and we could just type or write them out each time. But around 1972, Don Abrams let us use his company's Addressograph machine that used individual metal plates embossed with names.

Above: I am operating the Roneo mimeograph machine at a mailout in my house in 1971. From 1969 to 1979, I estimate that I turned that crank at least 600,000 times.

Top right: Lou Rissland at the same mailout. Lou maintained a keen interest in Poricy Park over all the years he and Marcia were involved, and helped with many managerial decisions. He was a salesman for the Avery Label company, and had retired from the Army Reserve as a full colonel.

Lower right: Gail Abrams at the mailout. She and her husband Don were frequent hosts for our meetings in the early 1970s. They moved to Little Silver in 1981. You'll meet Don on page 29.

Soon after, Jim Knowles (who joined our committee in 1971) put our mailing list on IBM punched tab cards and had labels made in the Bell Labs computer center. I later used a UNIX-based mini-computer system at Bell Labs. After we acquired our own desk-top computer in 1979, we put the mailing list on this computer. At first, we printed labels using a Perkin-Elmer impact printer, and then went to an Okidata dot-matrix tractor-feed printer. After that came the laser and ink-jet printers that are in common usage today.

Boustrophedon!

I first had the Okidata dot-matrix printer in my home so I could write the software for it on my own time. It had the feature, now common, of having the print head move back and forth, printing one line left-to-right and the next, right-to-left. You have all seen this.

But not everyone had seen this in 1984, which was around the time we acquired this printer. It was also the year that Cathy's father turned 80. He was at our house one day, and I wanted to impress him with this wonderful technology that allowed a printer to print backwards. So, I had the computer print something while he watched.

"That's not new at all. It's *boustrophedon*."

E. Vincent Dwyer was a chemical engineer by training, a N.Y. Telephone management person by profession, but a classicist by love. He taught Latin in the evenings and we still have his dictionary. He had a wonderful grasp of things ancient.

Boustrophedon comes from the Greek. The "bo" at the beginning is derived from the word for ox or cattle (hence, *bovine*), and the rest of the word is from a Greek word for "turning." Hence, the word means "as the ox turns." This is how you plow a field – you go one way, turn your oxen around, and then go back the other.

In ancient times, there were some forms of writing that actually did that. A scribe would write one line from left to write, and then drop down a line and write the next the other way. In that style, the second line was meant to be read from right-to-left, that is, in the direction it was written, but today, all lines (in many languages) are read left-to-right.

Hint: If you want to find how to pronounce it, you may need an unabridged dictionary.

Henry and the Death of the Roneo

As the years progressed, the Roneo became crankier and crankier (heh, heh). The drum cloth needed cleaning and replacing. The gears were worn. And the print quality began to deteriorate.

For several years, Cathy and I had wanted to take in a fresh air child for two weeks in the summer, and we finally did that in 1979. Henry was a 9-year-old black child from Staten Island. In that summer, our boys were 15, 13, and 10.

Henry had a great time. But he was a handful! He liked everyone and had more energy than all of us combined. He got up at dawn and tried to wake everyone else up so he could start the day. He never stopped; he was always in motion.

It was Sunday, July 15, 1979, the day of our annual church picnic in the early afternoon. The weather was fine. Around 11 am, I decided to try to clean the mimeo and print something. I did this outdoors, of course, and wore old clothes.

The mimeo did not cooperate. It kept getting clogged and throwing out grey, illegible, blurry sheets. As I continued, I got covered with ink.

Meanwhile, Henry was sitting still (!), watching this calamity. After I was simply filthy and after parts were strewn all over, he spoke up: "Hey – How come they gave you this job?"

That was the end for the Roneo. We had a good time at the picnic.

Acquiring the Land: The Fossil Beds

Land acquisition was finished by 1973, just three years after the sewer settlement. After 1973, things got complicated because three major efforts proceeded simultaneously:

- Developing programs.
- Building the Nature Center.
- Restoring the historic buildings.

We'll get to those items later. But we'll start with acquiring land, and we can treat the Fossil Beds as a case by itself because the PPCC was not directly responsible for the acquisition, although we did help with the development of the area.

Early Plans for Fossil Beds Acquisition

In April 1969, just before the Sewerage Authority sought easements, the Township filed an application with the U.S. Dept. of Housing and Urban Development (HUD) for $80,125 as partial funds for acquiring the 40-acre Fossil Beds tract.

Later on, when New Jersey Green Acres became available, the Fossil Beds were included in a block grant application for additional funds. Eventually the grants were approved and covered most of the cost of $132,000 for the Fossil Beds at the closing on July 30, 1973. It was purchased from Sylvia and Louis Kaplan and John Berman, none of whom were known to members of our committee.

There Are Lots of Fossils

A frequent question asked is whether we were concerned that we would run out of fossils. They are, after all, irreplaceable.

There are probably billions of fossils underlying this section of Monmouth County. At this location, Poricy Brook is confined to a narrow stream, instead of being in a floodplain, because it must pass under the Middletown-Lincroft Road bridge. Hence, it cuts down to this layer and exposes fossils.

Ed and Maxine Flanagan at the Fossil Beds, Oct. 1969.

The sewer line's passage through this area was never at issue, since it would not cut into the bank. It would, however, cut down into the fossil layer bringing even more to the surface.

Even before acquisition, we frequently held fossil hunts in the stream bed. I personally confess to a lack of burning interest in the fossils, and their attraction was always a bit of a mystery to me. But not to many others, especially Frank Lescinsky, who with his wife Lethe were the usual leaders of the fossil hunts. In 1973, Frank wrote a very good brochure about the fossils, which is reproduced in part as an appendix here.

Fossil Bed Work Parties

Initially there wasn't much at the Fossil Beds. No sign, no delineated parking lot, and this was mainly because the Township didn't own it. But in 1973 (the year of acquisition), when Jim Duke was Director of Parks and Recreation, he made a deal with us. There was a landfill in Belford that had some utility poles in it, and if our committee would go out and cut 75 sections of 6-foot lengths, he would use them to line the parking lot when it was constructed the following year.

November 10, 1973 was a cold, clear day. There were six of us in the work party (I took the picture), and the things I remember best were (a) Marcia's

coming out in mid-morning with hot coffee and cocoa, and (b) descending on a diner on Route 36 afterward and consuming huge helpings of mashed potatoes and gravy. This was hard work, and if you don't believe it, try moving a full-length utility pole so you can put it in a position to cut it up.

On May 18, 1974 we had one of several work parties in the Fossil Beds. The Township installed the poles we cut, each mounted vertically to delineate the parking area, and they also had made raised beds for plantings. Some five dogwood trees were planted, as well as many bushes. It really looked fine when we had finished.

Well, like so many other work projects on public lands, the plantings deteriorated over time. The trees died over the next several years, the bushes were not maintained, and today there are few remnants of the nice landscaping we had provided. But the area still looks tidy and is given frequent use.

The Fossil Bed log cutting project in Belford, Saturday, November 10, 1973. Adults from left: Don Abrams, Jim Knowles, Lou Rissland. Photo: Pete Brady. I regret that the youths are unidentified.

Ken Albrecht at the Fossil Bed work party May 18, 1974. (Diane Lehder is in the background.)

A fossil hunt. This one was held Sept. 30, 1973. Frank and Lethe Lescinsky conducted many of these.

Normandy Park

At the start of 1978, the newspapers announced that funds had been received to construct the "Poricy Park Sports Complex." Huh? We asked John Campbell, then Parks and Recreation Director, about this and he told us that they planned to build this in the topland section which was part of the Fossil Beds acquisition. We had no problem with this except for the name, because for several years we had represented Poricy Park as a nature preserve. So, we asked John to pick another name, which he and the Recreation Advisory Committee did. That's how "Normandy Park" was created. It contains lighted courts today and is also used for summer evening concerts.

Having thus concluded our history of the acquisition of the Fossil Beds, we can turn our attention to the major sections of the park.

Where We Stood in August 1970

Nowhere. That's where the Township stood in August 1970 in acquiring land (with the exception of the Fossil Beds). But our organization had certainly been trying to make it happen.

In all of the flyers which we had mass-distributed throughout the Township, we had stressed the value of the area. We had also done a preliminary analysis of the revenue the land would produce from property taxes on houses vs the cost of leaving the land idle and not having to pay the cost of educating the school children.

On September 23, 1970, we issued 4,000 copies of a brochure, "Poricy Park: Here Today, Gone Tomorrow?" It had ten photographs and eight pages of text. We mentioned the land acquisition funds available from federal and state sources. And we asked the readers to write to the Township Committee.

It was of course the Township Committee that would have to act on this. They had to be *persuaded* to do it. Unlike the Sewerage Authority, which could be held accountable and challenged in courts, the Township Committee had to act on their own good will. And, they had to purchase the Gebhardt Farm, as we stated in the flyer:

"**Despite the worthwhile steps already taken toward preserving the Poricy area [Fossil Bed funding application and acquiring some very small tracts], the real hang-up in creating Poricy Park is the 90-acre Gebhardt Farm which occupies a key position in the center of the area. This farm is currently for sale, and consists of open fields completely isolated from the developed areas of the Township...[but] this concept of 'park' as an area that preserves a rural atmosphere is quite contrary to our present Township government's concept of the word... One official stated that 'The Gebhardt Farm is simply too large to develop and maintain.'"**

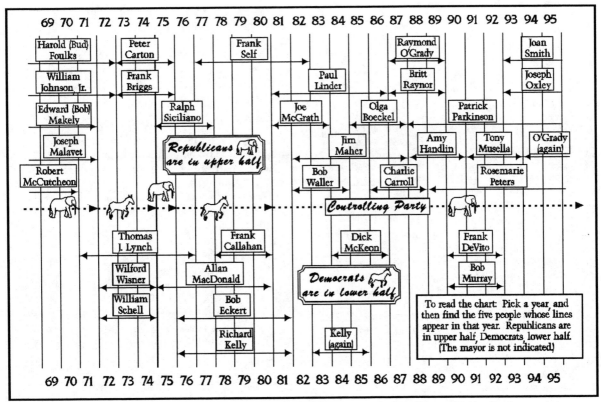

The following people are shown on the chart with their years of service:

69	70	71	72	73	74	75	76	77	78	79	80	81	82	83	84	85	86	87	88	89	90	91	92	93	94	95

Upper half (Republicans):
Harold (Bud) Foulks · Peter Carton · Frank Self · Raymond O'Grady · Joan Smith · William Johnson, Jr. · Frank Briggs · Paul Linder · Britt Raynor · Joseph Oxley · Edward (Bob) Makely · Ralph Siciliano · Joe McGrath · Olga Boeckel · Patrick Parkinson · Joseph Malavet · Jim Maher · Amy Handlin · Tony Musella · O'Grady (again) · Robert McCutcheon · Bob Waller · Charlie Carroll · Rosemarie Peters

Republicans are in upper half

Controlling Party

Lower half (Democrats):
Thomas J. Lynch · Frank Callahan · Dick McKeon · Frank DeVito · Wilford Wisner · Allan MacDonald · Bob Murray · William Schell · Bob Eckert · Richard Kelly · Kelly (again)

Democrats are in lower half

To read the chart: Pick a year, and then find the five people whose lines appear in that year. Republicans are in upper half, Democrats lower half. (The mayor is not indicated.)

The Middletown Township Committee Members During the Founding of Poricy Park

Those Darn Fossil Beds Again

We go back to January 1970 when we had urged acquisition of the land. The Township Committee said that they *were* acquiring the land, because hadn't they applied for funds to buy it? And, they thought that they had, because in their minds, and in the minds of many of the public, the Fossil Beds *were* Poricy Park, and our committee's efforts were focused only on that acquisition. We had to get everyone out of those beds and think *farm*.

That Infernal Sewer Line Again

And, the Township Committee, and many members of the public, were at first supporting the Sewerage Authority, and some thought that the PPCC's efforts to secure land was just a front to get people to back us in our battle to reroute the sewer line. We also had to get everyone out of the sewers!

A Chart of the Township Committee

Shown above is a chart indicating members of the Township Committee over a 27 year period.

Our walk through the "park" with the Township
Committee, Sat., Feb. 28, 1970. From left: Mayor "Bud"
Foulks, Committeemen Bob Makely and Bob McCutcheon, Hank Flanagan, and teachers Gloria Lehman and
Carol Moremen. There is also a view of several of the
decrepit buildings which were subsequently torn down,
but the barn was saved! (Also see photo on page 111.)

The Hike with the Township Committee

On Saturday, February 28, 1970 we managed to
persuade three of the five-member Township Committee to go on a tour of the proposed park area.
They are identified in the photo, as well as two of the
teachers that were with us. Not shown are two
other teachers: Steve Slovenz and John Dowling.[9]

The idea behind the hike was to get the *teachers*
to conduct it. As Hank put it, "Tell them what you
tell the kids. Don't hammer away at the value of the
area. Instead, tell them what they're looking at, and
try to get them to appreciate it and even enjoy it.

"And, above all," Hank told us all ahead of time,
"There are two words I don't want to hear today:
fossils and *sewers*."

Chrys Flanagan prepared a lunch in their home,
and I recall that two of the Committee members
attended it. It was a nice day, a nice walk, and I
think almost completely nonconfrontational. It also

---

[9] I was there too, but it was my fate to appear rarely
in early photos since I was usually the photographer.

wasn't very effective. As Dwight Richardson put it
several months later, what the Township Committee
wanted most of all from us was to go away.

And, it was the following Friday that Mayor
Foulks showed up at the Water Policy hearing and
testified as a witness for the Sewerage Authority, as
previously described on page 18.

Hikes, Bumper Stickers, Petitions

But we didn't go away. We continued to
conduct public hikes through the area, perhaps four
a year, we distributed bumper stickers, and in April
1970 we circulated petitions.

I remember going into one neighborhood on a
Sunday afternoon with Diane Lehder to get petition
signatures. I took one part of the neighborhood and
she took the other. After perhaps an hour, we met
and decided "The hell with it," and went home. It
was not a good experience. People were naturally
defensive when a stranger rang their doorbell. They
had never heard of Poricy Park. Some had mean
dogs. Some didn't have to have dogs to be mean.

Well, at the Township Committee meeting on
Tuesday, June 23 we presented the petitions to the
Township Committee. There were 2,000 signatures,
so this will give you an idea of how many of us were
involved at this time. Friends, children, lots of
people helped.

The presentation was a mildly stiff occasion. We
were still locked in battle with the Sewerage
Authority; the settlement was a month away and
was still in doubt. The committee's response was
simple: "We already have 21 parks." (You can finish
the thought — "We don't need another.")

And then there was Ben Schaffer, the director of
Parks and Recreation, at the Planning Board meeting
on Monday, August 3. He didn't make a public
statement, but we spoke with him after the meeting.
His response was that "The Gebhardt Farm is far too
much land for the Commission to hold idle."

Bob Makely and Brady's Pipe Dream

But we were making some slight headway. Committeeman Bob Makely, who had attended our February walk, was an acquaintance of the Risslands and Marcia persuaded him to meet with us in her home on Friday, June 19, 1970. Bob had discussed getting grants for land with Dick Seuffert, the Township Administrator. At our meeting, Bob made the point that we had done some things that had offended the Township Committee and that we should be more moderate in our approach, lest we lose ground. I remember responding that "How can we lose ground when we're already on the floor on our backs?" Dwight discussed public education and the possibility of summer programs. The meeting was cordial, but it was just another small step toward selling the Committee.

A day or so later, Bob Makely called up Marcia. As Marcia frequently recounted the conversation, "Marcia, I know you're all trying to do something nice for the Township, but you're pushing too hard. Tell Pete Brady that he's asking for too much, and that the Gebhardt Farm is a pipe dream."

Hank's Resignation

On Sunday, August 23, 1970 Hank came over to my house and, without any preliminary social remarks, said to me "Pete, I am resigning from the Poricy Park Citizens Committee." He handed me a handwritten draft of his resignation letter, which we revised slightly, and then I typed it up and mailed it to the twenty-or-so current members of the PPCC. Here are the relevant paragraphs:

> The PPCC has, since its formation, done far more than just move a sewer line. It has alerted the Township to the value in the Poricy area, it has helped establish conservation as a real force in the Township, and even has caused the Township to become seriously interested in acquiring the Boy Scout Tract. Much work remains, though, in other undeveloped land not only in Poricy, but also elsewhere in the Township.

> I am sorry to say, however, that theses efforts have resulted in a tremendous deterioration of my personal affairs, which must be put in order. I therefore feel I must resign from the PPCC. The PPCC is endowed with able personnel and will ably continue its work without me. I therefore feel that my departure will not seriously hurt the work of the committee.

> My interests are still directed toward civic affairs, and in fact, I have been elected president of the River Plaza Civic Association, which has just been formed and is in considerable need of help...

Over the next year, several people asked me why Hank resigned. If there was a hidden reason, I never learned it. I know that I never suggested it to him, nor did I want him to resign. But at this time, the committee was heading in a new direction, that of acquiring land, and we were beginning to negotiate to purchase the Cotton Tract. Hank and I both saw an immense amount of work ahead, and I don't think this is what Hank would be able to personally invest in for the next many years. I remember his remark to me that night in August: "It's going to be uphill all the way."

We called a meeting for the following Thursday. Hank and I felt that Dwight Richardson was the obvious choice as our next chairman. Marcia replaced Gayle Richardson as treasurer, and I remained as secretary. We never dealt formally with Hank again except in a few skirmishes with the Sewerage Authority, but we remained good friends.

Hank's Paid Newspaper Letter

Hank and many others were upset over the way some things were going on in the Township. On Thursday, October 29, Hank printed a full-page letter at his expense in the *Courier*. It was reprinted the next day in the *Register* with the heading, "Paid as a Public Service by Middletown Democrats." There was nothing subtle in this letter. It was done entirely on his own; at least, the PPCC had no hand in promoting it. It is reproduced in part on the next page.

(As it appeared in the *Courier*, October 29, 1970)

To Citizens of Middletown:

One cannot become involved in the affairs of Middletown Township to any extent without having awakened in him a deep concern for the future of our community. Events of just the last two weeks should be sufficient to awaken the same concern in any Middletown resident. Three are cited:

1. October 21, 1970, learning of the alleged damage to the Poricy Fossil Beds as cited by the Conservation Commission, Mayor Harold H. Foulks stated "Why don't people call me when these things come up?"
   Fact: [At this point Hank recounted the numerous times people did contact the Mayor, and continued with] Not only did the Township Committee ignore the pleadings of Middletown Citizens but when these citizens turned for help at the State level the Mayor, appearing on behalf of the Township Committee, appeared in Trenton and testified against the citizens.

2. In a recent campaign speech, Robert McCutcheon, incumbent committeeman, stated that the federal government recommended an ultimate goal of 600 acres of parkland and open space in our Township. [Hank then quoted the figure stated by the National Park and Recreation Association of 3,000 acres.]

3. The missing Township funds. [Here, Hank cited a well-publicized scandal of missing Township funds, involving Mr. Schotte, president of the now defunct Eatontown National Bank, in whose desk the F.B.I. had discovered a note with the words "Middletown $55,000." This money had apparently bypassed the Township's treasurer's office.]

Hank concluded his letter by endorsing Tom Lynch for Township Committee and urging all to vote for him. As part of his credentials included at the bottom of the letter, Hank is identified as "founder and past chairman of Middletown's Poricy Park Citizens Committee."

Bud Foulks' Reaction

There isn't much room for ambiguity in that letter. As I previously pointed out, if you look carefully at what Bud Foulks stated in Trenton, he was not really testifying against the citizens, but he was indeed the Authority's witness.

A year later, Bud had become a strong advocate of our cause and a friend of Dwight. He confided in Dwight, "I was really beginning to come over to your side and to promote the park, and then I saw Henry Flanagan's letter. At that point, I said to myself, 'P--- on Poricy Park.'"

The Township's Position in Sept. 1970

Here is where the Township stood in September:

- The Township Committee: "We already have 21 parks."
- Mayor Foulks: "P--- on Poricy Park."
- Committeeman Bob Makely: "The Gebhardt Farm is a pipe dream."
- Committeeman Bob McCutcheon: "I don't know where we are going to get the money and we can't afford that project at this time." (At the Oak Hill Assn. September 22 and the River Plaza Civic Assn. October 14.)
- Ben Schaffer, Director, Parks and Recreation: "The farm is too much land to hold idle."
- Recreation Commission: "We could not even consider development of this park for the next ten years." (*Register*, 11/25/1969) Further, a member of the Commission had privately told Hank that they would not develop a tract that contained a significant body of water.

It didn't look very hopeful. But, we did have a few things going for us. Just a few.

The Cotton Tract

Acquiring the Cotton Tract was not just a good move. It was also a *necessary* move. With 20-20 hindsight, I believe that had we not acquired the Cotton Tract, Poricy Park would not exist today. The Fossil Beds might have been acquired, but the Gebhardt Farm would be covered with houses.

The Nature Conservancy

Our first contact with The Nature Conservancy was when I called them on March 16, 1970 for general information about their organization. At that time, they were still relatively unknown and had been involved thus far with saving only two tracts in New Jersey.[10] They had only their national office in Arlington, VA, but they did have representatives in different areas. I had called them for information on saving land, and asked what it would take for them to acquire our parkland, especially the farm. Their policy at that time was that they purchased land only to hold it for a short time so they could then turn it over to another agency. And, they would have to be reimbursed.

Since then, The Nature Conservancy has established regional offices and they even hold some parcels and operate nature centers. But not in 1970.

So, this did not seem promising.

Our Walk with E. Leigh Cotton

But then, in early summer we looked again at the undeveloped tracts in "Poricy Park" and thought that we might be able to acquire the 14-acre Cotton Tract. Dwight set up a meeting in late July with the owner of the property, E. Leigh Cotton.

The Cotton Tract, January 2, 1971.

Cotton was 73 years old in 1970, when he told us he was "too old to retire." He had bought his farm on Nut Swamp Road in 1934. His father had worked for Mrs. Payne Whitney, at Greentree Stable, where Christian Brothers Academy in Lincroft stands today. Cotton had always worked with horses and was a jockey in California at 12 years old.

---

[10] The first two were William Hutcheson Memorial Forest, Somerset County (1955), and Valhalla Hemlock Glen, Morris County (1968). The Cotton Tract was the third (1971). There were 66 in NJ as of December 2004.

Frank Lescinsky with E. Leigh Cotton and his sister Vera Cotton at Cotton's home, December 10, 1970 when we interviewed him about the history of his property.

During World War II, the Navy had taken some of his property to build the ammunition road. (See map facing page 1.) He still had farm property along Nut Swamp Road between the Navy Road and the tract labeled "Nurseries 33 acres" on the map. The Navy Road had made the back 14 acres inaccessible; you had to go through the McLean Orchard (now Colts Glen) to get to it. So, Cotton never used the "back 14." In 1962, Cotton sold the land around him for the Cotton Ridge development, but retained his home and the back property.

In early August we walked through the back 14 acres with Leigh Cotton. We were very impressed with the tract, because it contained several kinds of terrain. It included marshland, topland, and banks. It would be a nice teaching tool for nature.

At that time, undeveloped land in Middletown was going for about $5,000 per acre. (The Board of Education had just purchased a nursery as a site for High School South for $4,500 per acre.) We had, of course, told Cotton ahead of time that we were interested in buying his property but had not discussed a price. On the walk, we finally asked him how much he wanted.

"Well, the Township has it assessed for seven, but you can have it for five."

I remember afterward talking with Frank Lescinsky, and we had both done the same thing. We mentally multiplied 14 acres by $5,000 to arrive at $70,000. A tall order, but maybe we could somehow do it. But then Cotton continued to talk about land values, and it became clear that the price he stated was not per acre, but *$5,000 total*!

The Option

Early next week I made an appointment with Herbert Hiller, The Nature Conservancy's New Jersey representative, to tour the site with us on August 21. He told us that we needed to get a lawyer to represent his organization, and then to get an option for the property. On his word, the Conservancy could approve this without a Board vote if it was for less than $50,000. They would then loan us the funds for the closing, unless we could raise the amount ahead of time. Further, The Nature Conservancy had no trouble dealing with small parcels. They recognized the value of saving small tracts of open space.

The Nature Conservancy was a blessing to us:

- They would hold the property themselves and take responsibility for insurance and other administrative measures.
- They were a nonprofit organization and could accept tax-deductible gifts for the property.
- They were a national, recognized organization and would bring prestige to the effort.

Dan O'Hern agreed to be our attorney. On September 9, 1970, The Nature Conservancy signed an option to purchase the 14-acre property. We immediately sent out a press release.

This purchase was the major turning point in both the public and political acceptance of our cause. The results were not immediate, but several things happened in the next few months to signal that things were changing.

Editorial: The *Daily Register*, September 14, 1970

Poricy Park Project Moves

Middletown Township – and indeed, all of Monmouth County – will have acquired a valuable asset when the Poricy Brook area becomes public property. We say "when" rather than "if" because the enterprise and determination of the Poricy Park Citizens Committee strongly indicate that the park will become a reality.

Having won its fight to keep the township sewer line out of the bank of Poricy Brook, the committee is not sitting back on its laurels. Its action last week in taking a purchase option on 14 of the 300 acres sought for the park is the kind of overt effort that will keep the project alive and moving....

[Two paragraphs omitted here.]

Purchase of the tract should – as the PPCC points out – demonstrate to the Township Committee the sincerity of area citizens' desire to make Poricy Park a reality. The Cotton Tract would be the first portion of the park acquired for public use.

The Poricy Park group is to be commended on its objectives and its efforts to date. It deserves the support of township residents and officials, and all the rest of us who stand to share the benefits of its foresight and its enterprise.

Raising the Funds

We announced that we were now receiving donations to purchase the Cotton Tract.

The funds did not come pouring in. However, an early contribution came from the East Keansburg Betterment Association (now North Middletown), which is about as far away from the park area as you can get in Middletown. We highlighted this contribution in press releases to address the occasional criticism we were receiving that this was just a park for the Oak Hill Area.

In late November we received a very significant contribution, not so much because it was $500 (very helpful, indeed), but more important, because the donor was Bill Johnson, Jr., a member of the Township Committee.

But we needed more to achieve our goal, which was $5,000 for the land and, we figured, perhaps another $2,000 to handle closing costs and miscellaneous expenses. By early November we had received only $2,500 in contributions.

One day, I stopped by Marcia's house on the way home from work. She was our treasurer at the time, and we went over the funds trying to figure out how to raise the balance. We thought, "Those funds are on people's dressers in loose change. Could we do it with $5 and $10 amounts? How do we get people to part with relatively small amounts?"

MIDDLETOWN OFFICE

KEANSBURG-MIDDLETOWN NATIONAL BANK

MIDDLETOWN, N.J.

November 27, 1970

Poricy Park Citizens Committee

The Keansburg-Middletown National Bank is always ready to help all organizations in projects that affect the improvement and preservation of our community. With that thought in mind I am indeed happy to enclose herewith our check in the amount of $500 and hope that your project is a huge success.

Very truly yours,
(Signed) William C. Johnson, Jr.
Executive Vice President

A Bottle of Good Scotch

So, we distributed 1100 copies of the letter shown above to the River Plaza and Oak Hill area.

The response was impressive. About 200 contributions came in the range from $2 to $250 with the median being $10. I guess the bottle of Scotch at $10 set the standard.

And, I <u>know</u> you have had fun with the prices for those items. But, for verification, in 1963, when I was dating Cathy who lived in New York City, we had Sunday dinner in Lüchows on several occasions.

Handing the Cotton Tract deed to the Township on December 14, 1971. From left: Lynden Kibler, Chair, Middletown Conservation Commission; Dwight Richardson, Chair, PPCC; Mayor Harold ("Bud") Foulks; Committeeman Edward ("Bob") Makely.

The 7-course dinner was $4.95. (Alas, both Lüchows and the 7-course $4.95 dinner are long gone.)

By February 1971 we had raised $6,779, which was more than enough to cover costs for The Nature Conservancy. They held a balance for us of $1,262. (More on that balance in a few chapters later.)

The Nature Conservancy closed on the property in early 1971, and the Cotton Tract was conveyed to the Township in a ceremony in December 1971. The property has deed restrictions such that if it is over-developed with structures and, in essence, not left in its natural condition, it will revert to the Nature Conservancy.

The Significance of the Cotton Tract

It often happens that people donate land for public parkland. But it is extremely rare that citizens raise funds through public subscription and donate the land to their local government. I believe that the fact that this happened at all, plus the magnitude of the involvement (200 contributors) had a major impact on our government officials.

George Fricke: His Map and His Mill

Gayle Richardson at Thorne Middle School in May 1971 with the map made by George Fricke.

We take a break from our narrative and describe the unusual career of one of our volunteers.

George and Catherine Fricke lived on Wilson Avenue in New Monmouth, and George got involved in Poricy Park in its first year. In July 1970, George agreed to make a large map of the Poricy Park area on plywood to be put on an easel, which could be set up as a display. He did a fine job and the map was used for many years.

George had a job in Newark, which involved chemicals as I recall. He had to take the first train out of Middletown every morning just after 6 am.

Around 1974, he had a dramatic change of life. He sold all he had and purchased a nearly defunct mill in the tiny crossroads of Harmony, Maine, and moved to nearby Cambridge, Maine.

The mill, operating since 1821, is reputed to be the oldest woolen spinning mill in America. I saw the mill in 1977, after George had worked on it 12 hours a day, seven days a week for about two years. It was called Bartlett Mills and is now renowned for making specialty yarn of very fine quality.

Its chief feature was a *mule spinner*, a building-wide contraption holding perhaps 100 spindles, which rolls back and forth, each spindle operating much like a simple drop spindle. George said that he believed it to be the only such machine in use in our country at the time. In 1996, my wife and I saw a nearly identical mule spinner in commercial operation at Trefriw Mills in northern Wales.

Cathy Brady with David, Stephen, and Jeremy watch George Fricke demonstrate the mule spinner.

Cathy Brady and George Fricke at his mill, July 1977.

The Commitment to Buy the Farm

Poricy Park got a lot of publicity in 1970, at first from the sewer battle, and in early fall, from our option to purchase the Cotton Tract. I really do think the bumper stickers helped too. (You can forget about the petitions.) I think the Township Committee was beginning to take us seriously.

The McCutcheon/Lynch 1970 Election

For several years prior to 1970, it was assumed that whoever ran on the Republican ticket would get elected to the 5-member Township Committee. In 1969, just as the PPCC was getting started, Bud Foulks and Bill Johnson were easily reelected. The terms are for three years. For each of two consecutive years two seats come up, and on the third, one seat is available. 1970 was that third year for one seat. Bob McCutcheon was running for reelection.

Our committee was determined to stay away from endorsing anyone. We realized that we had to work with whomever won. Hank, as I described earlier, printed a full-page endorsement of the Democratic candidate Thomas J. Lynch. He did this on his own, but it was right after he left the PPCC and it appeared to some that he was representing us.

Tom Lynch was a friendly down-to-earth man who worked, I recall, at Western Electric. He took a favorable interest in our project and attended one of our hikes.

The election was a stunning defeat for the Republicans. Tom Lynch defeated Bob McCutcheon 9560 to 6159. This, for a town that had routinely elected Republicans. It wasn't even close.

As reported in the *Courier*, the Republicans gave two reasons for the defeat: sewer construction, and the Eatontown Bank scandal involving a township government official who was alleged to have taken Township funds and used them for personal purposes.

I think the Poricy Park issue may have cost the Republicans some votes, but not enough to swing the election. Our problems with the sewer line made the front page several times, but people didn't need us to be concerned with sewers. People were personally involved with the sewer installation all over town because easements were being sought everywhere, and nearly everyone would have to pay for a plumber to install a hookup to the system..

Bob McCutcheon practically made his opposition to purchasing the Gebhardt Farm a plank in his campaign platform, repeating his statement that the Township could not afford it and he would not support it. This might have cost him a few votes, but again, not enough to make the difference.

The election contained a sad event. Bob McCutcheon was suddenly taken ill right before the election and died soon afterward. He never lived to see the Gebhardt Farm purchased by the Township and saved from being developed for housing. But a developer named a street in a housing development near Poricy Park after him: McCutcheon Court.

Fund Raising with Personal Contacts

During fall 1970, members of our committee visited several people on fund-raising calls to see if we could get some significant contributions. We were going beyond the $10 bottle of Scotch.

We were helped enormously by Stanton Whitney who, with his wife Janet, lived on Cooper Road. The Whitneys were dedicated conservationists and proved to be crucial to our success. I recall Dwight, Marcia, and me visiting the Whitneys when Stan would write down lists of people he knew we might call for an appointment. We could use his name.

Some of the visits went nowhere, but some were memorable. Here are two of my favorites.

Williamson Thomas and Sergei Rachmaninoff

On a beautiful Saturday morning in October 1970, Dwight and I went to see Williamson Thomas. He lived on Locust Point Road in a house that was right next to Clay Pit Creek, which is an inlet from the Navesink River. It remains one of the prettiest houses I have ever been in.

Thomas told us that the house was a hotel in the early 1930s, and for a brief interval, Sergei Rachmaninoff stayed there and invited friends, many with musical talents, to visit him. Thomas had heard that informal concerts were given there.[11]

Williamson Thomas became a regular supporter of Poricy Park, but I remember him best for the very nice visit we had with him.

Don't run over the flowers!

We generally went out in pairs to visit people. Most visits did yield contributions, although not always large. The visits were usually successful because if people were not interested in contributing, they generally refused the request to see them. Such refusals were common enough, but we just kept at it.

Carl Peterson was unknown to me before this whole thing started. I contacted him after he had written what I felt was an effective letter to a newspaper endorsing this project. He later agreed to join our personal contact visits.

I had arranged to visit a woman in late afternoon and I brought Carl with me. I drove. Her house had a circular driveway lined on the inside and outside edges with flowers. As I entered the driveway, Carl said, "Pete, don't run over the flowers."

The visit did not go well. Our hostess was clearly not impressed with our project, and it appeared that she generally did not give to causes. I wondered why she agreed to see us.

Our visit was over and we got into my car. As we started to move outward on her driveway, Carl said, "*Now* you can run over the flowers."

---

[11] This was the New Amsterdam Hotel. A photograph of it appears on p. 107 in *Middletown Township, the Old Photograph Series*, © 1994 by Randall Gabrielan, Alan Sutton, publishers.

The Visit with Bob Stanley

One of the names Stanton Whitney gave us was that of Robert C. Stanley, Jr. Dwight Richardson and Lou Rissland arranged to visit him at his home on Navesink River Road in early November 1970.

Had we had the slightest knowledge of politics and civic affairs, we would have immediately known who Bob Stanley was. He was very active in the Republican Party, but is probably best remembered today for the significant work he did in developing the Monmouth Medical Center in Long Branch. Lou and Dwight knew little or none of this when they visited Bob.

Lou and Dwight asked for, and got, a contribution for the Cotton Tract, but they stressed our desire to acquire the Gebhardt Farm and establish a park.

According to Lou, Bob was candid about his frustration with the local Republicans. He felt that they had lost touch with the people, and were blind to the benefits of a project such as Poricy Park. Bob said he would help as much as he could, and he would write to several people he knew in government and politics and get them behind this project.

At that time, Dwight was chairman of our committee. Bob asked Dwight to draft the letter that he would sign. After whatever modifications Bob would make, he would send it out.

I did see Dwight's letter once, and I regret that I did not make a copy of it. Dwight doesn't have a copy either. Neither of us saw the final letter that Bob sent out nor does either of us know who received it. But it was very effective. This is, of course, speculation, but one of the recipients might have been Bill Johnson, Jr., of the Keansburg Middletown Bank, who sent us his contribution in late November. I think, however, that Bob's letter had a far greater benefit than stimulating contributions. I believe it was the single key that unlocked government resistance to acquiring the land for Poricy Park, and in the next section I will show why I believe that.

Our Meeting with Joe Azzolina

In early January 1971 Dwight and I went to see Joe Azzolina. Again, we were not acquainted with him, but we were told he had some influence with the people in local government and might be able to help us.

We met Joe at his home on Borden Road early on a Sunday evening. Neither Dwight, Joe, nor I today remember the reason we went to see him! It may have involved some difficulties we were having with the sewer line installation. But it doesn't matter today, because that was not the significant part of the meeting.

We sat in a tight circle in Joe's living room and made our case for whatever we wanted, and we were ready to leave. Joe stood up and asked, "What are you guys drinking?" "Huh?" "I'm offering you a drink. What will you have?"

I don't remember what he poured, but after we all were settled again in our chairs, Joe said, "Now, what do you guys want?" One of us restated the problem that we had brought with us, but Joe interrupted: "No, I don't mean that. What are your long-term plans for your entire project?"

We were there for almost another hour. We went over each of the tracts in the area and explained what was in them and their value as a nature preserve and teaching tool. We had, by that time, detailed cost projections of acquisition and development, and we also had cost comparisons with providing schools should the area go to houses. We talked about the New Jersey Green Acres program; the 1961 funds had long been exhausted but another bond issue was being considered for the coming November (1971). Joe was a NJ State Assemblyman at the time, and he said he would make some contacts at the state and local levels and see what he could do.

Green Acres

Before proceeding with this account, it is worthwhile to clarify what we mean by *Green Acres*.

The term "Green Acres" is used colloquially to refer to any dedicated open space, but I am going to use the formal definition here. New Jersey had a special Green Acres fund which was obtained from periodic bond issues, and which was used for open space acquisition and development of both state and local lands. If a property was obtained through Green Acres assistance, it could have a sign put up on the property that indicated that. There are restrictions on what can be done with the property, such as what percent of the land can be built upon.

Thus, as we will see, the Gebhardt Farm became a Green Acres site, but the Cotton Tract is not, because no Green Acres funds went into it.

The Green Acres Division of the NJ Department of Environmental Protection has a web site showing the nine bonding referenda passed from 1961 through 1995. In 1998, voters approved a referendum creating a stable source of funds for preservation, thus supplanting the Green Acres bonding program.

The early Green Acres bond issues which are relevant to this story are:

- 1961. $60 million. This had been exhausted.
- 1971. $80 million, of which $40 million was for local land acquisition.
- 1974. $200 million, of which $100 million was for local acquisition and development.

The Letters that Joe Azzolina Wrote

On January 21, 1971, Joe wrote to Joseph Barba, Deputy Commissioner DEP, and asked about pending applications for Green Acres from Middletown Township. I am quoting this letter here because it indicates a major new direction in our local government's position toward land preservation.

January 21, 1971
Joseph Barba, Deputy Commissioner
Department of Environmental Protection
Dear Joe:

Can you please let me know what Green Acres applications are pending for Middletown Township?

I am enclosing the attached brochure, "Poricy Park: Here Today... Gone Tomorrow?" This is an example of citizens who are actively trying to improve their environment.

The Poricy Park Citizens Committee (PPCC) have done their homework and their views deserve serious consideration. The PPCC has had a series of significant accomplishments during the past fifteen months. They have succeeded in the courts against a Sewerage Authority to cause them to reroute a planned sewer line and thus save more than 2500 trees. During this past year they have alerted a large segment of the population to the need to further conserve the Poricy area. Their commitment to purchase for the Township one of the tracts of land in the threatened area with citizens contributions is a unique and forceful expression of the will of the people. The many letters received from the public, recognition from national conservation groups, and editorial support from all local newspapers demonstrate a broad base of support that should not be ignored.

I'm becoming more and more convinced that conservation is the politics of the future. I, too, am extremely interested in the preservation of open space and conservation in the Poricy area of Middletown.

I would appreciate any information about what the state is willing to and can do to help preserve this area and also what can be done on the federal level.
Sincerely,
Joseph Azzolina

On February 9, 2005 I discussed this letter with Joe. He agreed that he could not, on his own, have composed all of it because there are too many detailed references to events of 1970, and also because there was an enclosure of our brochure of September 1970. He must have gotten the brochure from us,

maybe even from me. And, I suspect, much of the content of the middle paragraphs might have come from Bob Stanley (and originally, Dwight). Bob Stanley knew Joe well in those days, and Joe would have been a near certain recipient of Bob's letter.

I also do not remember receiving a copy of Joe's letter; I just recently found it buried in my files. And, along with that letter was another Joe wrote, this time on March 30 to the Township Committee. I will quote a portion of this one:

March 30, 1971
Members of the Middletown Township Committee
[Three paragraphs omitted.]

It appears very likely that a 50 million dollar Green Acres Bond Issue will appear on the ballot in November. [It actually became $80 million.]

Therefore, I suggest, if you have not already done so, and if there is considerable interest by the Township Committee in acquiring the Gebhardt Farm, the committee should file the necessary applications as quickly as possible for the Gebhardt Farm and any other tracts of land in the Poricy Brook area.

As I understand it, the applications are filed in numerical order as received. I have also been informed when new Green Acres monies become available, the applications will be processed in the order they are received....
Very truly yours,
Joseph Azzolina

The Resolution of Intent to Purchase

At the time, we knew nothing of these letters, and we were just plugging away with our hikes and publicity and looking into the Colts Glen development application (which turned out to be a major effort). Out of habit, several of us attended the Township Committee meeting on April 13, 1971. We were stunned during the meeting when the Committee passed a resolution of intent to purchase the Gebhardt Farm!

Poricy Park When It Was Fun

The London Branch of the PPCC

Marcia kept a folder labeled "Poricy Park When It Was Fun," into which she tossed an occasional item. The folder contains items almost exclusively

Martin Davies and Brian Champness, members of the London Branch of the PPCC, stage a demonstration in London, June 1971. Note bumper sticker. This photo appeared on the front page of the July 11, 1971 *Register*.

from the first 15 years of our involvement. One item is the story of the London Branch of the PPCC.

Brian Champness was on the staff of University College London doing work in speech research, as I was doing at Bell Labs. Brian came over to the United States to work on a special project for a few months, and we became good friends.

Brian took a keen interest in Poricy Park. He went on one of our hikes and attended some Township Committee meetings. He was sitting with us when they announced their intent to purchase the Gebhardt Farm.

When he was returning to England, he asked if he could do anything to thank us for our hospitality. We said, "Yes. Organize a London Branch of the PPCC and stage and photograph a public demonstration. Be sure the photo makes it obvious that you took it in England." Thus, the photo at left.

The *Register* shortly thereafter published the letter below. And, years later in December 1980, Brian and his family visited the Nature Center.

Derby Road, South Woodford, London E 18
To the Editor:

The members of the London Branch of the Poricy Park Citizens Committee were most excited to find our pictures on the front page of the newspaper – and an American newspaper at that! In our demonstrations for Poricy Park, we attracted considerable interest and comments from people who were concerned with conservation and ecology.

We are pleased to hear from our colleagues in Middletown that Poricy Park is as healthy as ever and we wish all residents every success with their future park.

The Middletown PPCC has also sent us the entire front page of the July 11 Daily Register, which we have put on prominent display on a bulletin board, where it continues to attract much attention.

Yours faithfully, Brian Champness
President, PPCC (London Branch)

Following the defeat of the Republicans in fall 1970, the Democrats and other candidates could smell blood. It made for an interesting year.

Alice Maxwell, Raine & Murphy

In those days, the *ADvisor* was a free weekly newspaper tossed on driveways, and Alice Maxwell was one of their writers. She was often interesting, and she tried to print dirt whenever she could find it.

On May 3, 1971 we had a particularly difficult evening at the Planning Board meeting. (You'll hear about that later.) The discussion continued in the hallway outside of the Town Hall meeting room.

Dwight and I were standing among a small crowd of people and were approached by a woman we did not know. "I'm Alice Maxwell, and I'm a reporter, and I'm determined to get to the bottom of your organization."

"What do you mean?"

"You people say you're trying to make a park, but someone is sponsoring you and has other goals."

"No, all we want is to have things done right in forming Poricy Park."

"Well, I happen to know that the Haskells once owned one of the tracts next to the pond." (Which was true; they owned the "Boy Scout Tract" (see map in front) and had given it to the Boy Scouts to sell it.) "Someone told me that BLAA–anche Haskell wants to get something out of this. I'll bet that BLAA–anche is funding your group." (I can't do justice here to the way she pronounced "Blanche.")

"We don't know Blanche Haskell."

"I'll just bet you don't. I think she's behind this and she is using you. I'm going to get to the bottom of this." And, in a voice that could be heard over to the next county, "I SMELL A RAT!!!"

After Alice left our presence, I asked Dwight, "What was that all about?" "I don't know, but I'll bet we haven't heard the end of this."

And we hadn't. But before I continue, I will say who Blanche Haskell was, which I found out only in 2005 when I was doing research for this book. She was the widow of Amory Haskell, Sr., and she owned "Woodland Farms," which people commonly referred to as "The Haskell Estate," a large tract in the center of Middletown. The property was used for an annual "Hunt," a horse race to benefit charity. There was (and still is) concern that it would be turned into a town house development. (Blanche eventually sold the property, but it still remains intact.)

Walter Raine and John Murphy were two independent and aggressive candidates who had entered the race for Township Committee. One of them called Dwight, referred to our encounter with Alice Maxwell, and asked if we would come to see them at Murphy's home.

At the meeting, they went on the attack. They were convinced that we weren't what we said we were and that we had some kind of force behind us. "You people are much too professional. We've never seen a local bumper sticker campaign so effective. You hand out professionally-printed flyers all over town, and they must be expensive to produce. And the school presentations (see prior photo of Gayle Richardson at Thorne). If we knew you were doing that, we'd have gone to the Board of Education and had you stopped, because you're using the schools to further your political agenda."

We spent the next 45 minutes going over our finances, telling them about our $80 mimeograph machine, our work with government agencies. They finally were mollified and agreed to leave us alone and to get Alice Maxwell off our backs.

In November, Murphy and Raine came in 5th and 6th in the six-way race for two seats. Democrats Will Wisner and Bill Schell won, and incumbents Bob Makely and Joe Malavet were out of office.

The McLean Orchard, circa 1962, taken from a point above the Fairview Cemetery and looking SW toward Thompson Junior High School (now Middle School) in upper right hand corner. The McLean farmhouse and pond is in the center. (A photograph of the farmhouse appears on p. 37 of Vol. I of *Middletown Township* © by Randall Gabrielan, 1994.) The farmhouse was demolished to make room for the Colts Glen development. The outline of E. Leigh Cotton's "back 14-acres" is clearly delineated toward right center , adjacent to the Naval Ammunition Road. Poricy Brook (actually, Poricy Marsh) meanders along the back of the orchards with its banks intact, supporting large trees on each side. The entrance to the Gebhardt Farm is at lower left, and is so narrow that it has a separate set of railroad crossing lights. (At that time, there were only lights, not gates at this crossing.) Later, the Township will acquire the lower left corner of the orchard and make that the entrance to the farm. See key map on next page for identification of certain landmarks.

The Battle of Colts Glen

The *Daily Register*, Friday, January 27, 1967

Historic Orchards Sold for Housing

The McLean Orchards Estate, 126 acres located on Oak Hill Road, has been purchased by Johnstowne Building Corporation, of which John L. Fitzgerald of Rumson is president, for a subdivision of quality and distinctive homes....

The large farmhouse was the location of the film about Helen Keller, "The Miracle Worker."

McLean Orchards was one of the few farms in New Jersey which has been owned by the same family for more than 200 years and in continuous use for farming. It was originally owned by Joseph Stillwell, great-great uncle of Edith McLean and the late Sydney McLean. The farm is part of an original 500-acre estate owned by Mr. Stillwell, extending from Route 35 on both sides of Oak Hill Road to Middletown-Lincroft Road.

On the back of the farm ran Poricy Brook which emptied into the Navesink River. On this brook in 1720 was built the second grist mill in Middletown. The Lenape Indians paddled up the brook in their canoes to have their corn ground into meal.

In the year 1776, English records show that the British fleet blockading New York harbor sent small boats of light draft up Poricy Brook to the Stillwell mill to buy their meal and flour. Mr. Stillwell, at the point of a gun, was forced to hand over the meal. Loyal as he was to the colonies, he found it difficult to help the enemy.

Through the years the McLeans have found many Indian relics to show that the land around here was well-covered by Indians. They found different colored arrow heads and tomahawks. Near the brook were found mounds of oyster shells, indicating that the Indians must have come up Poricy Brook to feast on oysters which they brought with them from the Navesink River.

Additional information regarding McLean Orchards can be found in "Ellis History," a historical journal.

A few pages ago we left the Gebhardt Farm in the hands of the Township, which had passed a resolution of intent to purchase it. The actual deed transfer would not occur for another 2½ years, and in the meanwhile, several other things would happen. So, we will return to the farm later.

When we sat in Town Hall in April 1971 and heard the Township Committee pass their resolution, we had no idea that we were about to enter a battle similar to the one we had with the Sewerage Authority. We would need an attorney, engage in several formal hearings before Township bodies, and end up in court in Freehold. Several local, state, and federal agencies would get dragged into this. And it was nearly all because of one man – Frank Blaisdell.

But I'm getting ahead of the story.

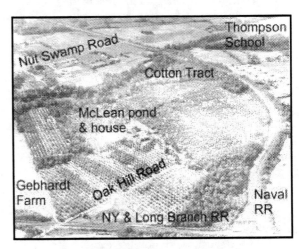

Key map to the photo on previous page.

John Allison and Clausland Mountain

In 1970, during my contacts with The Nature Conservancy, they recommended we talk with John Allison of Rockland County, NY. He was involved with a citizens' project to save Clausland Mountain and had mustered support to raise funds, generate publicity, and do all those great things.

Dwight and I arranged to meet John for lunch in a restaurant in northern New Jersey on October 30, 1970. John gave us several useful pointers for saving land, but Dwight and I always remembered and often repeated this quote from him: "You will get your strongest support – and your strongest <u>opposition</u> – from the people that live closest to your park."

John was half correct. The part about the opposition. Our support came from people over a wide area, including some close to the site, but not in greater amounts than from the rest of the town. (The major exception was the essential support from people close to the brook in dealing with the Sewerage Authority during our first year.) We'll soon get to the opposition from those close to the park.

An Early Meeting with the Developer

On January 21, 1971, Frank Lescinsky and I met with John Fitzgerald and Bob Sharkey in the model home at the Colts Glen housing development. They were the managers of the Johnstowne Building Corporation. They told us that they had discussed purchasing the Gebhardt Farm with Jack Cavanaugh, the owner of the farm, but that they knew we were interested in creating a park, and maybe they could reserve a strip of land for us along the top of the bank at the bottom edge of the farm.

No, we replied, we're not interested in a strip of land. We want the whole farm.

This was not music to their ears, but it turns out that we were about to become a more immediate problem for them.

Bernie Finan of Red Bank was our attorney during the controversy over the Colts Glen development. He was recommended by Dan O'Hern, because Dan could not take the case. Bernie and I have since become lifelong friends. He is shown here in 1995.

Status of the Development

Soon after the 1967 purchase of the McLean farm, the developer drew up plans to build some 165 houses in three sections of 35, 65, and 65 lots. He soon proceeded with Section I directly on Oak Hill Road using septic tanks, but he was not allowed to start the next sections until the sewers were installed. He also cleared the way for the main roads through the property, and in so doing, knocked down many trees along the south bank, creating severe erosion. In January 1971, about 20 homes of the 35 lots in Section I were occupied.

This photo, taken in early spring 1971, shows what Conservation Commission Chairman Lynden Kibler called the "Grand Canyon of Poricy Brook." It was one of two major gullies created in preliminary construction by the Colts Glen builder. In the photo are Carol and Mike Huber. Mike is standing at about the location of the front door of a typical house; the yard would extend 2/3 across the marsh. Carol was the Water Resources Chair of the League of Women Voters. Mike has had a long and productive career in conservation. Prior to retirement in April 1990 he had served as Chairman, President & CEO of the J.M. Huber Corporation. He has served as a trustee of the Monmouth Conservation Foundation, the American Littoral Society, NJ Chapter of the Nature Conservancy, and other environmental organizations. He played the major role in donating 255 acres along the Navesink River to the Monmouth County Park System.

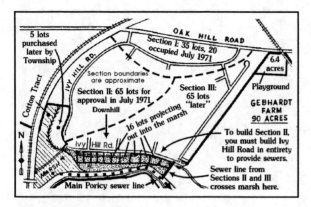

The Colts Glen Housing Development

The Basic Problem

In one sentence, Ivy Hill Road was planned to be too close to the fragile bank of the Poricy Marsh.

In the builder's original plans, there were around 16 houses planned with lots extending far out into the marsh, whose construction would cause serious erosion. In the wild and wooly days of allowing anything to be built, this plan would probably have been routinely approved. (My former house on Marcshire Drive, built in 1966, was in the middle of a small stream, and when the sump pump failed we had up to 3 feet of water in the basement.)

But Colts Glen was a little more complex. Section I was a done deal. The builder now wanted to build Section II, 65 more lots. No problem, no erosion, looks fine. The only trouble was, nobody could flush a toilet until sewers were installed, and to install sewers, the builder needed to nail down Ivy Hill Road in Section III, because that's where the sewer pipe would run to get to the marsh crossing. Once he built that road, he would have to come back later with his Section III plan to build 16 houses into the marsh, and we feared the Township might let him do that based on hardship.

We saw a simple solution. Consider Sections II and III as one unit of 130 houses. The Township was about to approve a *cluster zoning* ordinance which would allow the builder to have the same number of houses, but on slightly smaller lots, and in this case pull all the lots in Sections II and III north, away from the bank. Lots first planned for a half acre (22,000 sq. ft.) would be reduced to 18,000 sq. ft.

Why not let Section II go in as planned and then worry about clustering Section III? You couldn't occupy Section II houses until the sewers were in, but perhaps you could start to build them, and in so doing, you would have frozen the Section II layout. Now you are left with only 65 houses to play with in Section III, in which case the cluster zoning ordinance wouldn't work because you don't have enough room to squash 65 Section III houses north of a relocated Ivy Hill Road. The lots would be too small.

But the builder had already laid out his development, with surveyed land and maps. He didn't want to do it again for the 130 houses in Sections II and III. Further, his entire development for all three sections had been approved some years ago as a sketch map. He planned to stay the course.

But he stayed the course in the face of some growing concern among officials and experts:

1. April 13, 1970. Township Engineer Richard Schultz of T&M Associates wrote the builder about the existing erosion, asking him to fix it.
2. November 5, 1970. Neal Munch, District Conservationist for the U.S. Dept. of Agriculture wrote Lynden Kibler, chair of the Middletown Conservation Commission, stating that he had examined the gullies, which he stated were caused by the builder. (An important point, because later the builder would deny that he created the gullies.)
3. February 8, 1971: Township Engineer wrote the builder again, and said he still had done nothing about the problem observed in the prior April.
4. February 26, 1971. I wrote to the builder, with copies to all other parties, pointing out damage and urging cluster zoning of the development.

5. March 31, 1971. Lynden Kibler, Middletown Conservation Commission, wrote NJ DEP stating that no corrective action taken yet.

6. April 1, 1971. Township Engineer Richard Schultz met with the builder on site. The builder had taken some measures, but as stated by the engineer, the problem "is not corrected but has not become much worse."

I apologize for what may be an indulgence in presenting that whole list, but I want to make it clear that this was regarded as a serious problem by several agencies, all of which had communicated this to the builder and Township authorities.

Despite all these warnings, the builder proceeded with his application for Section II. The introduction of the resolution to approve the development was scheduled for the Planning Board meeting May 3, 1971.

The Birdwatchers and the Homeowners

At the May 3 meeting, the resolution was simply introduced. The hearing would be in June. But by this time, the homeowners in Section I of the development had gotten wind of what was happening and several had their minds fixed on the idea that cluster zoning would destroy the value of their neighborhood. They had a spokesman, Robert Scales, who delivered a speech (considerably condensed here):

"When we bought our homes, we were shown plans that had houses on half-acre lots throughout the entire development. We thought we were buying homes in a prestige area. Now we are told that cheap houses will be built on small lots. Our investment is being threatened. We have a big investment here. These people (pointing to our group), they have no investment here. WE ARE AGAINST CLUSTER ZONING!!" (Loud, prolonged applause from the homeowners.)

It was decided, after further arguments from our committee and some Planning Board discussion with the builder, to postpone the introduction for a month, during which time the warring factions could

The *Courier*, May 6, 1971

"It's our money the bird-watchers are stealing."

"It's our money the birdwatchers are stealing" was a red-headed lady's comment as she left with her partisans in a three sided tussle over proposed cluster zoning of a development in Monday's Planning Board meeting.

The development is Fairview Oaks [Colts Glen] where one section borders the Cotton Tract recently purchased by conservation-minded citizens as part of a hoped for Poricy Park.

The first section has been developed off Oak Hill Road and is known as Colts Glen. Developer John Fitzgerald was seeking permission to build on 65 lots in Section II ...

Residents of the development, led by Robert Scales of Ivy Hill Road, a former president of the Keansburg Board of Education, turned out in force to object to any cluster zoning of sections 2 and 3, a move conservationists led by Dr. Lynden Kibler, chairman of the Conservation Commission, and the spokesmen for the Poricy Park Citizens Committee advocated strongly.
[Article continues]

hold private discussions. After adjournment, the arguments continued in the hallway. Several people asserted that there was no value in saving "an ugly, stinking swamp," and all were convinced that cluster zoning would be economically disastrous for them.

Bernie Finan and Our Strategy

In April we had engaged an attorney, Bernard Finan from Red Bank, who had been recommended by Dan O'Hern. Bernie was an enthusiastic birder and lover of the outdoors. He attended the Planning Board meetings with us, and now we had to determine what our posture should be at the June meeting.

We did hold a meeting with Dwight, Bernie, myself, and representatives of the builder. We decided that maybe the best strategy would be to let the builder get Section II approved and then, later, when he had to get Section III approved in order to build houses in Section II (because of the need for sewers), we could confront him directly on the lots in the marsh, and the Planning Board would never allow him to build there. It was late in the evening and we congratulated ourselves on this brilliant plan.

The next day at work at Bell Labs I shared this with Diane Lehder, who, along with others in our group, had been attending the meetings and following this closely.

"That is just plain STUPID. That's no solution at all. Don't you realize that when Section III comes up, those same homeowners, now armed with their victory over us in Section II, will come back in even greater force, possibly along with people that have bought contracts for the Section II homes? And, the builder will claim that he will use the utmost care in the marsh lots, and Planning Board will give in and grant him his application as long as he promises to do things carefully. It must have been pretty late at Dwight's bar."

This probably sounds like a back-handed compliment, but I will say that one of Diane's greatest talents was the ability to recognize the obvious that everyone else was blind to. I attended meetings with her, both in Poricy Park and at Bell Labs, where she practically leapt to her feet while others were all agreeing on something and pointed out the flaws in their reasoning. And in this case, she was of course right. We had to adopt another strategy.

There were many meetings and phone calls in May, and they included some people that might have been able to resolve this. One was Marshall McDowell, a Planning Board member, who tried but could not get the builder to move the road. Another was the Planning Board's professional planner, Robert Strong, who was in favor of clustering and wanted to draw a sketch map of how it would work.

But all this came to naught because of the position of the chairman of the Planning Board.

Frank Blaisdell

Frank Blaisdell had a long career in public service. He was a trustee of Riverview Hospital, Red Bank, for 25 years. He served in many capacities in Middletown government and was Mayor from 1954 to 1959. He was now Planning Board chairman. [12]

He also owned a lumber yard on Bridge Avenue in Red Bank (now out of business). His business did well in the construction boom after World War II.

During the sewer controversy, Ed Schumann and Jack Buzzi were stubborn and often wrong, but they were always *polite*. Not so Frank Blaisdell. I attended at least ten planning board meetings while Blaisdell was chairman. He was arrogant and autocratic to at least some members of the public, including me. And, I made it a point to return the favor. He and I were openly hostile to each other.

At the June 1971 hearing, our attorney suggested that we have a licensed stenographer record the proceedings in July. Blaisdell rejected this; "We don't take testimony at these hearings." This lack of a record proved to go strongly against us later on.

Virtually every professional person involved with construction projects and land management, all the Township agencies that were involved, and even the Board's professional planner not only advocated relocating Ivy Hill Road by cluster zoning the development, but also offered to help in the redesign. So, why didn't the builder go along with this?

I do think that Blaisdell was the key figure here. He was known to favor builders over the environment, and I witnessed times when he ignored the recommendations of the Environmental Commission when developments came under review. My guess is that the builder believed that he need not change his

---

[12] The career of Frank Blaisdell is described in an interview with his son Bruce in an article by Gloria Stavelli, *The HUB*, May 30, 2003.

plans, and that his original plans would get approval despite opposition from various groups and even from a few members of the Board. He might have believed that because he had Blaisdell on his side, he didn't need to make any changes in his plans.

The June 7 meeting was pretty much a rehash of the same material. The PPCC had put out an all points bulletin urging people to attend it, and it was packed. The Colts Glen homeowners were also well represented and restated their position against cluster zoning. The major point we made, which was agreed with by some Planning Board members, was that you have to consider Sections II and III together because of the sewer lines and the roads. At that meeting, Bob Makely, a member of both the Planning Board and Township Committee, is quoted by the *Daily Register* (June 8) as saying that the board would be "making a terrible mistake if it approved one section without the other."

No decision was made, and the issue was rescheduled for additional discussion in July.

The July 6 Planning Board Meeting

The Little River Campground is located near Mt. Mansfield in Vermont, and our family took our vacation there in the first full week in July 1971. So, I missed the Planning Board meeting on Tuesday, July 6. The next evening, I found a phone booth at the edge of a field and called Dwight.

After a little hemming and hawing, Dwight gave me the bad news. The Planning Board approved the builder's plans by a vote of 4-3.

There was essentially no record of the meeting. Some of the letters sent to the Planning Board might be on file, but there was no recorded testimony. But there was the text of the resolution.

The resolution is a masterpiece of self- and public-delusion. I call it that, because the people that voted "yes" had to have something that justified their vote. It's full of "whereas-es," as in "Whereas the Planning Board has considered the reports of its engineer and planning consultant." What a joke.

The engineer (Dick Schultz of T&M Associates) and planning consultant (Robert Strong) had both recommended clustering to move the road. Yeah, the board "considered" these recommendations and then they trashed them.

The builder also agreed to give the Township some of the land south of Ivy Hill Road, provided that the Township give him back the 6.4 acres on Ivy Hill Road he had previously donated to the Township for a playground. The Recreation Commission immediately (July 13) wrote a letter to the Township Committee opposing it. (These 6.4 acres later became the main entrance to Poricy Park.)

The PPCC printed the entire resolution, annotated with our comments, and sent it out to our mailing list of a few hundred people in Middletown. We urged them to attend the Township Committee meeting on July 27. You see, the builder still needed the approval of the Township Committee.

It All Comes Down to Lawyers

Here was the vote to approve the Planning Board resolution:
FOR: Blaisdell, Lynch, McDowell, Speck
AGAINST: Foulks, Makely, Azzolina
ABSENT: Mallet, Colby

Blaisdell, Lynch[13], and McDowell comprised a triumvirate and were expected to vote in a block. Foulks, Makely, and Azzolina had shown support for the park by working toward purchase of the farm. So who was Alan Speck, the swing vote?

Alan Speck was a regular citizen, appointed to the Board. Having seen him at several meetings, I believe he was always trying to do the right thing. He later told Dwight that he voted for the resolution because the Board's attorney, William Bassler, told everyone in caucus that an approval would avoid a lawsuit from the builder. This whole thing, like so many others, came down to lawyers.

---

[13] The Thomas Lynch that was on the Planning Board was not the same Thomas Lynch that was serving his first year on the Township Committee.

The July 27 Township Committee Meeting

There was a stenographer present at the July 27 Township Committee meeting, and testimony was taken. There was also a big crowd. There were only a few witnesses. Each person was called to the microphone, stated his/her name, was interrogated by the attorney that called the witness, cross examined by the other attorney, and then was subjected to cross examination by members of the Township Committee. The two attorneys representing the opposing sides were Bernie Finan for the PPCC and Gerald Goldman for the applicant, namely Johnstowne Building Corporation. The transcript is 94 double-spaced pages long.

The main issue was the erosion already caused by the builder and the potential for more erosion resulting from further construction of Ivy Hill Road. A related issue was whether Sections II and III were locked together. Cluster zoning was never mentioned. In fact, we never heard from the Colts Glen homeowners again about that subject.

The hearing began with lawyers wrangling over just what authority the Township Committee had over the builder's application. Then there was testimony from the Township's engineer over the erosion, the substance of which has been covered here already. What I do want to include here is a portion of the remarks of Dwight Richardson, PPCC Chairman. This may give the reader insight into why Dwight was such an effective leader in our cause.

I have taken the liberty of abridging and slightly editing Dwight's statement, as follows.

Dwight: Mayor Foulks, I'm sorry we are having to put you through this this evening.

Mayor Foulks: That's all right. We are interested in this, too.

Dwight: As you know, we are opposed to this particular development going in with the problems that have already occurred and the problems that we feel are going to occur with the approval of Section 3 linked with Section 2. The Township engineer and many other people felt that these two sections ought to be locked together. I think we all have that opinion now, so I want to talk about them in terms of these original plans.

Now, the developer planned to build about 130 homes in Sections II and III. This is about 100 acres, just to give you a rule of thumb. Now, we object primarily to the 24 lots along the marsh. This is the area which many of you are familiar with, that is, characterized by its adjacency to the Poricy Brook basin flood plain and drainage basin.

Now, this is a very beautiful area. I think it might be useful to paint sort of a word picture for you. Certainly Dick Cole sitting out there could do a much finer job on this as a naturalist than I can, somewhat as a layman in this area of conservation. The brook and flood plain and marsh represent a real ecological treasure as far as the Poricy area is concerned. It's part of an 80-acre fresh-water marsh that has many fine attributes to it, that has nourishing grasses down there.

It has water, is covered with water most of the time in many seasons. That water as it flows supports wild life, small mammals, ferns, many species of birds. For an encroachment and building on this area it would be a travesty, because we would lose a very fine resource as far as this community is concerned.

Now, we have our main objection as far as this particular original plan is concerned. The one which our lawyers strived to get out in English is that the Ivy Hill Road is just too darn garn close to that bank....

Dwight continued with details on the size of the bank, and the difficulty of the Township's enforcing of easements should they try to spare the bank with easements along back yards of the homeowners whose homes were built close to the bank. Dwight's testimony and examination ended on page 65 of the transcript.

The hearing continued and finally they came to statements from other witnesses including the League of Women Voters, the River Plaza Civic Association, and myself, all of whom supported our position. There was one Middletown resident that, in my opinion, made a particularly effective statement and he is quoted here:

I am Philip Jacobs from Robin Court. We've seen a very interesting thing here tonight. We've seen some real fine lawyers from North Jersey, and we've heard from a corporation. We sat here, now, several hours, and we haven't seen one bit of feeling from the corporation or its lawyer that they have any cognizance of the problem that the Poricy Park Committee has been trying to develop here. We have an area of valuable land, ecologically valuable if not for any other reason, which we are trying to protect.

This corporation is a faceless proposition. These people were sent down here to work for them. They're probably the only people in this room that are making a salary for sitting here tonight. All of us poor slobs are just citizens that did our work during the day. It seems to me that the Township Committee just has to recognize that this corporation is out to get the best proposition it can for itself. Otherwise, these people wouldn't be here. I haven't seen any evidence that they give a damn about this whole Poricy Brook environment. They really don't know anything about it, because they have been in North Jersey all this time and we are down here. You have to have a feel for this darn garn[14] thing to be receptive to what the committee here is trying to bring to your committee, so I would hope in your deliberations that you consider these points.

The Township Committee concluded the meeting by announcing that they would make a decision on August 10, 1971.

The Township Committee's Resolution

On August 10, the Township Committee, by unanimous vote, reversed the recommendation of the Planning Board, and they thus denied the builder's application for Section II.

There are nine specific clauses listed for their decision. I will quote just the first:

Clause 1: Because Sections 2 and 3 of the subdivision are inextricably bound to each other, it is impossible to consider Section 2 without Section 3, and both sections should be submitted as a unit.

The resolution continues citing the erosion damage, the difficulties of enforcing conservation easements, and the near impossibility of a proper design of Section 3 if Section 2 is approved as submitted.

One might think the story ends there, but it now became a game of moves and countermoves. A lot like a chess game.

Builder Sues, Applies for Section III

Soon after, Johnstowne Building Corporation sued the Township, asking the court to overturn the rejection of the Section II plans.

At the same time, the builder applied for approval of Section III. But with a modification. He removed the disputed houses south of Ivy Hill Road from the application, calling this area "Section IV." He would build the rest of his development, and come back later to apply for Section IV. Ivy Hill Road would go ahead as planned. The hearing before the Planning Board was on September 7.

This time, at the Planning Board hearing, there *was* recorded testimony. Here is a portion of Dwight's remarks:

Regarding Ivy Hill Road, the builder is asking the Planning Board to give approval for constructing houses on one side [the north side] of a road that is one-third of a mile long and asking you to ignore what's going to happen to Section IV, that is, the other side of the road, until some future time. We feel that it is an abrogation of the Planning Board's responsibility if you look at only one part of the tract.

I would draw your attention to the fact that there hasn't been a single lot-line changed. There hasn't been a single road changed.... So, we encourage you to look at the problem from the standpoint of the whole area.

The vote was to deny the application, seven to one. The single vote to approve Section III came from the Board Chairman, Frank Blaisdell.

---

[14] I can't believe that both Dwight and Philip Jacobs said "darn garn." Perhaps they said "doggone" and the stenographer recorded "darn garn"?

As with all applications, this one still had to go before the Township Committee. In the Committee's resolution to affirm the Planning Board (ie, to deny the application), they again reiterated that you can't break up this development into intermediate sections; it must be considered as one unit. On the idea of breaking out Section IV and applying for it later, here is what they said in their resolution:

The applicant indicated in the testimony before the Planning Board that it was his intention to wait until the improvements were fully installed on Ivy Hill Road at which time he would take another look at the lots south of the road and get a better idea of whether or not a problem would be created... Sectional planning and a "let's wait and see" attitude is the antithesis of good and comprehensive planning and that position will not be taken by the Township Committee.

Put in plainer terms, the Township isn't going to let the builder sweep this issue under the rug.

The Builder's Day in Court

The trial for Section II was held on March 1, 1972. The attorneys were Gerald Goldman, representing the builder, and Robert Otten representing the Township. Judge Merritt Lane presided.

In the pre-trial hearing on February 1, Lane ruled that there would be no new testimony taken, and that the trial must be confined to the existing records.

The trial began at 9 am. There was the usual posturing of lawyers and arguments about which exhibits could be entered. At 10:55 the arguments began. Lane clearly understood the issues, and even seemed to be arguing the Township's position:

Lane to Goldman: Don't you see that the Township Committee is trying to help the builder? They're saying, consider the whole development at once. Move the road and get the conservationists off your back. What if you build in Sections II and III and then come in with lots south of the road judged to be unbuildable?

Goldman: That's a risk we'll have to take. We're prepared to discuss alternate issues.

Lane: The municipality contains practical men. They realized that if Sections II and III are built, Section IV would be applied for later and "some soft-hearted judge in Freehold" will grant the builder's right to use the land. We're dealing with proper planning in an area that has ecological significance. We're dealing with the <u>future</u> – that's what planning is all about.

Well, this went on until lunch, and they resumed at 1:30. Judge Lane made this curious statement:

Lane: I have carefully reviewed everything. Today was just the frosting on the cake.

Then, it became apparent what he meant. He read a lengthy decision, obviously prepared ahead of time. I suppose he was required to listen to people in the morning, but it was all to no avail. At the end of his reading, he stated that the Township Committee had no right to allow new testimony (at the July 27 hearing) and they must be limited to the record from the Planning Board, however inadequate it might be. In that record, there is no evidence to support the Township Committee's overturning of the Planning Board resolution. The Township Committee's denial of the builder's application was "arbitrary, capricious, and unreasonable."

And thus, the builder was given approval to go ahead with Section II.

A Chess Game: Our Queen is Captured

In the corridor outside the court room, we were in shock. And then, the builder, John Fitzgerald, came up to our (new) chairman, Jim Knowles, and made this remark: "Sometimes you need a decisive event like this to change direction." What a puzzling thing to say.

I stated earlier that this became a chess game. I am not a chess player, but I do know the rules for moving the pieces. You try to ensnare the opponent's king while protecting your own. You have different pieces to use with varying degrees of power. The most powerful piece is the queen, and it's not a good idea to lose it.

Well, the builder, with the court decision, had captured our queen. But meanwhile, we had some other pieces that had encircled him while he was pursuing our queen.

The builder's biggest problem was that he could never sell a house until the sewers were installed, and that required putting them in Ivy Hill Road, and he would have to get approval for his Section III to do that, and the Township had come down hard on his idea to temporarily ignore the lots on the south side of Ivy Hill Road. This would just be another round of continued battles, delaying him at least a year, even if he succeeded.

So, he did a curious thing. He voluntarily had the whole development redesigned to conform to the cluster zoning ordinance. He moved Ivy Hill Road north, and donated 16 acres of marshland to the Township. By the next year he was in the business of selling houses.

Was it Worth It?

A lot of time, effort, and money went into this one. The 16 acres has almost never since been used for park programs; we had thought it might be a passageway between the farm and the Cotton Tract, but it just didn't work out. But once again, as with the sewer line, we saved the bank from destruction and the marsh from being destroyed by erosion.

There was another gain. For the first time in anyone's memory, the Planning Board's automatic acceptance of a builder's plans had been challenged on ecological grounds by an aroused citizenry. I know that this did have some influence on further building projects. In particular, the nurseries on Nut Swamp Road, which backed onto Poricy marsh, were later developed and our committee worked directly with the Planning Board in modifying the design of the developments to keep the bank intact, even to the point of slightly reducing the number of houses.

Marcia was fond of writing doggerel, especially when addressing the folly of government.

POWER TO THE PEOPLE

We have a Town Committee
(That's the democratic way)
But what can be the use of it
Is more than I can say.

It holds its public meetings
Where the voters air their views
(Whether relevant and pertinent
or just to cry the blues).

The funniest thing about it
Is that it makes decisions
About such things as zoning laws
And major subdivisions.

That this municipality
Is run in Township Hall
Has no basis in reality;
We have no say at all.

It seems our representatives
Were voted in in vain.
Who calls the shots in Middletown?
No one but Merritt Lane.

Will Wisner and the Five Lots

Will Wisner and Bill Schell began their terms on the Township Committee in January 1972. Some of us knew Will, and we asked him to consider buying a few lots backing onto the Cotton Tract from the builder at building lot prices. These lots would be included in the Green Acres application the Township was preparing for the farm. Our reason was that the Cotton Tract would essentially become just an extension of people's backyards, should houses be built there. Will got the Township Committee to agree to do this, and the builder sold the Township the five lots for a total of $50,000.

November 1971. One of several hikes we led to introduce people to the future park. The photo was taken on the SW corner of the Gebhardt Farm. I can identify only a few people, but these few were influential in our cause. PPCC Chairman Dwight Richardson is the tall man 3rd from left at rear. Marcia Rissland is 3 people to our right of Dwight in back row, blond hair and no hat. Three more people over with lower right of face obscured is Jim Knowles, future PPCC chairman. Will Wisner, just elected to the Township Committee, is in center back row, black hat, glasses. His wife Marion is the tall woman two to our right of Will. Far right back row is Bill Pfefferle, standing next to his wife Eleanor (glasses). Eleanor served on the Board of Education for many years and was helpful with development of our programs. In the back, to our left of Eleanor (to our right of man with glasses) is Bernice Trombino, a long-time member of the PPCC, whom you'll meet again later. I don't know the dog's name.

Spot the Shanties!

1978 aerial view of the Colts Glen development, from one of the standard photos prepared by the Monmouth County Planning Board. Ivy Hill Road has been moved away from the marsh and the north bank is intact.

All 161 houses (the final count) are built or under construction. Can you draw the line separating the elegant estates of Section I and the "cheap houses on tiny lots" in the clustered section? No fair cheating and looking at the sketch map a few pages back!

The newly constructed Nature Center and parking lot are at right.

If you can't lick 'em, join 'em.

Perhaps the builder had the last word after all. This advertisement appeared in local newspapers sometime in 1973. The text that appeared below the drawing is not shown in our picture, but this is the first paragraph:

> "You'll find no look of "sameness" about a Colts Glen home… or the beautifully landscaped ground on which it stands! Steeped in history and rich tradition, the site of Colts Glen at Middletown is surrounded by lovely old farms, "green acres" and developing Poricy Park."

At right: We had a party for Dwight when he moved out of Middletown in 1985. He's the man in the back. I chose this photo because it's my only photo of Ruth Ann Knowles (left), and my best one of Hank Flanagan. Cathy Brady is next to Hank.

Dwight Moves Up

When Will Wisner and Bill Schell joined the Township Committee in January 1972, the Democrats took control. They immediately appointed Dwight to a 6-year term on the Planning Board.

The rest of us on the PPCC were dismayed. We had been strong adversaries of the Planning Board, and we felt that Dwight had to leave the PPCC. Dwight did not agree, but he did leave. Jim Knowles became our new chairman. Jim had been following events closely, especially those involving our interactions with the Township government.

Dwight remained a friend and helped us on several occasions. But the Planning Board was not a good experience for him. They soon undertook to revise the master plan for the Township, and this involved allowing some apartments to be built. Public hearings were held at which hundreds turned out and castigated the Board and Dwight personally. Dwight previously had a deep faith that people were basically good and would come around if you just were patient and reasoned with them. After six years, Dwight was a changed person.

Dwight now lives in Florida and we correspond, as in preparing this book. He is always welcome in my home. He can even bring his French horn.

A commuter train next to the farm. Photo was taken prior to 1957, when steam service ended on the NY&LB Railroad.

Purchasing the Gebhardt Farm

Mrs. Gebhardt died in August 1970, and her nephew, Jack Cavanaugh inherited the farm. He immediately sold the herd of cows and wanted to sell the farm. He reasoned that since the Board of Education paid $4500/acre for its new high school site, he should get the same for his 90 acres, namely $405,000. After the Township made its commitment in April 1971 to purchase the farm, there followed two years of negotiating and haggling, coupled with working with federal and state agencies on grant applications.

In October 1972 state Green Acres funding was approved for $332,000 for several tracts, including the farm. HUD funds followed in December for $239,662. In 1973, the Township entered condemnation proceedings, which were agreed to by Cavanaugh, to get a fair price.

On November 30, 1973 the Township closed on the farm in the office of Cavanaugh's attorney, John Pillsbury. Shown here are PPCC chairman Jim Knowles, Township Attorney Peter Frunzi, and Marcia Rissland. The recorded cost of the transaction on the deed was $530,000. That's real champagne in the glasses.

1972-1974: Years of Inactivity

When we all began our project in 1969, we never intended that we would become personally involved in the operation of a park. We thought we could write some letters, show up at a few public meetings, and then the Township would acquire the land and take charge of the park.

In our first few years, our committee remained an informal group of people who had occasional meetings when it seemed necessary. We had a mailing list of perhaps two hundred people. There was no concept of "membership" in the PPCC, nor was there an annual drive for contributions. By mid-1972 we had spent around $6,000 for the Cotton Tract purchase and maybe $5,000 for other activities.

So, in 1972 we had no real projects. The Township still owned only the Cotton Tract, with major land acquisitions a year ahead. We had been acquiring knowledge of the ecology of the area, and some of us visited a few nature centers to get an idea of what we might have in Middletown. But we believed that our basic work was done, and we would become just an auxiliary "friends" organization.

This situation would change gradually in 1974 when we began to work with the Township to design a Nature Center, and then drastically at the end of 1974 when we had to make a decision on whether we would jump into the deep water.

The years from mid-1974 to 1982 were nearly frantic, and while writing this, I felt I was trying to untangle a twisted rope of strings of different colors. Rather than proceed down the rope in chronological order, I have untangled it and will tell the entire story of one "string," back up, and in like manner, tell the other stories separately, as follows (also see the diagram on page 142):

1. Developing educational programs.
2. Managing the land.
3. Constructing the Nature Center building.
4. Restoring the historic buildings.

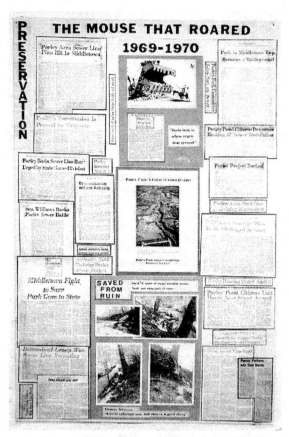

To prepare for a wine & cheese party in 1980, Marcia prepared a set of six posters illustrating "How to Make a Park." The first is shown here. When she got to the end of the Colts Glen battle in 1972 in the 4th poster, she included a panel stating "The fighting stops. So does the press coverage."

But coverage did resume later with opening of the Nature Center, the establishing of public programs, and restoration of the historic buildings.

The Educational Programs

The Poricy Brook marsh in summer 1971.

Mrs. Leistner and My Epiphany

It was a hot, muggy day in summer 1970, threatening to rain. I had arranged to meet Mrs. Leistner, whom I would escort into the marsh, which later became part of the Cotton Tract. She, in turn, would identify the plants that grew there.

My only photograph of her is in the group photo taken in October 1969 pictured on page 3. She was an elderly German woman with an extraordinary knowledge of botany. She knew some of the plants only by their German names, but that did not dampen my enthusiasm for what she was finding.

I had no idea what to expect. I had never paid much attention to wildflowers, and to me the marsh was a mostly grassy area in which you would sink into the water if you didn't watch every step. (And, that's what a marsh really is!)

The next hour was one discovery after another. "Look here – this is a monkey flower! Very rare. It's related to the snapdragon." (And, a while later after we had seen about 50 of them, I asked her why she called it "rare," and she responded, "Well, it isn't rare here but it is in a lot of other places.") She told me that Queen Anne's lace was really just a wild carrot, completely edible. We saw vervain. Spotted jewelweed, which she told me could be crushed and the juice used to stop itching. (It really works.) We must have seen 30 species of flowers. We also looked at trees, bushes, and an occasional butterfly. I took photographs of everything. Except her.

It began to rain. We extracted ourselves from the marsh and bid each other good bye. I saw her a few times since, but not in such a setting.

Mrs. Leistner gave me a gift. It was an epiphany for me; my eyes were opened. I took up an interest in plants and eventually acquired more than 20 books on the subject. (My Peterson guide to wildflowers is dog-eared.[15]) Roadsides, forests, and vacant lots were transformed into gardens for me.

And, I wanted to share this gift with everyone else. I hoped that someday we could bring other people down into this marsh and get them to love the small, wild places that abound all over.

---

[15] Roger Tory Peterson and Margaret McKenna, <u>A Field Guide to Wildflowers of Northeastern and North-Central North America</u>, Houghlin Mifflin, Boston, 1968 (and later editions).

The Great Swamp in northern New Jersey

Marshes and Swamps

The simplest way to tell the difference between a *marsh* and a *swamp* is to look at what is growing in it. A marsh supports *grasses*. It is wet all the time, but shallow so that grasses can take hold. There may be a few trees growing in it, but they die out before they get large because their roots cannot tolerate being so constantly wet. Certain kinds of trees do grow here, notably the black willow. The grasses in a marsh support food for wildlife and also slow down the water flow and allow the water to seep into the ground and recharge aquifers.

A swamp supports *trees*. It is flooded on occasion, generally in the spring, but at other times it can be fairly dry. There are enough trees that they shade out grasses. The Passaic River flows through the Great Swamp, pictured here.

There are small sections along Poricy Brook that are wooded and swampy, such as one area of the Cotton Tract next to a small stream. This area contains skunk cabbage in the late winter. But most of the area between the stream banks east of the Navy Road is marshland.

The Cotton Tract Booklet

We had been learning all these fine things about marshes and wildlife, and we shared our knowledge on our occasional hikes and talks in schools, but we wanted something more concrete to use as a teaching tool. We decided to publish a booklet.

In December 1973 we still had funds in the Nature Conservancy account left over from the Cotton Tract purchase. We asked if we could use the funds to publish a book about the property they had helped save. They agreed, and asked only that we put their logo on the book.

Jack-in-the pulpit grows in flat, poorly drained topland in the Cotton Tract.

By this time, I had taken many photographs of trees and flowers. I would write the text. Marcia was a good illustrator and agreed to do the drawings. Diane Lehder would help edit and publish the book. Producing this book was our main activity in 1974, up to September.

The red-tailed hawk and the striped skunk, two of many drawings Marcia made for the Cotton Tract booklet.

Mixed Reviews

We mailed the booklet in November 1974 to everyone on our list, which consisted mostly of people that had previously contributed. We had a great sense of pride in the booklet. We asked for a contribution to help defray the cost of printing it.

We got some contributions, but also some negative responses. "It's lovely, but it's not the reason we contributed to your cause. We didn't want you to get into the printing business. We wanted you to create a park."

A friend of Diane's was not so subtle. He told her that he was furious over this, and that he would never contribute again.

One purpose of the book was to use it as a teaching tool for school classes coming to the area. We gave some copies to the Board of Education and some teachers, and the schools did eventually order 75 more copies. But this never developed into a standard program.

The Nature Conservancy, at least, was pleased with the book and told us that it was the best guide they had seen thus far for any of the tracts they had helped to save.

Despite the mixed reception the booklet got, I still feel it was worth it for ourselves, and it kept us going in 1974. Reading the book thirty years later, it contains a wealth of information which had required us to do a great deal of research to assemble. Much of this information was incorporated into later nature programs.

Professor Fischer and the Glacial Erratic

Richard Fischer, through his students, had the most profound effect of anyone on the development of the programs in Poricy Park.

I finally met Professor Fischer in March 1978 on the Cornell campus when our family was visiting the area. At that time, we had been corresponding for more than three years by phone and mail. He wrote that he would meet us on a path between two particular buildings and we should wait by the glacial erratic. "You can't miss it."

I guessed that a "glacial erratic" was some sort of fissure, or a cliff, or a canyon. But when we got to the path, we saw nothing that looked geological in nature. It was just a path between buildings. I finally sat down on a rock next to the path.

"Ah. You must be Pete Brady. I see you found the glacial erratic." "No, I don't see it." "That's because *you're sitting on it!*"

A glacial erratic is an isolated item that was dropped by a glacier as it moved through the area.

Diane Walton and Meacham Lake

We had several chance meetings with people that proved fortuitous to our cause, but the one with Diane Walton was truly an act of providence.

For years, we took our vacation by camping with the children. We had heard about the fine campgrounds in the Adirondacks, and, in summer 1974, picked one from a map. We chose Meacham Lake because it was the one that was the farthest north, and we would experience solitude.

We arrived on Saturday morning. Here's a tip. *Never* arrive on a Saturday morning. It's jammed with weekend campers, who will depart the next day. Arrive on Sunday and take your pick of sites.

But what about northern solitude? Take another look at a map. Meacham Lake is only an hour or so from Montreal. The campground was filled with French Canadians, who are masters of partying into the night. So much for solitude.

Anyway, on Tuesday we took a nature walk, which was led by an enthusiastic and knowledgeable Diane Walton. I asked where she had learned her skills, and it was from Professor Fischer at Cornell. She told me how to contact him.

I called Professor Fischer and said that we were trying to establish a nature center, and possibly even have the Township hire a naturalist, and could he suggest someone we could talk with? He immediately suggested Peter Brooks, a former student, who had just started working for the city of Englewood, NJ. "He was one of my finest students. By all means see him."

Peter Brooks and Allan MacDonald

Our meeting with Peter Brooks was the single most important event in setting up our whole course of environmental study at Poricy Park.

In those days, there was frequent turnover on the Township Committee with at least one new member each year. In November 1974, Republican Ralph Siciliano and Democrat Allan MacDonald had been newly elected. (See chart on page 31.) It was our practice to have a reception after each election and share the wonders of Poricy Park. The 1974 reception was held at my house on December 4. We said we had an appointment in Englewood with Peter Brooks, and could they join us?

Ralph couldn't make it, but Allan agreed to go.

Englewood was very similar to our setup, except that they were maybe three years ahead of us. They had a 150-acre park and were about to build an interpretive building for about $300,000.

- When they first got the land there was a power vacuum with no plans for the area. (Ditto Middletown in 1974)
- With no plans to use it, it was becoming overgrown with weeds and briars and in five years would become a jungle. (Ditto)
- You must actively use and manage the land, else it will become a wasteland. "The best defense is a good offense." (Ditto)

December 11, 1974, at Englewood with Peter
Brooks (left), director of the Flat Rock Brook
Nature Center, Township Committeeman elect
Allan MacDonald, Marcia Rissland, Diane
Lehder, and Pete Brady (who took the photo).

- School teachers are generally not trained in
  environmental science. You can't just have
  most of them come in and run their own
  programs. You need your own trained environmental teachers familiar with the park.

I think the most important part of the meeting
centered on the structure of the school programs.
Quoting Peter Brooks, "Too often a 4th-grade teacher
brings a class to a park and is met by someone
wearing a Smokey-the-Bear hat. They start down a
trail in the woods. 'Oh, look, see that hole in the
tree? That's where a great horned owl lives. He
comes out at night.' And maybe they do see
something with more substance, sometimes.

"Anyway, next year the same kids are in 5th
grade and their teacher brings them to the park and
are met by the same naturalist, who takes them
down the same trail and repeats the program."

Peter continued by giving us a blueprint for the
proper design of school programs. He said that you
should construct a set of different programs high-
lighting different features, in different seasons, each

geared to a particular grade. Maybe 6th-graders
come in the fall, 4th-graders in winter. Get study
materials out in the classroom ahead of time.
Volunteers can be good teachers if they are trained
well.[16] Set a fair price for the programs and be sure
you don't go broke running them.

What we all did not know is that this advice was
being heard by a future Mayor of Middletown.

Our First School Class

On the following February 11, we took a sixth-
grade class taught by Esther Pavelka through the
Cotton Tract, studying "Signs of Life in Winter." The
trip was written up in *School News*, April 1975:

> Mrs. Diane Lehder of the PPCC explained that "this
> is more intensive than an ordinary 'visit a park' field
> trip. The essential feature of this program is that one
> (and only one) special topic is selected for intensive
> study. In this case, the students sought out anything
> that showed life in winter. They found buds, insects,
> worms, animal tracks, and many other features.
> Similar programs already exist in a few other New
> Jersey localities." [Such as Englewood.]

Teacher
Esther Pa-
velka (right)
with Kim
Hendricks,
Stuart
McGowan,
and Janice
Brennan in
the Cotton
Tract,
Feb. 11,
1975.

---

[16] Such trained volunteers are called *docents* (DOE-
sent), a very common term in museums, but generally unknown to most people not in this field.

The First Year After the Champagne

In the year following our champagne toast on the occasion of acquiring the farm, the development of "Poricy Park" got off to a rough start.

By the fall of 1974, all tracts in Poricy Park had been acquired, the farm for one full year. Besides the Fossil Beds and the farm, whose purchases have already been covered, the Boy Scout Tract was purchased by the Township on May 2, 1974 for $60,000. This included seven additional acres on the east side of the railroad plus some acreage in the pond.

Most of the park tracts were intended to be left alone, and some were already in their final natural state, be it forest or marsh. The Boy Scout tract, formerly a hay field, started in 1969 as nearly cleared land, but it was "going back to nature." The only piece that required management was the farm, but this was the major section of the park.

The farm had not been actively used since early 1971. So, in late 1974, we were four years into Peter Brooks' prediction that "in five years it would be a jungle."

And, the PPCC was an independent group of citizens with no credentials or authority to do anything in the park, nor did we want to. We were clear in our intent that the Township should run the park.

Our First Visit to the Farmhouse

On October 2, 1973, Marcia and I, accompanied by Lou and Cathy, set foot in the farmhouse for the first time. It was eight weeks prior to the Township's closing on the property.

The house was occupied by Roger Stolen and John Worlock, two engineers from Bell Labs. Somehow they survived, despite a temperamental water pump, a water heater on its last legs, and a coal furnace that had to be stoked by hand. They gave us a tour and served us mead. None of us had had mead before, which is a fermented drink made from honey.

The furnace, water heater, and coal bin.

These tenants survived another winter in the farmhouse, and then the Township evicted them in early 1974. The place was up for grabs. In August 1974 some of us met Jim Froelich at the farmhouse. He was a Township employee, in charge of keeping track of real estate. He wanted to move in, and in fact, he did move several pieces of furniture there.

And, all this time the barn was ignored.

Jim Duke and Denise King

Herbert ("Bud") Bradshaw had been the acting Township Administrator in 1973 and up through fall 1974. His competence is attested to by his success in negotiations for the Gebhardt Farm.

Jim Duke was director of Parks and Recreation during much of 1974. He, therefore, was in charge of developing the farm. It was the intent of the PPCC, and most of the public that had supported us, that the park be developed for environmental study.

Jim took two steps during summer 1974. In April, he had perhaps an acre of the farm plowed under and rented garden plots. This move was hailed by newspapers, stating that rather than let such a property remain idle, this was a creative step toward public usage.

At this time, we were not involved with the farm, and when we heard about the garden plots we thought they were a good idea. It's right there in mimeographed black and white in our May 1974 newsletter: "The PPCC is delighted with this innovative use of parkland."

The second step he took was to hire Denise King, a student at his own alma mater, Penn State University, to come in and open the farmhouse for whatever summer programs she wanted to run.[17]

The garden plots were a dismal failure, but they were repeated the next year. (The reason they were repeated the next year was because a member of the Recreation Advisory Committee lobbied for them.) The area became littered with debris, including plastic scarecrows. Crops were stolen. Woodchucks were poisoned. And, the only source of water was the farmhouse, some distance away, and if the hose was left running the pump would blow a fuse or otherwise fail. This happened several times.

Denise King was a much better idea. She kept the farmhouse door open to anyone that wanted to visit. She developed a following of a handful of "groupies," teen-age boys that hung around with her and explored the area to see what was there. And, she ran several programs throughout the park. She was there 10 weeks. It is to my great regret that we spent almost no time over there with her.

But she did spend some time with us. We were preparing the Cotton Tract booklet at that time, and she dropped by on several occasions to talk about the future of the park. A major task assigned to her was to prepare a report on the park development.

The report is comprehensive, and she had contacted more than 20 community leaders to get their advice. She included details of the design of the programs she had run, budget estimates for the first three years, and costs to develop the facility. She estimated $75,000 to renovate the old buildings (very close to what it did cost) and $100,000 to

Denise King was Poricy Park's first naturalist in 1974, and we never took her picture! So, I did the next best thing – I tracked her down to the Rolling T Ranch, a 25-acre ranch in southwest Colorado where she and her husband Stephen Stovall raise lambs, with a few head of cattle and some horses. After leaving Poricy Park and graduating from Penn State, Denise developed more than 18 park sites across the country. She is now looking into the history of nearby cliff dwellings. She and Steve have four children and five grandchildren, and is shown here with her grandson Sam.

construct a nature center (that proved to be low).

This report might have had an impact if Jim Duke, Director Parks and Recreation, and his assistant Greg Trotta, had not both announced their resignations around September 1. And, at the same time, George Smith became Township Administrator, replacing Bud Bradshaw.

---

[17] Yes, we had a Duke and a King managing the park.

George Smith in the Fall of 1974

George Smith, who became administrator in fall 1974, was our cross to bear for two years.

We met George on September 12 at the home of Township Planner Bill McCann. The meeting was all cordiality. Welcome to Middletown.

At that meeting, George Smith agreed to:

- Put the position of director of the Nature Center in the 1975 budget.
- Make repairs to the farmhouse and barn, which were falling apart. (We weren't talking about an historic restoration, which we regarded as out of reach at that time. We just wanted them repaired.)

Smith never did put the director of the Nature Center in the budget. He also did nothing about the buildings – at least, not for the next several months, until we raised hell about it.

George Smith moved into the ranch house at the top of the hill. He had a beautiful view of the farm from there. And, to enhance the view, he proceeded to turn the farm into the Township leaf dump.

In the fall of 1974, a steady procession of trucks rolled down the hill to dump leaves in full view of the farmhouse. We complained. It continued.

We attended the public hearing on the 1975 budget, held at 10 am, Nov. 27, 1974. We learned that there was no Nature Center director in the budget, and that Smith was "looking into getting estimates" for repairs to the buildings. (He wasn't.)

Regarding the leaves, his remark was quoted many times since among ourselves: "Yes, we are *storing* the leaves there."

Regarding the buildings, he still did nothing by mid-January 1975, despite direct intervention by our new committeeman, Allan MacDonald.

The Recreation Advisory Committee

The Recreation Advisory Committee (RAC) had the charter to work with the director of Parks and

The leaf dump, looking south from the farmhouse.

Recreation and give whatever support and advice was needed.

The RAC was in a difficult position with the PPCC. We were a self-appointed outside group and had no chartered authority from the Township. They therefore felt that the PPCC should not be dealing directly with any of the Township officials. Rather, we should be going to them, and then they would take their own position on items. And that sounds correct from an administrative point of view.

The problem was that they had not been involved in the events of the past five years. We had fought two battles to save stream banks, one of which gave 16 acres of marsh to the Township, and we had purchased a 14-acre natural area. We had studied the area and even written a book about it, and had conducted many programs with the public and schools. We had visited other nature centers to see how they operated. And, we had a loyal following of hundreds of citizens. The RAC members had not been involved in any of this.

What they did do, and probably did well, was represent the *active* recreation interests of the community. They wanted ball fields, soccer fields, possibly a centrally located recreation center. The existing facilities had to be maintained, and the work crews assigned. There were major events during the year, especially the Middletown Folk Festival, which had begun in 1968 (and was to continue through 1984, 17 years in all).[18]

In some phone calls members of the RAC had with Frank Lescinsky and me in early 1975, they indicated some concerns:

- Isn't Poricy Park going to be duplicating the role of the Monmouth Museum? The Monmouth County Park System?
- Who is responsible for the park development? The PPCC or Parks and Recreation?
- Just what is the official role of the PPCC, if indeed it has any?
- How come the PPCC gets to meet often with members of the Township Committee and we see them only occasionally?
- The PPCC should be going through the RAC, because the RAC is responsible for recreation in Middletown, not the PPCC.

Most were sensible concerns. But some were not. Our meetings with the RAC were difficult at times because they made unreasonable requests, such as some members' withholding approval for a plan for park development unless it included road access from Nut Swamp Road. (This would involve building a bridge across the marsh and acquiring land on the south side of the marsh for right-of-way.)

In the two-year period of 1974-5 we did not achieve harmony with the RAC, particularly because there was no director of Parks and Recreation, a vacancy that would continue through April 1975.

But we did meet with them, perhaps seven times in the 12 months beginning in fall 1974. We also kept up our own campaign, because we were the only ones trying to do something about the deteriorating condition of the farm.

The Township did help bridge the two groups by appointing one of our members, Lethe Lescinsky, to the Recreation Advisory Committee.

---

[18] To the credit of the tireless labors of Dick and Marlene Levine and their folk musician friends.

All Is Not Well

We went back into the business of raising a public outcry. We distributed more than 600 copies of a 7-page flyer, complete with photographs. It went to our mailing list of 312 names, to 220 names of Middletown residents on the list of the Monmouth County Historical Association, and 100 names supplied by the Middletown Township Historical Society. It is significant that we were still limiting ourselves to Middletown, and not yet thinking of this as a *regional* park.

Well, the Township Committee did get letters. 38 of the writers sent us copies. Some are on carbon paper, some hand-copied. The people were upset. So was the Township Committee. They were *angry*. But not about the farm. They were angry with us.

This 7-page flyer was sent to more than 600 people. Here are the opening paragraphs.

Poricy Park: All is not well.
January 15, 1975

Dear Friend of Poricy Park,

In the year since the Township of Middletown acquired the major properties in Poricy Park, there has been, on balance, a notable lack of progress. This is especially true of the Gebhardt Farm area, which is intended to be the focal point of the whole park. Simple, necessary, important tasks have not been done. Basic maintenance on the farm has been neglected, and there has actually been abuse of the farm by the Township's using it as a leaf dump. The 200-year-old buildings are in a near state of collapse. Even more serious is the fact that the Township has essentially taken no action to apply for Green Acres development funds to establish the park as an environmental education center.

For the first time in three years we are asking you to write again. This is our trump card, our last resort to get this project moving again. YOU must let the Township Committee know that you are there, you are concerned, and you are watching.

The barn in December 1974. One dubious advantage of having part of the roof removed is that it gives you a daylight view of the construction, with hand-hewn beams and pegged joints. These two pictures were included in the "All is not well" brochure, along with a photo taken in early 1972 showing that the roof was intact then. (You can also see the intact roof in 1969 on the back cover of this book.)

Through the opening in the center you can see a portion of the "cat house," which Marcia so-named because it was the home of about 20 semi-wild cats. It burned down in August 1975. (The cats escaped the fire.)

The following is one of the letters sent to the Township Committee in response to our flyer "All is not well." It was chosen from the 38 copies of letters that were sent to us and that Marcia saved.

January 24, 1975

Township Committee:

How long is Middletown's largest park to be subjected to neglect and abuse on the part of the Township? As a long-time supporter of the Poricy Park Citizens Committee, I am indignant that the Township has used both the Fossil Beds and the Gebhardt Farm as a dump for leaves. It is an insult both to the Poricy Park Citizens Committee and to the hundreds of Middletown residents who have supported and contributed to their aims.

How long do you suppose a vacant house and an empty barn can remain immune to vandalism? Time passes, and nothing gets done. If there is a bottleneck in the administration, the time has come when it should be located and dealt with.

Lois H. Rhamstine

It turns out we had made an error in our flyer. The Township had requested Green Acres funds for park development, which included the Nature Center. But, we didn't know it. And, maybe they didn't know it until after they received our flyer.

In August 1974, at Jim Duke's request, a consulting firm, COMPASS (Community Planning Associates), had included the Poricy Park Nature Center in a letter of intent to Green Acres. It wasn't a formal application, but it did get us in the queue. Jim Duke resigned right after this, at about the same time George Smith was hired, and Smith might not have known about it. Of course, he might have checked into it on one of the occasions during the fall when we had asked about Green Acres funds.

Jim Knowles had been the chairman of the PPCC since January 1972, and he had a good grasp of the ways things can get screwed up in management. One comment he made on a few occasions, and which I have tried to take to heart ever since, is that people can do things that seem to be deliberately harmful to you when all they are really doing is bureaucratic bungling. You can misread into their actions motivations that really aren't there. In this case, it wasn't that the Township was refusing to apply for Green Acres funds, but that there was organizational confusion during the fall of 1974.

Anyway, we showed up at the Township Committee caucus on February 4 and they brought up the letters they had received. They said, "We're not saying these are form letters, and they do appear to be individually written, but they kind of look as if they came from the same source." Well, they came from people that had read our flyer and seen the photos. Yes, they were rather similar.

The result of all this was that the Township did put a roof on the barn. Unfortunately, it leaked, creating an even worse condition, because the dampness caused mildew and rot to occur during the summer.

Bob Bramley's Article

We had sent our flyer to the newspapers, and it landed in the hands of Bob Bramley of the *Daily Register*. Bob had interests in many things. For example, he was a woodworker and displayed his craft at the Middletown Folk Festival.

Bob did some research into the history of the buildings and wrote the article on the next page. This in turn caused Marcia to start her own research on the buildings, which we will describe later.

We will show the Bramley article on the next page, but we will stay for now with the role of the PPCC in conducting programs. Because 1975 marked the point where we began to operate the park ourselves, rather than request to have the programs conducted by the Parks and Recreation Department.

Excerpt from the *Daily Register* (Red Bank), January 10, 1975

Historically rich Gebhardt Farm is deteriorating, causing concern

by BOB BRAMLEY

Historic values are trickling away at the Gebhardt Farm, members of the Poricy Park Citizens Committee (PPCC) warn.

"When the Township acquired the Gebhardt Farm in 1973, it obtained not only open space for the community, but also a farmhouse and barn constructed in the 1700s. The buildings have great historic value. They are also, unfortunately, in poor condition," says Paul T. Brady, secretary of the PPCC.

Owned by Soldier

The historic value of the 18th-century farmhouse and barn is made vivid in the story of Joseph Murray, a private in the 1st Regiment of Monmouth County, New Jersey Militia, in the Revolu-

tionary War. Murray, who came to this country with his mother Elizabeth Murray from Londonderry, Ireland, was the owner of the Gebhardt Farm as early as May 9, 1767, when he granted a mortgage deed to the property of Lydia Compton.

He was still in possession of the farmstead June 8, 1780. Taken prisoner of war by the British in January, 1779, Murray had escaped by January 1780. In June of that year he was serving in Col. Asher Holme's Regt. of Monmouth Militia under the command of Lieut. Garrett Hendrickson.

[Here are omitted several paragraphs on the story of Joseph Murray, because the same story is told in an appendix in-

cluded here, "A Notoriously Violent Rebel." Bramley's article continues after that:]

Changes hands

The farm was owned by William Mears of Rumson when it was sold in 1940 to Albert H. Gebhardt, a New York City diamond broker. Working on the farmhouse after he had acquired it, Mr. Gebhardt found between the bricks of the main chimney a colonial coin which had evidently been placed there by the original owner.

The concern of members of the PPCC has been heightened by the continuing deterioration of the farm buildings, especially the barn, from which part of the roof is missing, with the old hand-hewn beams

HISTORIC LANDMARK This farmhouse on the Gebhardt Farm stands vacant and deteriorating since the tenant left last year. The stone porch reportedly once showed bloodstains left when a former owner, a Revolutionary War soldier, was murdered in 1780. (Register Staff Photo.)

open to the weather. And standing idle, the buildings are subject to the attacks of vandals and constitute an attractive and dangerous nuisance to all children, the members maintain.

"The buildings are a hazard to children who persist in playing on them, and who climb three stories high on the exposed roof beams of the barn ...

"The Township has also chosen to use the

Gebhardt Farm as a dump for leaves, which also contain plastic bags and nondegradable debris. The PPCC has objected to this to no avail. Poricy Park is one of the township's most important assets. It cannot withstand the township's continued neglect and abuse," warns Mr. Brady.

Marcia's Call to Arms

In October 1994, at a seminar in the farmhouse, Marcia was asked "When did you actually realize the history of the farmhouse? How far along were you on Poricy Park when you took this interest?"

Marcia replied, "It wasn't until we made a public stink [in January 1975] about the condition of the barn and a newspaper reporter named Bob Bramley wrote an article about it, and he was the one that produced the article from the *History of the New Jersey Coast* and wrote it into his newspaper article, and that's when I got interested in Joseph Murray. People had him living up on Kings Highway. So I had to get to work and find out where did he really live? Well, he lived here, and that's when I got interested in this house."

Poricy Park: Open for Business!

In the first few months of 1975, we still had no director of Parks and Recreation. We did manage to have a few meetings with the Recreation Advisory Committee and also with an architect about the design for a Nature Center building. That project acquired a life of its own and will be covered later.

But, initially in 1975, we held to our position that the Township should run the park and conduct the programs.

Well, things didn't go anywhere. The Township abandoned its plans to make the farmhouse habitable, and they could not rent it out. It appeared that the Township would not again hire a summer naturalist, as they did with Denise King. And then we had a meeting of the PPCC on March 24.

March 24, 1975: Let's Do It!

At that March 24 meeting, I suggested to our committee that if the Township would not run programs, perhaps we could. We had run several sample programs with schools and the public, and we had contacts with colleges that might give us leads on hiring a naturalist.

So, with less than $1500 in our treasury, we decided to hire a summer naturalist ourselves. The naturalist would operate out of the farmhouse, which we would fix up as best we could.

The next day, I called various people in the township government, including Township Committee members Allan MacDonald and Peter Carton, and they saw no problem in our doing this. Marcia would check on the condition of the farmhouse.

Our decision on March 24 permanently changed the mission of the PPCC. We were no longer an auxiliary group; we were going to run the park. And, we were no longer going to be limited to Middletown support. We had to go beyond the Township; to a wide area of Monmouth County for funding and program attendance.

We Meet John Campbell

On the same day of our fateful decision we learned that John Campbell would be our next director of Parks and Recreation.

On August 1, 1991, on the occasion of John Campbell's' retirement, the *Asbury Park Press* published an account of John Campbell's accomplishments in his 16-year service in Middletown. The article was titled, "His Care Made Parks Grow." He had guided the parks from a budget of $244,000 in 1975 to the 1991 level of $1.2 million. (In 2004 this figure was $2,064,890.[19])

In the article, Jim Truncer, Director of the Monmouth County Park System, said: "Middletown has the most comprehensive parks and recreation program in Monmouth County at the municipal level, and that's a tribute to Mr. Campbell's leadership."

Campbell himself is quoted, "With about 1,000 acres of parks and ball fields, the township has long taken an aggressive approach to preserving open space. The first thing I observed when I came to Middletown was that somebody had very good foresight in setting aside open space."

Our group met John Campbell on May 8, 1975. We made a presentation covering the history of the PPCC, the Englewood program philosophy which we had adopted, our upcoming summer programs, where we were thus far with plans for a Nature Center, the present condition of the park, the leaf dumping, and the embryonic Green Acres application for funds for park development.

In this book, I introduced Marcia Rissland on page 15 and then went on to other topics, mainly because Marcia did not really come into her own until later years. I'm going to do the same thing with John Campbell. He never got directly involved with

---

[19] Source: www.middletownnj.org

our programs; his main effort was in park development and, especially, in building the Nature Center, which we'll cover here soon. So, I'll go on telling about our programs.

Starting Your Own Business: S.C.O.R.E.

On Saturday, April 15, 1978 I attended a full-day seminar at Brookdale College on the subject of starting your own small business. It was attended by more than 100 people, and was arranged by the Service Corps of Retired Executives, or S.C.O.R.E. The topics covered included getting incorporated, what a "partnership" and "sole-proprietorship" are, insurance, and other related items.

But the talk I remember best is the opening statement of the president of S.C.O.R.E.: "Welcome to our seminar on starting your own business. We will cover many topics here, which we hope will be useful as you embark on this journey. But the main thing we hope to do is to talk you out of it."

He went on to give statistics of new business failure rates: half fail in the first year, and 90 percent fail in the first five years.

That was excellent advice, but unfortunately for me, it came three years too late. In 1975, none of us knew what we were really getting into — except Jim Knowles, our chairman, who was more experienced at business than we were. He saw it all coming. He didn't try to talk us out of it, but he sure made it clear what the long-term implications were of offering to run the programs ourselves.

With the hiring of a naturalist, we were starting a small business. He would be our first employee. We needed several kinds of insurance — liability, theft, employee disability and unemployment. We had to get NJ State sales tax registry. (Some people think that because you are a tax-exempt organization, you don't have to collect tax on what you sell. Not true; you do have to collect it, but you don't pay sales tax on what you *purchase*.) We needed a phone. We needed new sources of income. We needed to file annual returns to the IRS and State.

And, we needed a naturalist.

The Summer of 1975

I again called Professor Fischer at Cornell and asked if he knew someone that could be our naturalist in the upcoming summer. He, and some other people we knew, gave us some people to contact, and then Fischer called back and said that the New York State Dept. of Environmental Conservation had suddenly cut back on their summer program, leaving some people with no summer jobs. And one of these people was Woodward Bousquet,[20] an excellent student who was just graduating and would enroll for a master's degree in the fall.

By the end of April, we had hired Woody.

And, at the beginning of April, Marcia got the keys to the farmhouse.

The summer of 1975 was an exhausting and extraordinary experience for all who were fortunate to live through it. It involved converting an old, run down house into a pleasant environment for people to visit and attend programs. It required coordination of dozens of volunteers to staff it and work behind the scenes. Business matters had to be attended to. We had to advertise the programs. The Township had to provide services it had never provided in that tract before. The programs themselves had to be developed, and the naturalist had to be provided with assistance to run them. And, we had to pay for all this. Heading these tasks were:

- Preparing the farmhouse: Marcia Rissland
- Publicity, volunteer coordination: Diane Lehder
- Business matters and printing: Pete Brady
- Assisting Woody with program development: Lethe and Frank Lescinsky

I also note here that we were beginning to plan for the Nature Center building. In June 1975, we reorganized with Frank Lescinsky as chairman. Jim Knowles had put in three and a half years of fine service as chairman.

---

[20] Appendix C is a guide to pronunciation of names.

The cellar contained the skeleton of an upright piano. Most people couldn't resist strumming the strings as they walked by. It leaned against a wall separating the cellar hall from the open hearth kitchen. The wall and piano are gone, but the melody lingers on.

Beginning in May 1975, Marcia assumed responsibility for putting the farmhouse in useable condition. There was no thought of restoration then. But what many do not realize is that Marcia also assumed partial responsibility for the management of the entire farm, even though the Township government didn't know it. We'll see this play out over the years.

First, the farmhouse. It was full of junk, which had to be cleaned out before you could begin to think about making it "nice." Oil-soaked rags were all over the cellar. Broken glass, miscellaneous scraps of wood, coal left in the bin, and layers of dirt were everywhere. It was unclear in what year the bathroom had last been cleaned, but the toilet did work. Kind of. (The plumbing eventually became my responsibility.) Marcia began by making trips to the farm (less than two miles from her house) and moving many of her own belongings there, especially tools. Some of the tools she donated, some got "lost." She also moved furniture. The desk we used for three years (where Lois Kurz is seated on page 78) was Marcia's. There were table lamps. Kitchenware. Then, came the phone calls, sometimes several days in a row, to get the Township to pick up the trash.

Finally, she got to the point where she could schedule work parties, one of which was held on Saturday, May 31. Many people showed up; the photos here show some of them. That work party continued into Sunday. On another occasion a Boy Scout troop came over, and on another, a Girl Scout troop.

The basement in Marcia's house gradually turned into a staging area for things designated for the farm. On the work party days, many brought power tools. It was a group effort, but during some weeks Marcia was at the farmhouse nearly every day.

On May 24, Marcia took Township Administrator George Smith on a tour of the farmhouse. This was prior to the May 31 work party, but after Marcia had gotten rid of a lot of junk. She stressed the dangers of the dilapidated sheds in which children played, and asked that they be torn down, and that garbage be picked up on a scheduled basis. He said he'd get those things done. We would repeat those requests many times that year.

At right: Girl Scouts clean debris from the cellar. Their nice clothes suggest that they may not have known what they would be getting into.

Fixing Up the Farmhouse

May 31, 1975. Lunch at the first of many work parties held at the farmhouse over the next many years. From left: Jim Knowles, Lethe and Frank Lescinsky, Al Oppegard (seated, rear). Then clockwise from rear: Louis Rissland Jr. (standing), Lois Kurz, Marcia Rissland, Diane Lehder, and Laura Rissland.

Jim Knowles, Louis Rissland, Frank Lescinsky, Pete. I am stripping decades of paint from the door with a lye solution. Behind Jim at left is super shed; at right, the cat house. We had a decadent nostalgia for those buildings.

Diane Lehder was in from the start. She was a good strategist during the sewer battle and Colts Glen hearings, and her training in psychology was well suited toward public relations. In summer 1975 she scheduled the volunteers and was thus responsible for running the office. She moved to Ohio in fall 1975, but returned three years later and rejoined the board, where she served many years, some as chair of the PPCC. She and her husband Will now live on Kiawah Island, SC.

At right: Lois Kurz holds down the office in 1975. She also holds down the papers when the wind blows in the windows. Nice views out the windows. Lois was an official of the Girl Scouts of America and was valuable for her experience in working with youths.

The Volunteers

In April we asked for volunteers to sign up. We listed categories of clerical worker, trail guide, and program aid. For clerical workers, we said that "We offer warm, inviting, makeshift, temporary accommodations in a house built prior to 1700." (We were too early by a century on that one, as you'll see later.)

Our kick-off volunteers' meeting was on Thursday, June 19. It was a dark and stormy night. Really. There was a severe thunderstorm, and the wind and rain blew through the windows. It was quite a night. But, all met Woody and got a pep talk.

We had 36 volunteers that summer. Among those recruited were Peggy O'Connor and her daughter Maureen. Peggy was involved on our committee for several years, helping to coordinate volunteer tasks.

Those on trips and nature-related duties did a good job, and continued to do so into the future. However, staffing the office was a little more difficult for volunteers to handle. Some were not adept or knowledgeable enough to handle complicated questions from visitors, or callers. (And some were, such as Lois Kurz, pictured below.) The lesson we learned was that we needed a paid, office person to keep the place open and handle inquiries.

Woody Bousquet and Friends

The 1975 Summer Programs

Woody tried to teach us all he knew. He almost succeeded. And he almost succeeded in burning himself out. It was an exhausting eight weeks, and many of us couldn't keep up with him.

Woody took us all over the 250-acre park. He was especially talented with children. He would have them go into the field and swish a net back and forth through the grass and then bring it up close to their eyes, and using a magnifying glass identify tiny insects we never knew existed. He did the same with sieves in Poricy Pond. He turned the foundation of the former silo into a turtle pen. There were aquariums in the farmhouse that contained creatures caught right here in the park.

Woody had an advantage in that much of the land was still *disturbed ground*, meaning that it had recently been dug up, such as the sewer line path through the fossil beds. Also, many fields still existed as fields and had not been overgrown with alien plants. So, the park was a rich environment for wildflowers that grow in disturbed or cleared areas.

He had a likeable way of getting his points across. "You know how to tell the difference between a fir tree and a spruce? Try to shake hands with it. If it pricks you, it's a spruce."

Woody did more than conduct programs. He understood that we were trying to get a nature center built, and he attended some of the meetings of our committee with the Recreation Advisory Committee and the Township Committee.

On August 5, Woody conducted a field trip for the Township Committee. Our goal was not so much to sell them on building a nature center, but rather, to have them acquire an appreciation of the value of dedicated open space. I wanted them to have the same experience I had five years earlier on my walk with Mrs. Leistner.

Woody on a trip with the Township Committee on the evening of August 5, 1975. Twp. officials, from right: Frank Briggs, Peter Carton, Ralph Siciliano, Allan MacDonald, (all Township Committee); then Chris Abbes from recreation. George Smith is at left. Then, PPCC: Marcia, Lethe, Frank, Lois Kurz.

Schedule of Programs in Poricy Park, Middletown NJ   July 1 to July 26, 1975

These programs are sponsored by the Poricy Park Citizens Committee, and are directed by Woodward Bousquet, who recently graduated from Cornell University with a degree in environmental education. Poricy Park is a Middletown Township park.

The Poricy Park Nature Center, Oak Hill Road, Middletown (201-842-5966) is open daily, 10 am to 8 pm. There are no developed picnic facilities (tables, fireplaces), but cold soda is available, and visitors may enjoy bringing sandwiches. A telephone is available (no charge) for making local calls only. There are no public rest rooms in the park. Children attending programs are responsible for their own transportation.

There is a registration fee of 50¢ for participating in most of the programs listed here. There are two courses, however, which have a fee of $10 to cover materials. Nature trail guides are not required, but are useful, and may be purchased at the Nature Center. Work sessions have no registration fee. They involve clean up, trail blazing, and maintenance. We need help!   Please -- do not bring pets to these

July, 1975   activities. Thank you.

Sun	Mon	Tuesday	Wednesday	Thursday	Friday	Saturday
		July 1 ft#1 9:30-11:30 Field flowers Gebhardt Farm ft#2 1 to 3 pm Fossil trip	July 2 ft#3 6 to 8 am Birds - farm ft#4 9:30-11:30 Pond life ft#5 1 to 3 pm Forest ecology Cotton Tract	July 3 ft#6 1 to 3 pm Flowers, Boy Scout Tract ft#7 7 to 9 pm Plants & people	July 4 ft#8 9:30-11:30 Insect Study Gebhardt Farm Work session #1, Gebhardt Farm, 1-3 pm	July 5 ft#9 10-11:30 Reptiles, amphibians. Gebhardt Farm ft10 1 to 3 pm Pond life
July 6	July 7	July 8 ft11:6 to 8 am Birds - Cotton Tract	July 9 Course #1 1:30 - 4 pm ft12 7-9 pm Fossil trip	July 10 ft13 9:30-11:30 Insects - Farm ft14 1-3 pm Forest - Cotton	July 1 Course #1 1:30 - 4 pm ft15 7-9 pm Flowers, Fos. Bds	July 12 no scheduled activities
July 13	July 14	July 15 Course #2 9:30 - noon ft16 1-3 pm Pond life	July 16 Course #2 9:30 - noon Course #1 1:30 - 4 pm	July 17 Course #2 9:30 - noon Work session#2 1 to 3 pm ft17 7-9 pm Flowers - farm	July 18 ft18 9:30-12 Birds - Boy Scout Tract Course #1 1:30 - 4 pm	July 19 ft19 6-8 am Birds-Cotton Tr ft20 9:30-11:30 Pond life ft21 1-2:30 Reptiles, Amps.
July 20	July 21	July 22 Course #2 9:30 - noon ft22 1-3 pm Flowers - Boy Scout Tract	July 23 Course #2 9:30 - noon Course #1 1:30 - 4 pm	July 24 ft23 6-8 am Birds-Fos Beds Course2 9:30-12 ft24 1 to 2:30 Reptiles, Amps	July 25 Course #1 1:30 - 4 pm ft25 7-9 pm Pond life	July 26 Work session #3: trail maintenance, Cotton Tract 10 am - noon

A schedule for July 27 through August will be available in mid-July.

The programs in the calendar are explained in detail on the reverse side. The symbol "ft" means "field trip." The meeting place for each trip is designated on the reverse side. Please be sure you show up at the right place!!!!

Here are the first four weeks of our 1975 summer programs. (I was still in the mimeographing business, and it was a trying experience typing stencils such as this one since it requires a special technique with fluid to correct errors.) Our volunteers and committee members went on many of these trips and learned as much as the children.

The 1975 programs were intensively photographed. Several people took pictures. My own method was to buy black and white film in bulk, roll my own canisters, develop the film and make proof sheets such as this one. Hundreds of photos were thus processed. At summer's end, we produced an 11×22" single-sheet flyer containing 15 of the best photos.

At left was one of Woody's favorite photos, which I titled "Pokeweed and Spring Beauties." Woody told me that he liked the photo because of my clever caption, and not, of course, because of its content. This is one of the rare cases in which we do have the names of the people in the photos: Nancy Washileski and Suzan Sprenger. For those of you who are not into wildflowers, the *spring beauty* is a small, 5-petaled white flower which grows in the spring in the woods. *Pokeweed* is a tall, summer plant which grows in open areas. Its berries are said to be poisonous, but the leaves are edible, even from full-grown plants, and we have sometimes served them to guests at our home. You must par-boil them for a few minutes, discard the water, and then simmer. They're like spinach, and I like them better.

Success: If we build it, will they come?

In summer 1975 we had 690 program-visits.

Attendance is a bit of an art form. Poricy Park kept track of *program visits*, where a program visit was counted when a person arrived at the park, participated in a program, and left the park. If this was a five-day course, each time the person came counted as one visit. This is a pretty accurate way of counting program attendance, but it gives a low estimate of *park visitors*. It doesn't count the family that comes just to walk on the trails or to have a picnic lunch.

One 1975 contributor whom we went back to in 1976 for another grant asked what the 1975 attendance was. We answered "690." "Yes, but were they all different people or were some of them repeaters?" To this person, if there were many repeaters, we weren't doing our job of reaching a lot of people in the community. But would it have been better had they all been different, and anyone who came to a program didn't want to come back?

Well, so much for philosophy.

As far as the programs themselves went, the summer was a smashing success with respect to education and enjoyment. But the BIG question was whether a full-time Nature Center with its associated programs would be a continued success in Middletown. Would it be worth it? Or were we leading the Township down the path to constructing a giant white elephant?

And, at the end of the summer, we didn't know the answer to that question.

We did learn that there wasn't a market for a "nature center building" to be kept open seven days a week for long hours so people can visit. Very few people came in just to look around. (We developed a name for one kind of person: a *cruiser*, namely, the person that drove into the park, drove down the hill, drove slowly around the circle, never stopping, and then drove out of the park.) And, in subsequent years, we scaled back the hours that the facility was just "open," with no programs scheduled.

There are two basic kinds of visitor sites. One is the community-oriented facility that is geared to the *repeat visitor*. The other is a tourist-oriented site that looks for many different visitors and is concerned with the "gate," namely, the number of people that come to the site in a given year.

For example, Mount Vernon is an excellent site, a "must see" for anyone touring the USA, and its main attendance is due to tourism. It does have locally-oriented programs, but these are not its prime attraction. In contrast, Poricy Park is not regarded as a major tourist destination, and we knew we had to build a set of programs that would keep the "locals" coming back.

To get more insight into running a local nature center, several of us piled into a station wagon on July 23, 1975 and visited the Schuylkill Valley Nature Center. It is within the Philadelphia city limits, but just barely; it's way out on the northwestern edge. We brought John Campbell with us, and met Dick James, a hard-edged director who was surprisingly candid about the difficulties you can face. It was a good trip.

(A few years later I attended a seminar on management of environmental centers. Dick James was present, and his opening remark was, "The first rule, above all others, is survival." We later had a few occasions in Poricy Park to apply that rule.)

Well, nobody was going to break ground for the new building in the fall of 1975. We had more time to prove ourselves, and we decided to continue the summer programs into the next several years.

In this narrative, I will now cover the next two years of summer programs, so that they will not intrude on our later narrative on what else was happening in 1975-78, namely improving the condition of the grounds and buildings, and planning for a new Nature Center.

Karen Matson was a friend of one of our PPCC members, Pat Lindmark. Pat recommended Karen for the position of secretary/receptionist for the summer 1976 programs. Karen was also a photographer and took several photos of programs, including this photo which remains one of my all-time favorites of any photos taken in the park. Conducting the charge, wearing the fancy T-shirt is Ellen Fisher, then an art teacher at the Nut Swamp School. She is a daughter of Duffy Fisher, who was well known as a house mover, and Deacon of the Union Baptist Church, very near my current home. We have shared the following story with two of Duffy's other children, Duffy Jr., and Patricia: When our grandson Erik was four years old, I took him for a walk behind the church, where we found Duffy Fisher's grave. On his tombstone is carved a drawing of a house on a flat-bed truck. I told Erik that Duffy moved houses, and asked him, "Why do you think a man would spend his life moving houses on his truck?" Erik answered, "Because the houses were too big for him to pick up and move with his hands."

"Teddy" was our 1976 summer mascot. Baby raccoons are affectionate and playful, but when they get one year old they become sullen and difficult, as Teddy did. After the summer, Teddy went to live with Marcia and eventually went into the wild. One time during the summer, when Marcia and I felt we weren't getting enough newspaper coverage, we took Teddy to the Middletown offices of the *Daily Register* and turned him loose.

The 1976 Summer Programs

Woody was unavailable for summer 1976, so we contacted others, and on March 8, Tom Smith of

Hightstown accepted our offer. He was a teacher with the summer available, had a bachelor's degree from Rutgers, and a Masters in Environmental Education from Glassboro.

Many of the photos during the mid-'70s were taken by Pat Deotte. Pat also served as treasurer of the PPCC for several years.

The design of the programs was essentially the same as the previous year, eight weeks, with similar trips except that Tom had his own set of skills and interests. For example, he was licensed to catch birds with a net. We also hired Karen Matson to be our secretary. We were off to a good start, and initially the programs ran well.

But things started going sour. Beginning with the fifth week of programs, Tom started to have difficulties with us, and he called in to cancel several of the scheduled programs.

On Sunday, our family went off to New Hampshire for our annual camping vacation. I don't know what it is about me and phone booths in New England. In 1971, I called Dwight from a phone booth in Vermont to learn of the bad Planning Board decision on Colts Glen. This time, I called Frank Lescinsky from a phone booth in Newport, New Hampshire on August 22 to learn that Tom Smith had quit on the 15th. The last two weeks of programs were covered by the regular volunteers as best as they could.

Unlike the fall of 1975 when we published a big spread of photographs, this time we put out a simple one-sheet flyer mentioning the success we had with the programs and asking people to support the park. The flyer had five photographs, one featuring Teddy.

At right: Marcia and Teddy.

The 1977 Summer Programs

We had better luck in 1977. Once again, Professor Fischer had a student, Mike Weilbacher, who was between his junior and senior year. Mike was a showman. He loved crowds and he got people involved in doing things. He introduced "Games Nite" in which adults and children would play nature-oriented games.

The format of the programs was by now familiar, except that they ran for only six weeks. There were four week-long courses, in (1) general nature study, (2) freshwater environment, (3) the forest, and (4) exploring bird life, plus many other single event programs. Program attendance was 1300, exceeding the sum of the prior two summers.

Mike also designed our first T-shirt. He was good at artwork, and came into his own in later years when we switched to an offset press for our calendar.

Mike and Woody Bousquet were friends, and like Woody, Mike tried to teach us all he knew in six weeks, thus nearly burning himself out. This may be great for the summer, but in the long pull it might be more difficult. We had to consider this in offering him the job next year as our first full-time naturalist of the new Nature Center.

Our program flyer still listed the farmhouse as built in 1703. Marcia had not quite yet found the 1767 mortgage that Joseph Murray took out.

Once again, we took a million pictures. The top one here shows, in back row, Dennis Barshewski and Chris Febo, two loyal steady volunteers for several years. (Chris had a friend, Tim Young, and both of them frequently rode their bikes from Keyport to come to the park and help in many ways.) At left in front is Barbara Maul, our secretary that summer and also for the first two years of full-time operation. Next to her are Mike and Marcia. The center photo shows Mike conducting one of his courses. They were well attended. Children loved him. In the bottom photo are two frequent volunteers, Carolyn Hickson and Pat Lindmark.

When our programs ended in August, we were one month from the September 8 groundbreaking for the new Nature Center. So, I'll back up now and explain how we got there. There were some bumps in that road, too.

1975 – 1977: Slow Progress on the Farm

The Cat House

The cat house burned down on August 26, 1975.

It was probably arson. It was also a gift to us, because it rid the farm of a festering eyesore and health hazard. It also served as a wakeup call to the Township.

Every open-air farm or museum seems to have cats. The Monmouth County Park System takes care of their cats, has them neutered, and keeps them healthy. Some cats remain for years, others just come and go. But those that stay are well cared for.

There were about 20 cats on the farm, and they lived near the barn in a medium-size shack which Marcia dubbed the "cat house." They were sickly and were not neutered, so they kept breeding. The prior owner of the farm came over to feed them, but that's all the care they got. They were elusive and not friendly. And, they were killing off the wildlife. They were a major complaint of our early naturalists.

After their house burned down, they hung around the barn. Marcia sought help from Township animal control, who did loan us humane traps. These would catch them and hold them unharmed. One at a time. Marcia would keep checking the traps and when she caught one, would drive it to the SPCA in Eatontown, and make a cash gift to them out of her own funds. It took about two years of nearly daily trap checking and monthly trips to Eatontown to get rid of them all.

There was one benefit to Marcia from this. She rescued two kittens from the scene and brought them home, and they became loving pets.

The State of Affairs on August 31

At the request of Committeeman Allan Mac-Donald, I wrote up a 3-page status report on August 31, 1975. Here are some paragraphs:

> The Township has been diligent in picking up trash at the farmhouse (after a somewhat erratic start in June). Lawn mowing has been a 50-50 proposition;

the PPCC has mowed the lawn around the house 4 or 5 times, and so has the Township.

> The outbuildings on the farm should have been torn down. We have requested this since before January. On May 24, my son slightly injured himself when he fell through the floor of an outbuilding, and by chance, George Smith arrived on the scene just at that moment. You may recall an impromptu visit you made to the farmhouse on June 7, when we again brought up the outbuildings. During the week of August 18, some neighborhood children broke into the side buildings of the barn, climbed onto the roof, disturbed some wasps, and were stung – one child was stung seven times. On August 26, one outbuilding burned down to the ground (leaving a charred mess which should be cleaned up). We are fortunate that more serious accidents have not occurred. Needless to say, we have been promised on several occasions that the buildings would be taken down.

> The most important maintenance item in the park at this time is the mowing of the fields. John Campbell is very much aware of this, and is trying to get it done. Jim Duke had much of the farm mowed in early 1974, but left out several large sections, and also mowed around (rather than cut down) the large multiflora rose[21] bushes that have taken over the fields. One field in particular was a mowed lawn in 1970, and is now a dense tangle of brambles more than six feet high. Apparently, the condition is so bad now that Township equipment is inadequate for the job and an outside contractor is required. We believe that the job can be done for a modest cost – perhaps a few hundred dollars – but the cost will increase drastically if the condition is not corrected this year.

> Another consequence of non-mowing is that a fire hazard is created. On March 27, 1975 a major brush fire occurred on the farm, and by coincidence, Fred Richardson and Harlan Hogan [Township employees]

---

[21] *Rosa multiflora*, native to eastern Asian countries, was imported in the 1930s for highway medians and has become a major invasive agricultural pest.

were on the farm at that time. Had the outbuilding fire of August 26 happened a few months from now, when the fields will be dry, the fire could spread to the farmhouse, which is only about 100 feet away.

The roof on the farm house is in very poor condition, and should be replaced (it is beyond repair). We have also found that the roof on the barn [which the Township put on last January] leaks considerably. Further repairs made in February were sufficient to keep the snow out, but rainwater gets in, and since the barn is closed up, the wood is rotting. I was in the barn yesterday, and the underside of the second floor is almost completely white from mildew and rot. [Note: at that time, the ceiling of the first floor extended over the entire barn. The center bay was not open to the roof.]

All during this time, we were working with John Campbell on the design of the new Nature Center building. This was keeping us busy enough, and we weren't active in land management. Until October.

Leaf Dumping – Again

On Wednesday, October 22, 1975 Frank Lescinsky happened to be on the farm and saw the leaf trucks roaring in, dumping leaves on the same site as they did the previous year (see photo on page 69). Marcia saw the dumping on the next day.

I called George Smith. He said he was not aware of any agreement that was reached on ending the dumping in the prior year, and he said that the Public Works Department told him there were no alternate sites anywhere else in the Township.

I then called our attorney Bernie Finan to see if the dumping was illegal and we could get a restraining order in court.[22] He thought we could get a temporary one by Wednesday, October 29, and it would cost us around $500. Instead, we prepared a press release, made public for the first time here in this book.

---

[22] "Legality" centers on whether land acquired with NJ Green Acres funds can be used for dumping.

[Hand-carried to Committee members Monday evening. It was never released to the press.]

October 27, 1975

To: The Township Committee
The following press release will be distributed to the newspapers on Tuesday, October 28, at 6 pm unless something is done about the conditions described therein. We are sending this to you ahead of time in good faith, as we do not want to send this to the papers. PLEASE correct this situation. You can reach us now to discuss this (list of our people and phone numbers).

Draft of Press Release

The Poricy Park Citizens Committee is outraged at learning that the Township of Middletown is once again dumping leaves on the Gebhardt Farm.

"They did this last year," stated PPCC Secretary Paul T. Brady, "and last year's dumpsite is still an acre of wasteland of soggy leaf piles. What really hurts is that we just met on October 10 with the Director of Public Works and suggested an alternative site.* He assured us that the leaves would not be dumped again on the farm, but he has reneged on his word."

Today, PPCC Chairman Frank Lescinsky personally saw trucks continuing to dump leaves on the farm and learned that it would continue through the fall.

Mr. Brady stated that "A few years ago, an enlightened Township Committee purchased the Gebhardt Farm with over a half-million dollars of Federal and State funds as permanent open space for recreation and enjoyment. We spent an entire summer conducting a successful nature study program of educating the public to appreciate the value of this land. Today, the township is converting the space into a dump. The PPCC is currently investigating the legality of using such open space lands for this purpose."

* This was the topland part of the Fossil Beds tract. This was several years before this was developed as Normandy Park in 1978. .

Tuesday, October 28, was a pretty busy day! At 10:15 am I spoke with John Campbell, who told me that we were making a <u>big</u> mistake in making this fuss over the leaf dumping. We were also trying to negotiate for the new Nature Center. "The Nature Center is the big prize. You are jeopardizing it."

At 11 am George Smith called Frank Lescinsky. The dumping had temporarily stopped, and the subject will be brought up tonight with the Township Committee. Smith did not like the Fossil Beds site as an alternative, because *it would look too ugly!!!*

Frank Lescinsky (left) with newly elected Bob Eckert (2nd from left), Dick Kelly (far right), & John Campbell, director Parks and Recreation. (12/4/1975)

At the Township Committee meeting on Tuesday evening, Lou Rissland explained the potential impact of a court order stopping the dumping, and so a meeting on the farm was scheduled for the next day.

The Wednesday farm meeting was attended by the foreman of the leaf crew, also Harlan Hogan (another foreman), George Smith, Lynden Kibler (Chair, Environmental Commission), John Campbell, Marcia, and me. They agreed to move the dump site to a more obscure area of the farm this fall, and then go elsewhere in future years (which they did!).

And then, the subject of mowing came up. Why is it needed on the farm? We went through a discussion of alien plants, how they take over fields, how the native plants and wildlife are forced out, and how easy it is to control them if you do it annually.

The Politics of Leaf Dumping

The upcoming election might have had something to do with the Township Committee's decision on leaf dumping. In the chart on page 31, we see that after three years of Democratic Party control, the Republicans had regained control of the Township Committee by a 3-2 margin. If even one Democrat won this year, control would switch back.

The leaf crisis was just a week prior to the election. Suggesting that the Republicans solved this to avoid bad publicity is speculation, but the fact is that both Democrats won anyway. Bob Eckert and Dick Kelly replaced Peter Carton and Frank Briggs,

defeating Peter's brother Larry Carton and Robert McEvilly.

At that time, the weekly *Courier* had on its staff "Tickie" (Lucille) Smith, who wrote a gossip column called "Heard around the halls," with a *nom de plume* of "Eve Dropper." Anyone in politics plunged into the paper right to her column to find out what was *really* going on. And, on November 13, 1975 she stated flatly that the first thing the Democrats would do would be to oust George Smith, this being a rumor that had circulated within the party. She was correct except for the "first thing" part. Smith lasted until the fall of 1976. And, it took a few more months after that to get him out of the ranch house.

It would be nice having Allan MacDonald as Mayor. Because in a phone call to me on March 14, 1975, he said, "During my three years on the Township Committee I hope I can show my appreciation of all the work you guys have put in by seeing that you get all you wanted."[23]

---

[23] This was directly in reference to constructing a Nature Center. Allan MacDonald served for 6 years.

January 1976. The PPCC-hired roofers work on the barn, and the demolished super shed is in foreground.

Mrs. Timolat and the Barn Roof

Following her husband's death in 1970, Mrs. Timolat continued to give us regular, but modest-sized contributions. Which was fine, because we weren't spending much money in those years.

But she took a strong interest in the park, and frequently called Marcia, and on occasion, me. She saw the decay occurring in the buildings and felt that underneath all those asbestos shingles and patchwork additions there were some lovely old farm buildings. She wanted them restored.

Well, Marcia told her, we can't get grants to do that until they are put on the National Register of Historic Places, which we were trying to do [as will be covered in the section on restoration]. But meanwhile, Marcia told her, the barn was actually in worse shape than it was before the Township put its roof on it.

Okay, said Mrs. Timolat, find a contractor, get an estimate, and she would cover the cost of a proper roof. This was at the end of October 1975.

After hunting around, Marcia came up with the S&W roofing company and their estimate of $2700. By November 24, we had the full amount. It took some modest red tape cutting to get the Township to authorize us to proceed with the project, but the

new roof was put on in January 1976. A few rotted rafters were also replaced. The rest of the barn remained the same, except that the contractor discovered severe framework rotting that had to be replaced at an extra cost of $500, which we covered.

In the course of getting estimates, one contractor told us that an asphalt shingle-on-plywood roof would last 15 years. It actually lasted 19 years.

And, at the same time, the Township took down super shed and some of the other outbuildings.

Super shed (tractor shed), March 8, 1975.

Let's see. We had the offer for the barn roof money around November 1, 1975 and the roof was finished three months later. During this time, while Marcia was dealing with the contractor, it was on me to get written authorization from Town Hall to have our contractor begin. This took: (1) at least five phone calls to George Smith, (2) two calls to John Campbell, (3) three calls to the Township attorney, (4) several calls to the roofer and his insurance company, (5) two calls to Township Committee members, (6) two <u>visits</u> to the Township attorney, (7) one visit to a Township Committee meeting, and (8) two visits to Town Hall by Cathy (Brady) to pick up the letter of authorization. Nothing to it.

Oh, one more thing. On my trip home from the Township Committee meeting, a drunk driver ran a stop sign and drove directly into my path. I crashed into him. Nobody was hurt, but my 1963 Rambler was totaled. I had to buy a new car. I chose a VW Rabbit. It cost about the same as the new barn roof.

Anyway, it was <u>three months from initial start of project (11/1/1975) to barn roof finished</u>.

The Roof on the House

Now, back in October 1975, we had discussed a new house roof with John Campbell. This time the <u>Township</u> would pay. Here is what followed:

- October 1975. John called a carpenter he knew, Charlie Norton, who said a good roof should run between $2,000 and $2,500.
- November 1975. Campbell wanted a second opinion. So, Marcia asked our own roofer in December (prior to his starting on the barn) what the house roof would cost (not including removal of the dormer). He said $2,450.
- January 1976. Campbell told PPCC that he would put request for $2,450 in budget. I passed this information on to our contractor.
- March 26, 1976. In a phone call with Township Attorney Peter Frunzi, he said that on March 1 there was a new law enacted that required any contract between $500 and $2,500 to get three

proposals. These could be non-formal estimates, but three were required. We had to do this with the house roof even though our estimate and budget request preceded March 1.
- June 1, 1976. Campbell asked if our contractor still was holding his price at $2,450. (Apparently he got his two other estimates.) I checked, and yes, his price was still the same, as long as the Township cleaned up the mess.
- July 8, 1976. Our contractor gets contract.
- Mid October. Our contractor has not started, we are now getting on <u>his</u> case. I explained that this is a <u>municipal</u> contract, good only for this year, and if they don't spend it, they lose it and cancel the contract. (For heaven's sake, this guy is a contractor. Doesn't he know that?)
- December 20, 1976. Work begins.
- January 19, 1977. North half of roof is done.
- January 25, 1977. South half of roof is removed, and dormer is gone.
- February 1977: PPCC pays additional $500, over the Township's contract, for dormer removal.
- Mid February 1977. Work is completed.

So, from mid-October to mid-February was <u>16 months from initial start of project to house roof</u>.

Support Your Local "Friends" Organization

Many parks, nature centers, museums, historic sites and other agencies are government funded, and they also have auxiliary organizations that raise funds to support them. Why, some people ask, should they donate money to these organizations when they are funded by tax dollars?

One answer lies in the above story. A nonprofit independent group can achieve small gains far more rapidly and efficiently than the government agency they support. So often, I have seen simple projects go through several layers of approval with associated delays just to satisfy bureaucratic and/or legal requirements. So, pick a friends group and help out!

The Firebombing

On Monday noon, May 2, 1977, I was in the Cotton Tract with some people, and one of the children mentioned that "there was an old house over on the farm with some broken windows." I decided to check on this after dinner.

I went over to the farm that evening with my 11-year-old son Stephen and walked around the farmhouse and was shocked to find that every window on the first floor had been broken, even some on the second floor by rocks having been thrown at them from the ground. The cellar sill windows were demolished, including the frames.

We went into the house and walked into the kitchen (on the first floor). It took about 30 seconds to realize the enormity of what had happened. On the kitchen floor were the remains of a glass bottle which had been the container of a Molotov cocktail. It had been tossed in and it had exploded, covering almost the entire surface areas of the floor, walls, and ceiling with thick black soot. Miraculously, nothing had caught on fire. The gasoline exploded when it hit the walls and then flashed out.

To her good fortune, Marcia was out of town. I called the police and Frank. Frank, Stephen, and I just stood there, stunned. The police were professional about this, took pictures, asked questions, but this was all in a day's work for them. We all knew there was no hope of catching the arsonists.

The alarm had not gone off.

The next day, Parks and Recreation people came over and surveyed the damage. I can't remember just when Marcia learned of this, but she often quoted their people telling her "not to worry, we will fix this up and take care of everything."

We had to fix up the farmhouse for the 1977 summer programs, and our first work party was scheduled for May 21.

The Township did take care of the worst of the damage. They boarded up the windows and soon replaced them. But it was Marcia, personally, who was at work daily, scrubbing the soot away, painting some surfaces, and doing many of the other tasks to recover from the bombing. (A volunteer, Clint Hasenohr, also made additional repairs to the windows during the next year.)

The Township asked us to keep track of our expenses for materials to repair the house. In August we submitted an accounting for $117.27, which was paid to us in December.

This incident opens the door to two more difficult topics: dirt bikes and alarms.

Dirt Bikes

Even before the Township acquired the park, kids had been riding minibikes through the tracts. This was particularly true of the Boy Scout Tract, which had a road that circled the property. We sometimes were able to stop the kids and talk to them, but it was a persistent irritation.

During 1976 it got worse. Kids on minibikes were replaced by gangs of youths on dirt bikes. These were heavy-duty all-terrain bikes. The gang members built their own trails with jump ramps, right on the farm, within sight of the ranch house which was still occupied by George Smith.

By April 1977 this had reached crisis level. The gangs came from different towns and set up all-day riding sessions on the farm. They brought alcohol and drugs. On April 20, Marcia and Frank met with Middletown Police Chief Joseph McCarthy and Captain Gleason, and the police agreed to give better surveillance and even try to catch the riders. Soon, Officer McClelland would occupy the now-vacant ranch house.

And, on the weekend of the bombing, the police did catch the riders. The police gave them a lecture and told them to leave. And they did leave. And they came back and firebombed the farmhouse.

The major dirt bike riding stopped after that, but there were still the occasional minibikes.

So, how come they didn't set off the alarm?

Burglar Alarms

The new Nature Center was opened in July 1978, and during its first two months of operation there were 15 false alarms caused by a variety of reasons: improperly installed equipment, poorly-designed equipment, human error, etc. That's just one of many statistics I kept over the years.

For anyone in the museum business, and especially in an open-air park with several buildings, alarms are a constant headache. This is especially true if several people have authority to open and close the buildings. In Poricy Park, there seemed to be nearly 15 such people at any time.

We had a "call list," of people for the police to call when an alarm went off. (We had two alarms, one on the Nature Center and one on the farm-house.) In my days of involvement, we rotated three families at the top of the list: Frank Lescinsky, Marcia and Lou Rissland, and myself. I was called many times, and the calls I best remember were in the middle of the night. There may have been up to 20 nighttime calls in an 18-year period, and that's just for me. Frank and Marcia also had their share.

I kept a set of pants and a shirt on a hook so I could dive into them and drive over to the park to meet the police. The typical time from phone call to getting back into bed was one hour.

The police were never happy to see me. But there was one time when, while we were checking out the nature center, one of the officers discovered our observation beehive.[24] He took a great interest in it, and wanted an explanation of how it worked. At his request, I found the queen, which can take from five to fifteen minutes.

Perhaps my favorite "night call" story was from Marcia and Lou. They were called at 3 am and opened the doors of their garage. As they were about to get into their car, Lou said, "Listen." And,

---

[24] Loaned to us and set up by volunteer Bob Appleby. This was always a popular exhibit.

although they lived more than a mile away, they could hear the siren on the farmhouse howling into the still night air.

At work (Bell Labs, then Bellcore) I learned not to tell people that I had been called out of bed. They always thought it was funny.

There were a few times that the alarm went off because of a genuine break-in. Maybe three times over 20 years. All the others were false alarms. When we complained to the alarm company, they went through a litany of reasons why it wasn't their fault. Their equipment "doesn't do that."

During my involvement, we went through five alarm companies. When we had had it with one company and switched to another, the new company would come in and size up the situation, and go through the following steps:

- They would look at what was already in place and declare that it was (a) obsolete and ineffective equipment, and (b) had been improperly installed.
- Then they would tell us that *their* equipment was far superior and that we would never have to worry about false alarms again.
- When we tried to explain our needs and some of the difficulties we might have with a new system, they would become arrogant and tell us that they were experts, had been in the business for 20 or more years, and they would install a perfect system, without our advice.
- When we asked what procedure we should follow at 3 am to try to determine what caused the false alarm, they would flatly state that we needn't worry about that, because we would not ever get a false alarm at 3 am, but on the one-in-a-million chance it did happen, just call this 800 number and they'll take care of it. (Q: "Will you come right over at 3 am to meet the police?" A: "We *told* you, that will never happen.")

And then, of course, their new system would behave just as badly as the old one did.

A Moment of Schadenfreude

After many years of having to take this from alarm companies, I had my personal moment of *schadenfreude*.[25]

On May 16, 1988 there was a particularly severe vandalism episode when several very large windows in the Nature Center were smashed. The alarm didn't go off. Then, the vandals went down to the farmhouse and broke several windows, again not setting off the farmhouse alarm system either. We were furious with the alarm company, and felt we should collect damages from them.

On May 26, we held a meeting in the Nature Center with the Township Attorney, several other Township officials, members of the Poricy Park staff, and two representatives of the alarm company. The Township attorney noted that the alarm contract held the company to only $50 liability for "defects" in the system, but he maintained that this problem was due to poor installation, and therefore the alarm company could be sued for damages. We then cited 25 false alarms that had occurred in 1986 and 1987. The alarm company stated flatly that none of these could have been caused by "poor installation." They don't do "poor installations."

The alarm company then told us of an option we did not know existed that had to do with the buzzer on the alarm keypad, and in their presence, I went over to test the option to see if it worked. It did. But in making this test, I inadvertently set off the alarm.

But I didn't know I had set off the alarm, because the siren within the building did not sound. So, a few minutes after we were all seated after the test, two squad cars drove up and four policemen got out and came into the building, quite irritated (as usual for this situation).

While the police were there, the alarm man went to the control box and found that the interior siren had been wired out of the system some time ago by their installation technician. This little demonstration of a flaw in their installation occurred in front of 14 people, including the cops. It felt good.

That's the end of my episode, but you might be wondering how this was settled. The alarm company installed at no charge several state-of-the-art glass breakage sensors in three buildings (Nature Center, farmhouse, ranch house). These would have cost $4,570. The PPCC paid for replacement of the windows, at $4,650. The Township agreed to cover from that point forward the liability insurance of the PPCC on its programs, thus sparing us the annual $3,000 cost of liability insurance, a major gain for us. The Township repaired the damaged windows in the farmhouse (which had been restored by 1988).

A Day in Marcia's Life

Life for many of us in the pre-Nature Center days consisted of trips to the farm and doing whatever we could to keep it in reasonable shape. Although others were involved, Marcia was the principal person doing this. Numerous problems arose involving maintenance of the (unrestored) farmhouse, emergency repairs to the barn, work parties, vandalism, and so on. We didn't keep exact diaries; therefore, much of what happened is lost to history. Which is a good thing, because it wouldn't make interesting reading to later generations. The incidents were okay to talk about over drinks at night,[26] but not to put in a book later.

But, there were a few times that Marcia, and sometimes I, did document things that happened, and I have selected one such account to include here. It's one day in Marcia's life, and it is included on the next page. For best enjoyment: Read the write-up from start to finish without skipping to the punch line!

---

[25] Malicious enjoyment experienced when observing the discomfort of others.

[26] Usually Laird's Apple Jack. Our tastes had improved considerably since "Duval" at Dwight's bar.

A Day with Public Works

Marcia's account of Tuesday, September 27, 1977. Public Works was scheduled to cut and remove trees and brush.

8:30 am: Marcia arrives at top of hill. Is immediately joined by Harlan Hogan (work crew foreman) who holds forth for 15 minutes about why nothing gets done.

8:45: John McGowan arrives (Director, Public Works).

9:05: First contingent of workers arrive, led by "Charlie." Carolyn [Lyn] Hickson [her photo is on page 85] arrives immediately after. Hogan, Charlie, and Marcia discuss what is to be done. Equipment consists of dump truck, pickup truck, brush chipper, and chain saw. Crew consists of Charlie and three CETA laborers.[27] Fourth laborer didn't show up. After several minutes of discussion and maneuvering of vehicles, the pickup truck which was towing the brush chipper got stuck in wet grass. After much spinning of wheels and loud exchanges, it was decided that it was time to knock off for the *de rigueur* coffee break. That is, a couple of men would take the truck and disappear to the vicinity of Route 35 and return with refreshment for the others. Lyn intervened and said <u>she</u> would go for coffee. They then said that someone would have to go back to the shop for a hammer, because the coupling that connected the brush chipper to the pickup truck was bent out of shape. Marcia announced that there was a hammer in the farmhouse and that she would be glad to get it. Marcia and Lyn departed, leaving the men sitting. When Marcia returned with the hammer, it seems that it was not so necessary after all. The coupling was uncoupled. While Marcia was getting the hammer, one of the men started the chain saw, and the rope broke off in his hand. This necessitated the departure of another man with truck and chain saw to get it fixed at the shop on Kane's Lane. Meanwhile, back on the farm, a couple of the laborers who were still left there complained bitterly about the sticker plants [probably tickseed sunflowers] with needle-sharp seeds which penetrate the heaviest trousers, and

27 Comprehensive Employment Training Act, pronounced "SEE-tuh," a federal program that paid local governments to hire people so they could be trained in new skills.

said they could not work there unless the stuff was mowed down. Charlie said he would go to Kane's Lane for the mower truck, but would wait to have his coffee first. Lyn arrived with coffee, soda, cigarettes, and change. The men had stood around awaiting this event for at least 20 minutes, doing absolutely nothing. After refreshing themselves at leisure, one of them finally pulled the rope on the mended chain saw, and at

11:00: The first tree was cut down!

11:15: Perceiving that work had commenced at last, Marcia told Lyn that she would go home to get some breakfast and be back by 11:45, when Lyn had to leave. Lyn said that the men would probably break for lunch (break what?) shortly thereafter, so Marcia might as well not come back until 1:00.

11:45: Lyn stopped by Marcia's house to advise her that the men had already knocked off for lunch. Nothing had been done, because the chain saw kept breaking down, and the truck was locked in gear. One of the men had to go out to get a mechanic, and came back without one.

12:45: Marcia went back to the hill. Two men were working on the truck, one was cutting up a dead limb with the chain saw, and Charlie was cutting figure eights with the mower. Marcia left word with the chain saw guy that she would be at the farmhouse.

1:20: Marcia saw a funeral cortege of Public Works vehicles departing: the ailing truck being towed by a pickup truck, and two other trucks following in attendance. She went to the hill to find out what was going on, but nothing was going on. Two men were sitting in yet another truck, sipping soda, smoking, and enjoying the scenery. They sprang to attitudes of virtue and one of them began pulling on the chain saw rope, without much effect. They then sat on the ground instead of on the truck.

1:45: Having seen a truck drive in and up to the hill, Marcia again went up. Charlie had returned from escorting the other trucks to Kane's Lane. He bitched

- 94 -

about the mechanics there who only fix police cars, said the sumac trees were not good for wood chips, said the mower couldn't cut half the stuff he was trying to get, etc., etc. He said it could be done in two days with a bulldozer.

2:15: Marcia had to leave.

4:20: Marcia returned. Men were gone. Trees were still there, also cigar packets, cake wrappers, soda cans, cigarette packs, bread crusts. And thus endeth the chronicle of how I spent my 25th wedding anniversary.

WHIMSEY

Alliterative Tools You Must Use to Preserve Poricy Park

Composed by Marcia Rissland while attending one of many Township Committee Meetings

Protest	Publicity	Promotion
Press Releases	Persuasion	Pressure
Propaganda	Politics	Persistence
Perseverance	Planning	Preparation
Photography	Prodding	Pushing

Illustration by Marcia Rissland from *The Cotton Tract* booklet.

John Campbell and the Nature Center

John Campbell arrived on the scene in April 1975 (we met him on May 8), at which time the idea of a nature center had been in the works for a few years, and we had even started talking about it with an architect. So, having a nature center was not John Campbell's original idea.

But the execution of having it designed and built was very much John's. He didn't do it all by himself, however, and in particular, the PPCC gave him encouragement, help, and at times, some difficulty.

Campbell's Hand in The Card Game

John was in a difficult position when he arrived, and looking back, I think he handled it well. Try to put yourself in his shoes. "John, welcome to Middletown. You're the Director of Parks and Recreation and you have charge of all the Township parks. Oh, I forgot. There is one park you're really not in charge of. That's our newest park, Poricy Park, and it's our biggest park (250 acres), greater than the sum of all the other parks put together, and you'll be responsible for its upkeep, but there's this group of upstart ecologists that insist on having the major say in the design of what goes into that park. Good luck!"

I don't play cards now, but I did once play bridge. If you're the declarer, you try to capture "tricks" by playing out your hand. Usually, the highest card played in the suit that is led on any trick takes the trick, but opponents will trump you if they can. This means that the lowly two of clubs can take a trick in which you have led the ace of spades.

With Poricy Park, John was dealt a hand with a lot of high cards. He had a staff, maintenance crew, a budget, and the authority to say what would happen in his parks. However, the PPCC had some independent funds, a lot of public support even to the point of having some influence on who gets into

town government, and by now, some experience in running educational programs and gathering information on nature centers. We were well known for blanketing the Township with flyers and bumper stickers. So, we didn't have many high cards, but we did have a hand with many trumps.

And, there was a third agency, the Recreation Advisory Committee, who had an undefined role in this project. They believed that they should be offering the principal advice and calling many of the shots, and were upset that an outside, independent group of citizens was taking a leadership role. To round out the bridge game analogy, they didn't have many trumps or high cards. And, some of them were helpful, and some were decidedly not.

Ernie Bostrom

Ernie Bostrom is a sad and entirely forgotten chapter in the history of the Nature Center. He deserves to have his story heard.

Bob Makely gave Poricy Park enormous support while he was on the Township Committee. He left the Committee at the end of 1971, but we remained in touch with him, and in early 1974 we contacted him to see if he could suggest a way we could get a start on getting a Nature Center built on the newly-acquired Gebhardt Farm. Bob suggested we talk with Ernie Bostrom.

Ernie was a partner in the architectural firm of Kobayashi and Bostrom, which was the firm that designed the Middletown Library on New Monmouth Road, which opened in 1971. Bob Makely had coordinated the library construction. Although Kobayashi probably made contributions to the design, the library was widely believed to be chiefly designed by Bostrom. (The Township later outgrew the library, and the remodeled library was opened in 2004.)

On February 20, 1974, Marcia, Jim Knowles, and I were joined by Bob Makely and Jim Duke

February 28, 1975. Middletown Township Planner Bill McCann, architect Ernie Bostrom, PPCC members Jim Knowles, Diane Lehder, and (not shown) Marcia Rissland and Pete Brady meet on the Gebhardt Farm to discuss plans for a Nature Center.

(Director, Parks and Recreation) in a meeting with Ernie. We were talking about a 2,500 sq. ft. building, which Ernie thought might cost around $75,000, take two months to plan and design, and around eight months to construct it. (The actual building would turn out to be twice as large and cost three times that figure.) This was just an informal meeting and Ernie told us he would have to do a more thorough design to get better numbers.

Nothing happened for a year. Jim Duke left in the fall, and there was no director of Parks and Recreation for several months, so we thought we'd try again to get this started. We must have had the Township's informal blessing, because we were joined by Middletown Planner Bill McCann. Bill, Jim Knowles, Marcia, Diane Lehder, and I met with Ernie on the farm on February 28, 1975 (photo). Later at lunch, Bill McCann thought we were talking about a building costing $200,000, not including landscaping, parking lot, and other external features. This was a pretty good estimate for what followed.

Ernie wrote a report on the general concept of a nature center and its role in the community, for which he charged $175. I can't remember who paid him for this, perhaps the Township. But on May 14, just a week after we had met John Campbell, Ernie joined John, Frank Lescinsky, and me for lunch and told us that the next step would be for a sketch plan from him, without construction details, and that would cost $2,000. The final plans would be $17,000. John said that $2,000 was okay from his budget, but the $17,000 would have to go for bids.

For the next several months, the Township jerked Ernie back and forth on the $2,000 sketch plan. About once a month, someone would tell us that it had been approved, which we would relate to Ernie. As late as September 19, 1975, Bob Makely, who was a Republican, told me that he had spoken with his friends on the Republican-controlled Township Committee, and it was settled, Ernie would get his $2,000 for the sketch plan.

But in early October, we learned that another architect, Bill Miller, who had Republican connections, had been chosen, thus ending Ernie Bostrom's brief career at Poricy Park. Later that month, it fell on me to give Ernie the bad news. It was a very difficult conversation.

What We Knew about Nature Centers

By fall 1975, many of us had visited other nature centers, as a group (such as Schuylkill Valley, already mentioned) and as individuals. (I had visited the Seven Ponds Nature Center in Dryden, Michigan, and others.) A major message we received is that you don't just build a building with one big room with a fireplace and restrooms and then conduct programs. Practically every site told us that were they to do it again, they would have more *administrative space* and more *storage space*.

We also got advice on the kind of equipment and sinks and drains you need for the kind of programs you run in a nature center. So, we were ready to talk with the architect.

Our First Meeting with Bill Miller

Bill Miller worked in the firm of James D. Witte, Architect, and although it is Witte's name that is on all the plans, it was Bill Miller that did the design of the Nature Center.

Frank and I met Bill Miller and John Campbell on October 6, 1975 at Bodman Park. We outlined the basic requirements: two large rooms, a kitchen off of one of them, three staff offices, rest rooms, a work room for maintenance, and as much storage space as he could provide. Maybe there would be a basement.

We then had our first sparring match with Bill Miller. He suggested we all drive over to Holmdel Park and see the "Shelter Building," which he designed, and which is the building of modern design next to the lake, with a large fireplace, refreshment stand, restrooms, and whatever else people need coming in from outdoors. Frank and I stated that each of us had seen the Shelter Building, and maybe it would be more appropriate to visit the Gebhardt Farm, where his new building would be situated. We also suggested that the modern architecture of his Holmdel Park building would clash with the colonial farm theme we hoped to have in the park someday. Miller responded, "Just because you have some old buildings on the property doesn't mean that they dictate the design of a new building." We agreed in part with him, and we certainly didn't want his building to look like the existing structures on the property! (Super shed, the decrepit barn, and the farmhouse covered with junkyard-scavenged material.) But, we said, we want the new building to be located so you could see the old ones from it for surveillance, and we don't want somebody to stand next to a restored farmhouse someday, look up at the Nature Center, and say "Who in hell put that thing up there?"

John Campbell was very good at smoothing feathers and we all went over to the farm. Bill would get to work. And, he did.

Plans 1, 2, 3, 4, ...

A few weeks later, Miller returned to Campbell with three plans (plans 1, 2, and 3), all of which Campbell rejected and sent him back to the drawing board. We never saw them. In the meantime, we were ingratiating ourselves with the Township government by making the fuss over the new round of leaf dumping (see page 87), so these were hectic times for us. We weren't exactly making friends with people in the Township government.

Miller came back to Campbell with plans 4 and 5, which Frank, Marcia, and I reviewed with Campbell and Miller on Monday, November 3. We did kind of like plan 4, with some modifications. The biggest problem was the placement of the rest rooms, which Miller said could not be changed because the redesign we wanted would not fit in the space allocated. (See next page.) We asked him to take another look and see if he could change them.

A week later, on Monday, November 10, Campbell gave Frank a copy of plan 4 to take home. It was for a 4,840 sq. ft. building, almost the way it ended up in final form. Almost. But Miller had not changed the rest rooms. At a general meeting of the PPCC that night we went over it, and there was much discussion with complete agreement that the rest rooms were badly situated.

Now, I am not a trained architect or draftsman, but I did trace the plans with the limited skills I learned in mechanical drawing class at Rensselaer. (8 am on Saturday mornings. Ugh.) I managed to move a few walls around and fix the rest room problem. Armed with this solution, Marcia and I met with Campbell, Miller, and some members of the Recreation Advisory Committee on Thursday, November 13. It was to be my last meeting with the RAC, because I disgraced myself and lost my temper. (As a result, the other members of the PPCC wouldn't let me join them in later meetings with the RAC!)

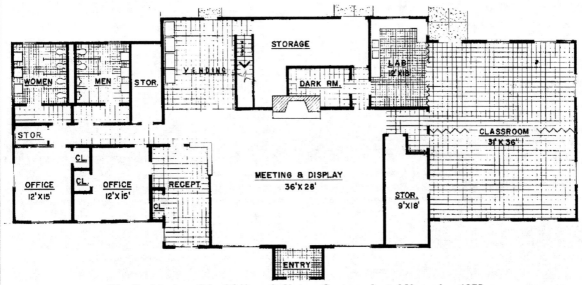

The final design of the 4,840 sq. ft. Nature Center, adopted November 1975.

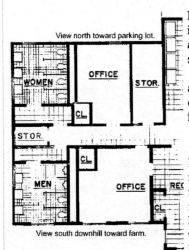

View north toward parking lot.

View south downhill toward farm.

The Final Design

Above is the final design, and at left is the next-to-last plan, as best as I remember it. In the plan at left, the men's room was given the best view in the park, and the office at top looked at the parking lot. Both offices abutted flushing toilets. Also, the plumbing for the toilets could not be shared, since the toilets were not back-to-back.

In the design above, the rest rooms have been moved to a more logical arrangement. (Incidentally, the "LAB" is actually the kitchen, but it is called a "laboratory" because "kitchen" might be viewed as inappropriate for a nature center. In practice, it was often used as a laboratory.)

The Basement

Marty and Betty Welt were active in the PPCC during the years the Nature Center was being built. They attended and hosted committee meetings and helped in several other ways. Marty was skilled in mechanical ways and later gave advice on the barn reconstruction. But his major impact on the park was to insist that the Nature Center have a basement. It was useful for storage, but it later kept all the severe problems with the heating system below ground, where they belonged. The basement is under the area at the top of the drawing from "vending" to "lab." The rest of the building is on a slab.

The Nov. 13, 1975 Meeting: Outburst

We began the meeting by trotting out the plan that Frank had been given on Monday, with several suggested modifications. Bill Miller balked at each change, especially moving the men's room. John Campbell was amenable to making some wall changes, but Miller insisted that my design shown on the previous page would not work. He was right – I had made a slight, but trivial error in drawing one of the walls, but one that was readily corrected.

At this point, one of the Recreation Committee people sensed that we were at odds with Miller and he immediately took Miller's side. He said that the Township had hired a professional architect, who knew much better than we did what he was doing, and we were going to accept his design exactly as is, like it or not, because that is the proper way to go about such things.

The meeting dragged on. After about one and a quarter hours, Miller had not budged an inch (literally and figuratively), and his supporter on the Recreation Advisory Committee was becoming more belligerent in his defense of the original plans. I cracked. I made an impassioned speech to the effect that I had put six years of my life into this project, had traveled all over the East studying nature centers, had been a major player in saving the biggest park in Middletown, had taken the trouble to learn what natural features were in the park, had been on and even led many field trips through the area, and we had not gotten any participation or help from the Recreation Advisory Committee, who didn't want to acquire the park in the first place [in 1970]. Apparently, nothing is going to change and we are wasting our time here, and I have therefore made my final contribution to this park and Middletown. If nobody is going to budge on this obviously flawed plan, then I am getting up and walking out and you guys can run your park all by yourselves.

It was not a bluff. I meant it.

It was John Campbell that broke the silence, and after further discussion, Miller agreed to move the men's room to the back side of the building.

I believe that the resulting design of the building and its placement on the land were well done. The building served our purposes, and it was not over-whelming when seen from the historic buildings at the base of the hill. I don't know what transpired between John Campbell and Bill Miller, but the combination of their efforts produced a good result.

But what we had at this time was just a sketch plan of the building, done so that an application for a grant could be sent in to NJ Green Acres. It would be more than a year before the plans would be done in detail sufficient for bids and construction. And, although the floor plan and appearance of the building served us well, the interior details of plumbing, heating, and air conditioning were later subcontracted. As we will discuss later, these internal features proved to be a disaster.

John submitted the plans with the application to Green Acres in December 1975. We now entered a waiting phase.

Green Acres Approval

As already mentioned, the NJ Green Acres bond issue of 1974 supported development of facilities (in addition to land acquisition).

On March 24, 1976 the Green Acres people toured the site with John Campbell. On June 1, Howard Wolf of Green Acres told me that they had all they needed for the application, and that John Campbell seemed "reasonably sophisticated" in his application procedures. But, approval could take two years.

It didn't take two years. At 5:20 pm on Thursday September 30, John called me to tell me that Green Acres had approved a grant for $161,000 for half of the construction cost of the Nature Center, including external improvements.

Funding: Memberships and Endowment

The first person I called right after hearing the news from John was Marcia. I told her that the Nature Center grant had been approved and then heard silence on the phone. Finally, she said, "Do you understand what this means?" "Yes. We had better start raising some real money."

Up to this point, we had been spending a few thousand dollars a year, except for special projects such as the Cotton Tract and the barn roof. We had to do something drastic to change that, and we had only a year or so to do it.

Jim Harrison was a colleague of mine at Bell Labs, and was trained as a psychologist. But he also had a good background in finances and was willing to spend a lot of time trying to figure out a budget for several years. We had to pay a full-time naturalist. Maybe the Township would give us a reception-ist/secretary. We finally came up with $25,000 per year. To us, this looked like Mt. Everest.

I just don't know how we did it. I was the principal person handling the financial planning. We had already established an investment fund (i.e., endowment), went on the road again to solicit one-time major contributions, and sent out many applications to foundations, many of which failed. I took four professionally taught fund raising courses, one of which was a godsend in that it showed us how to build up memberships.

I later became business manager of the park, a post I held until March 1993. So, I guess that I should know how we did it. But I really don't, and it would take days of plowing through records that I don't have access to in order to figure it out. Suffice it to say, by the late 1980s we were spending well over $125,000 annually to run the nature center.

There were a few high points. During the time that Patricia Contreras was director, we successfully applied for a National Endowment for the Human-ities Grant for $30,000 in 1982, and for an Institute of Museum Services grant for $19,695 in 1985. The NEH grant was non-repeatable, and the IMS grant was very difficult to obtain, and in fact, we failed to get it on two other tries. There were a few smaller grants, but none that could sustain the annual cost of operating the nature center.

When I left the business manager position in 1993, we had, for ten years, sustained an annual membership of more than 1,000 supporters, which included around 120 businesses. We had an endowment of $150,000. This took much detailed effort and many personal contacts.

I guess I have to go back to that S.C.O.R.E. seminar at Brookdale College in 1978. There is no magic bullet. To establish a business, you just have to put your whole lives into it, as did the people that were involved in Poricy Park in the late 1970s.

The Path Toward Groundbreaking

After receiving approval from Green Acres, the Township passed a bonding ordinance on Decem-ber 28, 1976 for $306,000 to build the Nature Center. It was on my 40th birthday. I think my major feeling was one of apprehension rather than delight. The architect went back to work, preparing detailed plans that would be used for bidding.

We saw those plans in February 1977. The first set of perhaps eight pages dealt with the floor plan and the elevation view of the building. Then, you turned the page and were faced with the details of plumbing, electrical, and heating systems, which had been subcontracted. We assumed that these were a necessary, but routine item and we paid little attention to them. In years to come, we'd learn a lot more about what was on those back pages.

Finally, in mid-March the plans went out to bid. There were some problems with the contracts and a re-bidding was required, but the final bids were opened on August 9, and the contract for the building was awarded to the Soldo Construction Company for $216,500. E. Palmer Bennett was awarded the contract for the parking lot and other exterior features for $95,109.

Groundbreaking: September 8, 1977

The newspapers contained the traditional photo, in this case of Mayor Allan MacDonald with his foot on a bright and shiny shovel digging into fresh, undisturbed soil, with the construction already well under way out of camera range, with bare dirt, bulldozers, and the inevitable portable toilet off to the side. He was flanked by Frank Lescinsky and John Campbell. Just for variety, I have chosen to show two different views here. The much-used portable bandstand housed whatever dignitaries they could assemble, and the group watching the ceremony consisted of whoever could get over there on a Thursday morning. The view is to the west, looking at the Colts Glen Development.

Lethe Lescinsky, Marcia Rissland, and Mayor Allan MacDonald at the groundbreaking.

What I best remember about the event was a brief conversation a few of us had with the contractor. We told him that we planned to start using the building in the next summer, and we asked if it would be ready in time. "Oh, don't worry about that! We'll be done and out of here before the end of November!"

Groan.

We went over to John Campbell and told him that there was no way we could run programs beginning in November. We had neither the money nor the staff. John seemed unperturbed. We soon found out why. He had had some experience in these matters.

The Ice Walk

November came and went, and so did December, and by January the slab had been poured and a shell of studs and joists was in place. No walls.

It was a brilliant, clear Saturday morning, and there had been about 15 inches of snow – a major storm. Then came a slow, light rain which froze on the snow, creating a layer of ice maybe 3/8 inches thick. Marcia and I had decided to go and check out the farmhouse. My son Stephen came with us. He was 11 years old.

Nothing had been plowed on the farm. We were able to park on Oak Hill Road. We started walking on the snow to the Nature Center. Stephen was light, with broad-soled boots, and he just walked on the layer of ice. Marcia sank in with about every fourth step. I crashed through with every step. We (well, I) were exhausted by the time we reached the Nature Center. Reaching the farmhouse was hopeless. But it did look OK from a distance.

As we stood in the framework of the new Nature Center, Marcia and I had a long moment of angst. Because we still did not know if we built it, would they come? It was a difficult and memorable morning.

Marcia's Role in the Nature Center

Just to review credits, the credit for much of the persuasion of the Township Committee to agree to build the Nature Center belongs to Allan Mac-Donald, who did this through 1975 as a Democratic minority member of the Committee. And, the credit for negotiating the funding, design, and contracts for the building belongs to John Campbell.

Having said that, and thereby having covered myself in case anyone feels I have forgotten those two people, I will state categorically that the day we moved into the building in July 1978, we were moving into a Nature Center equipped by Marcia.

Marcia is correctly remembered as the person that did the major work in restoring the historic buildings, but her role in setting up the Nature Center is never mentioned. I will now tell that story.

The construction got off to a slow start at the end of 1977, but after the worst of the winter, things picked up in 1978. Marcia was a nearly daily visitor to the farm, especially for the work she was doing on the barn, and she often dropped by the Nature Center. She became well known to the work crews and their supervisors. She sometimes brought coffee and refreshments. And, she often made suggestions on minor details such as design of electric outlets, placement of wood trim, etc.

I remember two incidents from the stories she told. One concerned the fireplace. She happened to be there when the masonry contractor showed her a sample of the "cheap-looking flagstone" (her words) that they were planning to use. She persuaded the contractor to ride around Monmouth County with her, visiting suppliers until she found the large, attractive rocks she wanted. The final results were just fine, as shown by the photo on page 145.

On another occasion, we knew that no appliances were included with the building, which meant that there was no kitchen range. Marcia asked me what we could do about this. Hovnanian was expanding Shadow Lake Village at this time, and I went over and asked if they had a slightly damaged range to donate to us, since they couldn't use it in their new condos. A week later, I drove over to the Nature Center with a range in my wagon.

Marcia then asked if the electrical contractor would help us out. Hovnanian donated the range, would the electrician install it for free? Agreed.

Furnishing the Building

Marcia's major work was in furnishing the building. The Township had contracted for an empty, unfurnished building.[28]

Marcia took on the task of equipping the building. She began by making a list, one of several she would make and distribute over the next half-year. One recipient of the list was local businesses, and an excerpt from the cover letter is shown below.

Letter from Marcia to local businesses.

February, 1978

To Merchants and Business People:

This year Poricy Park, a 250-acre natural preserve in Middletown, will have a new Environmental Education Center for the benefit of all residents of Middletown and nearby communities. The building is a result of a three-way effort by N.J. Green Acres, Middletown Township, and the Poricy Park Citizens Committee.

The PPCC is a tax-exempt nonprofit corporation of local residents dedicated to preservation of land and to education... Since the PPCC is responsible for equipping the building, we are seeking contributions of merchandise from local stores and businesses. Would you please look over the attached list? Any items, new or used, would be most welcome....

Sincerely,

Marcia Rissland

[The attached list appears here on the next page.]

---

[28] The Township did provide 100 folding chairs.

Items Needed for the Poricy Park Environmental Education Center

Prepared in February 1978 by Marcia Rissland

Tools & Hardware
Claw Hammers
Tack Hammers
Hand Saws
Miter Saw
Pliers
Assorted Screwdrivers
Wire Cutters
Assorted Wrenches
Picture Wire
Staple Gun
Yankee drill & bits
Metal Square
Metal Tape Rule
Carpenter's Folding Rule
Level
Pegboard Hangers
Portable Tool Chest
Drawers for Hardware

Art Supplies
Poster Board
Large Drawing Paper
Felt-Tipped Markers
Lettering Sets
Plastic 10" Triangle
Plastic T-Square
Poster Paints & Brushes
Scissors

Audio Visual
33 rpm Record Player
Cassette Tape Recorder
Portable Slide Screen
36" High Projector Table
Slide Files
Overhead Projector

Pet Supplies
Aquarium Tanks
  (leakers accepted)
Aquarium Equipment
  (filters, nets, lights, etc)
Animal Cages
Humane Live Traps
Carrying Cases (eg, cats)

Office Equipment
Desk Lamps
Waste Baskets
Free-Standing Bookcases
Filing Cabinets
  (2 or 4-drawer)

Miscellaneous
Heavy-Duty Shop Vacuum
Display Cases
Shelving Material
Postage Scale
Mover's Dolly

Kitchen Supplies
Large Teflon Frying Pan
Small Teflon Frying Pan
Saucepans
Stew Pot, Stainless Steel
Assorted Utensils
Tea Kettle
Plastic Garbage Pails
10-Cup Coffee Maker
Coffee Cups or Mugs
Mixing Bowls
Egg Beater
Plates
Pitchers, Large & Small
Dish Drainer

This was one of several lists Marcia prepared prior to our moving into the Nature Center. The last list, prepared around May 1, was six pages long and is annotated with comments on which items we had or still needed.

Marcia had much help from Ronnie Lander, a volunteer, who agreed to be the public point-of-contact for donated items. Marcia, Ronnie, Frank, and I met with John Campbell on April 10, 1978, to see what we could get from the Township and what we needed to do ourselves.

At the meeting, there was much left up in the air. It was uncertain whether there would be an alarm system, or what kind of locks would be on the doors, or whether trash cans would be provided outside, and how often they would be picked up. Light bulbs, toilet paper, and other janitorial supplies were going to be looked into. Curtains for windows still had not been determined. And, regarding the furniture and office supplies, that was the PPCC's responsibility, which we had always understood and

accepted. (Except for the Township's 100 metal folding chairs.)

In addition to scrounging and purchasing items, there were two other major sources of furnishings. One was the farmhouse, where we had run summer programs for three years. We believed (incorrectly) that we would be out of there at the start of the summer programs, and we could therefore move all our stuff up to the Nature Center at our "leisure" prior to start of programs in July.

The other source was Bell Labs, where I worked. At that time, the Labs was shifting from a workbench "soldering-iron bread-boarding" environment to one of computers and circuit boards. They were also getting new furniture. I was able to get them to donate lots of office equipment, including several

The barn on April 15, 1978. During the months that Marcia was working on furnishing the Nature Center, our contractors were rebuilding the barn, requiring Marcia to make nearly daily visits to the barn site. Both tasks took her full time, shuttling up and down the hill, and driving around town obtaining items for the Nature Center. We'll return to the barn later. I just wanted to include this so you'll know what Marcia did with her spare time. Note utility pole with transformer at far right.

desks, desk chairs, filing cabinets, an adding machine, other miscellaneous items, and a French typewriter. (We didn't make effective use of the French typewriter. *Quel dommage* (What a pity).)

Many of the Bell Labs items, especially the big ones, ended up in Marcia's garage, as well as other items we had obtained. She and Lou could forget about putting their cars there for a while.

My favorite Bell Labs story occurred in March 1979, after we had been in the Nature Center for several months. I was trying to get lab tables – those nice big ones that had electrical outlets built into the pedestals. These tables were rendered obsolete to the Labs when their research became computer oriented. I remember the call I made to Marcia:

"Marcia, regarding the tables, I just got a call from the Bell Labs donations person, and I have good news and bad news."

"What's the good news?"

"We're going to get our lab tables."

"Great! What's the bad news?"

"There are 18 of them, and they're going to be delivered tomorrow morning."

Bastille Day and Flypaper

We kept getting revised predictions of the day we could move into the Nature Center. It was at first April 1, then June 1, then maybe July. The contractor always seemed to have a few things left to do. The phones didn't work yet. Opening day seemed very elusive. So, we started our summer 1978 programs out of the farmhouse.

Finally, we <u>declared</u> that we would move into the Nature Center building on Friday, July 14 unless the Township denied us permission to do so. Marcia had previously moved most of her garage items over to the new building, and she had gone through the farmhouse, labeling items to be moved up to the top of the hill.

The denial didn't come, and we made our move. The weather was fine. Volunteers were at each end of the car caravan to load and unload. Marcia at first spent most of her time in the farmhouse acting like a drill sergeant and directing traffic there, and then began to move up the hill to be sure that everything ended up in the right place. It took the entire day.

At day's end, a few of us were standing in the Nature Center kitchen. Marcia turned to us and said, *"Well, the flies have captured the flypaper!"*

For many months – even years – Marcia continued to assume responsibility for the care and maintenance of the Nature Center. The Township eventually did furnish us with a maintenance person, part-time and occasionally full-time, but this did not end the need for cleanups after some programs, or occasionally looking through the freezer for dead animal carcasses that had started to petrify.

With her characteristic cynicism, Marcia put a sign on the refrigerator: "Please label anything you put in here with the date. Including the year."

The Dedication Ceremonies

The dedication, complete with ribbon cutting, occurred on Sunday, September 24, 1978, some two months after we had moved into the building. From left: Larry O'Neill, President, Middletown Board of Education; Freeholder Ernest Kavalek; four Township Committeemen: Frank Self, Dick Kelly, Allan MacDonald (Mayor), and Bob Eckert; Mike Weilbacher, Naturalist; Frank Lescinsky, President of the PPCC; Jim Gill, Chair, Recreation Advisory Committee; and John Campbell, Director, Parks and Recreation.

(In the picture, Jim Gill was fine as chair of the Recreation Advisory Committee. Our relations with that committee had improved greatly after 1975.)

I suppose I should leave the opening ceremonies unsullied by complaints. But, for the record, here is an excerpt from a letter I sent the Township Administrator, Joe Vuzzo, two days later (September 26):

Subject: Routine Cleaning of Nature Center
Dear Joe,

We understand that you had other commitments and were unable to attend the Nature Center dedication on September 24. The ceremony went well and the weather was beautiful.

The Nature Center was also beautiful. On the day before, almost 40 volunteer hours were spent cleaning the place, and people even brought vacuum cleaners from home. Windows were scraped, the rest room floors were washed, and dozens of other details were attended to.

After the ceremony, when everyone else went home, two or three volunteers spent another hour sweeping up all the dirt that was tracked in. The next morning (Monday), a sixth-grade class came back from a pond trip, carrying dirt on their shoes, which was also swept out by a volunteer – in this case, Marcia Rissland.

[The letter continues by asking for a Township commitment to perform scheduled cleaning and maintenance, which we did get in years to come, although at times the service had many periods of interruption.]

The Heating and Air Conditioning System

You might think that the heating/AC system in the Nature Center is something you really don't want to hear about. It's just one of many details in the construction of a building.

But there really is a story here, and the ending had financial implications for us that went well into the future. You might even find it entertaining.

The system was a forced air system, with a huge (7.5 horsepower, or 5,000 watt) motor running continuously, making an impressive noise and costing $5 or more a day just to run the motor. The motor/fan blew the air into two compartments, one with air conditioning coils, the other with heating coils. The heating coils contained hot water supplied by an oil furnace (gas was unavailable in 1977). There were six zones. When, in a particular zone heat was called for, a baffle dedicated to that zone caused the air to that zone to come from the hot chamber. (Or, the cold chamber if a lower temperature was called for.) There were at least 12 temperature-sensing devices, some outdoors.

In July 1985 I submitted a report to the Township Committee requesting that the entire system be taken out and replaced with three, standard home heating systems. Here is an excerpt from the beginning of the report:

> The Poricy Park Nature Center was opened on July 14, 1978. During the first summer, the A/C system experienced so many breakdowns that it operated properly for only three days. The first winter saw several dozen failures of the heating system. Even now, having eventually fixed installation errors, a complete breakdown occurs roughly every two months, with additional minor repairs needed every few weeks.
>
> During our history, about ten experts have examined the system, some called in on an official capacity, others were heating engineers who happened to be attending a program in the park and took an interest in the system. It is the unanimous opinion of all consultants that the system is far too large and complex for the building ...

I suppose I could leave it at that, but some of the stories really are interesting. Here are a few.

Christmas, 1980: The Ice Man Cometh

The Nature Center was designed with an unheated attic. The insulation is on the floor of the attic, and so the attic temperature is pretty much the same as outdoors. When the weather freezes, so does the attic.

Why, then, did the subcontractor architect for heating and plumbing air-mail the water pipes for the classroom (at one end) and the bathrooms (at the other end) through the uninsulated attic? That is, looking at the floor plan on page 99, the pipes come straight up from the cellar next to the fire place, and then go over to the far wall at left, where they descend to the sinks in the women's room.

Christmas Day, 1980 (Thursday) was very cold, and at the Nature Center was our park cat Albert, which I enjoyed feeding on holidays. As I drove into the parking lot, I noticed that it was a sheet of ice. Where did all that water come from?

It didn't take long to find out. The pipes had burst in the wall behind the sinks and water was roaring out of the building, and had been doing so for hours. I managed to shut off the water in the basement, and then the Township work crews had to fix the pipes. They had to cut a large hole in the exterior wall of the Nature Center. That hole stayed there, patched with plywood, for several months.

That was just one such incident. A similar failure occurred above the classroom ceiling in February 1979, and another time, much of the ceiling of the women's room came crashing down after the pipes burst above the ceiling. We tried to remember to leave the water running on freezing nights, and this spared us on several occasions.

Oil, Oil, Everywhere

The oil-fired furnace had a "collar" controlling the mix of air and oil going into the burner. This was badly out of adjustment, and the flame blew out in late fall 1978 But the oil kept flowing. The entire contents of the oil tank ended up on the cellar floor. The furnace technician declared that "Kids had monkeyed with the collar." Right. Kids got into the basement with special tools, loosened three bolts in hard-to-reach places, changed the collar setting and retightened the bolts.

And then there was the time that an oil delivery man was on his first day delivering oil, and his first assignment was to make a delivery to the Nature Center. He was inexperienced and apparently couldn't tell the difference between a sewer pipe and an oil pipe, and proceeded to dump 1,000 gallons of fuel oil directly into the Middletown sewer system. That one made it into the newspapers.

Three Wires to the Women's Room

Embedded in the labyrinth of controls, wires, pipes, and devices, was a miracle of simplicity, namely, the heat for the rest rooms. The diagram is shown below.

If this is too complex for some readers, not to worry. You will have a fine career ahead of you in design and installation of heating systems.

The oil-fired furnace is shown at left, and it provided heat for the main system. But, a pipe was tapped off the boiler and fed to baseboard heating pipes in both the men's and women's room. (There were no air ducts because the rest rooms were not air conditioned.)

The control for the heat was in the women's room. It was a simple thermostat with a single pole

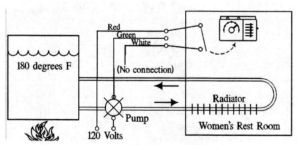

The Women's Room Heating System

on-off switch. When heat was called for, the switch would close, causing a water pump in the basement to operate, which would circulate hot water through pipes in both rest rooms. It just doesn't get simpler.

The wires to the thermostat were on a low voltage circuit (which by a relay (not shown) operated a 120-volt circuit). A two-conductor cable to the on-off switch would have worked, but the installer may have happened to have a reel of three-conductor cable. You will see that the installer should have connected the thermostat to the red and green wires, but inadvertently used the red and white wires, thus rendering the system inoperable.

This was a careless mistake, but was not a serious problem; just change the connections and you're in business.

Well, our first autumn in the new building arrived (1978), and so did cooler weather. The rest rooms were too cold, and adjusting the thermostat setting didn't do anything. Add this to the list of the many other problems we had been calling in.

The technician showed up, worked on the system for a half hour, and then left, declaring that the problem was fixed.

But it wasn't fixed, and the technician was called again. Same thing. Worked for a half hour, declared it fixed, left the building.

And it still didn't work, so on the weekend I decided to look into it myself, discovered the error and fixed it. My question is, what did the technician think he was doing when he "fixed" it?

And, you might wonder about the wisdom of having a thermostat on the wall in plain view of the public, especially school-age girls. Might they not mess with it? Indeed, yes they did, and it was often set to one extreme end of the scale or the other. I was also able to fix this by discovering a place for a setscrew to be installed to anchor the setting. I scrounged around in my tool box and found a screw that would fit. (My guess is that a set screw was provided with the unit and the installer just didn't bother to insert it.)

Talk to Cindy

There were many problems with the components in the system. Some of the technicians sent to correct the problems were stumped. One time while I was there, the technician told me that he was leaving because he didn't understand how the system worked. On another occasion, when nobody understood how one of the Honeywell controls worked, I ended up calling Honeywell and having them send us the specifications, whereby we found that the control had been installed improperly.

Early into our second heating season (November 1979), we were having trouble getting an adjustment set properly on the "adjustable inductor coil." (Whatever that was.) I called the service company, reached someone that seemed to know how this element worked, and he told me on the phone what I had to do to adjust it. Here is a faithful transcription from my notes taken during the call:

The adjustable inductor is the second coil after the fly-back transformer. Take out the two Phillips head screws on the top, slide the hood off. Look from the rear. On the right-hand side there is a donut coil on top. Then there are two tuning coils, the 2nd one in is on a white plastic square base. (On the right-hand side of the plastic form is a slug-tuned coil. Leave it alone.) On left side of base is a ferrite core. Tune this. Also on right hand side at rear there is an adjustment marked "focus" on G2. Diddle with the focus. If this doesn't work, call 555-1234 and talk to Cindy.

This is basically a good system.

Saturday, May 26, 1984 was a day in a Colonial Encampment, a major Memorial Day weekend program at the park. There were many visitors to the park, and it was hot, and the air conditioning did not work. We had turned it on earlier in May, and it broke down twice afterwards, the second time on May 25. So, on Saturday morning, I met the technician who would fix it.

Among other things, the sump pump on the A/C didn't work (which removes water that accumulates on the cooling coils), and the sump water was dribbling all over the floor. Another water pipe was leaking all over the furnace. And, the A/C died for no apparent reason, having just been fixed yesterday.

The technician examined the system and listed a variety of reasons why the system could have broken down in the last 24 hours. I told him that we hadn't had a summer in which the A/C hadn't failed at least four times. He acknowledged that there may be some problems, but he then said, and this is a direct quote, "You know, this is basically a good system."

Enough is enough. Replace it.

On July 28, 1979, after we had been in the building for one year, I sent a memo to John Campbell listing 22 problems we had had with the heating/AC system, some of which were still not fixed.

But some of the best problems were yet to come. The main switch to turn the system on and off was in the basement on a large control panel. It was metal, and was not properly grounded. I received a severe shock from it once, and so did a staff member, and the staff were then not willing to touch it. Beginning in 1982, large explosions began to occur in the basement every few weeks, filling the air with white, acrid smoke, and shaking the building to its foundations. Complete breakdowns were still occurring once every two months.

By July 1985, we decided that the system had to be replaced. I wrote a report for the Township Committee listing the sad history of our seven years trying to live with the system. We had talked with a heating contractor who estimated that for around $20,000 he could install three ordinary home heating systems that would do the job reliably, and should one of them fail, we still would have service in the other 2/3 of the building. We did a cost analysis and showed that the new system would more than pay for itself in a few years, as it would replace a horribly inefficient system which was costing us a fortune for fuel, electricity, and maintenance.

The Township Committee agreed. Yes, go ahead. BUT – it would have to go out for bids, and for that, we need specs prepared by a qualified expert. They recommended someone that we should contact to prepare a design for a new system.

The Expert's Recommendations

I met the consultant at the Nature Center on August 27, 1985. We went down in the basement and examined the current system. The consultant walked through and around the building. I showed him the 20 ton A/C unit outdoors and told him of the engineers that had assured me that 10 tons would have been sufficient. I told him some of the history of problems we had had, some serious ones still unsolved. Finally, the consultant gave me his assessment: "I'm not surprised you've been having trouble with this system. The problem with it is, *it isn't big enough.*"

He then went on to say that the A/C unit should be of size 40 tons, and gave several other huge size specifications for the equipment needed.

We went outside at my request, and I pointed to the ranch house nearby (photo on page 158). I said that the Nature Center was, at nearly 5,000 sq. ft., just about double the size of the house. "Why can't we install two or three home units, just like the ranch house has? One unit works fine over there."

"On, no, you don't understand. This is a *big, commercial operation.* You need industrial grade equipment with adequate capacity. It would be a serious mistake to use home units here."

So, we parted, and I was left in a state of dismay. By law, the Township could not install a new system without an expert's specifications, and here this guy was telling me that he would greatly increase our complexity, and almost certainly our headaches.

So, I spoke with John McGowan, Director of Public Works. He understood perfectly what was going on. This guy is going strictly by the book, and instead of a simple $20,000 system, his will cost around $60,000. And, he'll get a cut of that.

I then asked him, "What if we do it ourselves? The PPCC pays for the whole job, and we hire our own contractor?" "Well, I don't know, you'd have to talk to the Township Committee about that."

Our Own System

I went back to our own Board of Directors, and we came up with this offer: The PPCC will take care of the whole thing. But, in return, over the years, we would like the Township to "ramp up" on its annual grant to the PPCC, because we need help paying to keep this public building open six days a week. The cost details are not that important here; what is important is that they'd give us permission to do it, just like we put our own roof on the barn in 1976. And restored the barn. And restored the farmhouse.

The Committee was in agony. They questioned the legality of doing this. Shouldn't we get the Township Attorney's permission? "NO!" I said. "He'll also go by the book, and we'll be left either with the terrible system we have or one that's much bigger, more expensive to operate, and probably much worse. We're making a good offer to you."

More hand wringing and anguish followed in the next few weeks. Finally, in a call I made to John McGowan, he said, "I think you should just do it. I can't officially give you permission, but I think the best thing is just go ahead with it."

And, we did. We put in three new systems. We had to endure another winter with the old system, but the new A/C went in during summer 1986 followed by the heating system in the fall. There were occasional troubles with the new systems, but no more than a typical homeowner gets.

Restoration of the Farmhouse and Barn

Whistling Hill Farm, which we called the "Gebhardt Farm." Photo January 1971.

Numbers 1, 2, 3 indicate utility poles removed late 1979

Ranch house (Top of hill)

Site of Future Nature Center

Worker house, removed January 1976

Another worker house

West wing, milking stalls. Wings were demolished in 1978.

South wing, equipment.

1767 barn, restored 1978

"Super shed," torn down January 1976

"Cat House," Burned down August 1975

Murray Farmhouse, restoration finished November 1981

The Gebhardt Farm in January 1971. It was still privately owned but not farmed; the herd had been sold.

Another view in January 1971. This gives a better perspective on the location of the outbuildings. As with most farms, there were several outbuildings, but these were of no historic importance and were in poor condition. (There probably were outbuildings in the 1700s, but they were long gone.) The "×" in right foreground marks the location of the Murray Pond, constructed in 1982.

The Farmhouse: Not the Reason Why

In discussions I had during my research for this book, I was surprised to learn that some people (who weren't involved in our early days) believed that the preservation of the Murray Farmhouse was one of our principal reasons for preserving the parkland.

Not true! We had no idea of the real value of the farmhouse and barn. In our flyer of November 11, 1969, we vaguely stated "Houses of historical value exist on both the Gebhardt and Morris Tracts," and then dropped the matter for five years!

An Opinion from an Architect

Charles H. Detwiller, Jr. from Plainfield, NJ served as our consulting architect during the restoration of the farmhouse and barn. Here is how his first report begins, dated October 26, 1976:

I might as well open the report with a reflection of my immediate reaction upon approaching the site, as I came over the hill and first caught sight of the buildings. It was as if suddenly you were taken back into the 18th Century, seeing the unmistakable gentle lines and forms of the early barn and farmhouse, situated in an undisturbed setting of open fields and trees, completely isolated from the suburbia that has surrounded it. Truly an experience and something to go to great lengths to preserve.

What is a "Restoration"?

People often refer to any historic building as a "restoration," whether or not it is one. George Washington's home at Mount Vernon is not a "restoration," because it was always kept in a state of preservation. At times, it has required extensive repair, but that's not the same as restoring a building that had been changed significantly over the years. Mount Vernon always kept its original appearance.

On November 14, 1997, Marcia gave a talk[29] at

---

[29] This was at a conference of the Mid-Atlantic chapter of the Association for Living History, Farm and Agricultural Museums (ALHFAM), hosted by the Monmouth County Park System at Longstreet Farm.

an ALHFAM conference at Longstreet Farm (in Holmdel Park). Her talk was titled, "The Restoration of the Murray Farmhouse and Barn." She began her talk by defining some terms:

I need first to define some terms that are sometimes inaccurately applied to the things that are done to old buildings. Restoration is the removal of all later work to bring a building back to its appearance at some determined date, and using only materials and techniques original to that era. Reconstruction is just that – like some buildings in Colonial Williamsburg, building from scratch according to original blueprints. Rehabilitation is getting a decrepit structure into useable condition. Renovation is updating a building for more modern uses, or a more convenient layout. Refurbishment is more in the category of surface improvement – plaster, paint, replacement of damaged woodwork, etc. The most recent overhaul of the Murray Farmhouse, from 1975 to 1982, was a combination of refurbishment, rehabilitation, and restoration. Some of the 19th- and 20th-century changes were definite improvements and were retained. Others were architectural indignities and were joyfully demolished. That means that we kept or installed heat, a bathroom, a minimally modern kitchen, electricity, telephone, and intrusion alarms. Fortunately, the buildings were scornfully rejected by the National Register, and the Township government cared nothing about them. We could do pretty much as we pleased.

I call it "The unqualified doing the impossible for the uninterested."

You might detect a note of hubris, or perhaps frustration (or both) in Marcia's language. I'll say this just once. Marcia was a strong-willed person who charged right ahead when confronted by petty objections or indifference. She met a lot of both, and was outspoken in her opinions of people who got in the way. She did not usually make friends with such people. And, that's why the project got done.

Having shown that Marcia knew what was and what wasn't a restoration (and that I now know that too), I will refer to this project as a restoration, because that's what everybody has kept calling it.

1975-1977: A Lack of Direction

When a property with historic buildings is acquired by a preservation agency, it is customary for the agency to have some plan for development and preservation of the buildings. The plan, or at least, the general idea of a future for the buildings, usually exists at the time of acquisition. Thus, when the Monmouth County Park System acquired the Walnford property in 1985, it was understood that the grist mill (which had ceased operation in 1917) would be put back in running order, and that repairs would be made to the 1773 house to make it available for display and public tours. At that point, historians and architects did their work, contractors were brought in to do repairs, restoration, and so on. But the main point is, the general direction of that and most other projects was known ahead of time.

Not so with the Murray Farmhouse and Barn. All we wanted in the early 1970s was to have the Township acquire the farm and build a nature center and preserve the natural features of the area.

So, the old farmhouse and barn just sat there.

1975 began with the PPCC's "All is not well" flyer, which prompted Bob Bramley's article in the *Register* (page 73), which got Marcia started on her research into the history of the buildings. During the next year or two, here are the various forces that were in play regarding the future of the farm:

- Marcia wanted the house to be put in livable condition (that is, have an occupancy permit) so that it would have a tenant, for surveillance.
- The PPCC began running summer programs from the farmhouse, requiring much clean up and cosmetic repairs.
- The PPCC campaigned for the Township to put a roof on the barn, which the Township did. This temporary roof was replaced with a proper roof in January 1976 using PPCC funds.

- Similarly, we campaigned to have the house roof replaced, which was completed in February 1977 using Township funds.
- Other repairs and improvements were made to the buildings and property under the general umbrella of removing unwanted features (such as the old coal furnace).
- Mrs. Timolat was putting constant pressure on us (that is, on Marcia) to have the buildings properly restored.
- Marcia initiated the process of having the farm put on the National Register of Historic Places, which ultimately failed.
- John Campbell (and George Smith) took a firm position that the farmhouse should be in control of the Middletown Township Historical Society and ultimately become their headquarters.

The above events were happening simultaneously, and maybe the best way to present them is to pick them apart as separate stories.

We've covered the first four already, so we can review them just briefly here.

The idea of having someone live in the house evaporated when we decided to run summer programs. This was set in motion in spring 1975 with a major cleanup in May, with cleanups and work parties making cosmetic changes over the next three years. But this was not "restoration."

We also described here putting the roofs on the buildings. Again, this was not restoration.

We will now discuss some other improvements, in particular, the Project Heritage work effort, and the new electrical service to the buildings.

Project Heritage: February 1976

At the start of 1976 we learned of "Project Heritage," a program that employed people who were out of work, to supply labor for projects to improve historic buildings. The PPCC would have to supply the materials. Marcia contacted the people in charge, and in January 1976 met with the foreman and also Joe Scanlon, a trustee of the Middletown

Township Historical Society to determine what could be done.

The project was nearly out of control from the start. The foreman was eager to do major work, especially involving pouring concrete, which could forever preclude a proper restoration in the future. Scanlon made these suggestions: (1) pour an eight foot wide concrete footing under the 200-year-old open hearth fireplace in the basement, (2) set steel columns in concrete to prop up sagging beams (which was actually done years later, but well hidden behind wooden framework), and (3) replace the bricks on the basement floor with poured concrete.

Marcia was initially pleased to get some real work done after a year of frustration in trying to get anybody at all to help renovate the farmhouse, but she did see the difficulties these actions could bring. She made a counter suggestion that the work crew remove all the old steam pipes and radiators. There were some difficulties getting the people in charge to back down from the major items they proposed, but after some arguments, a more modest project was negotiated for.

Finally, work began on Monday, February 2, 1976. The workers put in several days of hard work. The steam system was removed, as well as other archaic features. Concrete was not poured. Friday, February 6 was their last day.

Electric Heat

The farmhouse did not have heat after the Township evicted the tenants in early 1974. This posed many difficulties, the most dramatic of which was the annual peeling of paint from many of the interior walls, as shown in the photo on this page.

This was remedied without much difficulty. In January 1978, Jean Ruck, an electrician from Port Monmouth, installed six baseboard electric heaters in the basement and first floor for a cost to the PPCC of $627. These were understood to be temporary, pending a complete new electric system, but the same heaters were later used with the new service.

April, 1975. Freezing winter temperatures caused paint to peel from the farmhouse interior walls. This was an annual event. The view is toward the south door. The small door at left was the original entrance to the cellar stairs.

These heaters did cause some problems with the old electrical service, which had to be adjusted somewhat to carry the increased load. But the more interesting problem the heaters caused was that they were part of the reason for rejection of a later application for a grant from the Institute for Museum Services.

In that application, filed in 1983, we mentioned that we had installed electric heat. One reviewer slammed us on this: "What kind of a so-called 'environmental organization' installs wasteful and inefficient electric heat?" We should have omitted the item entirely, but at least, we should have stated that the electric heat was a minimal system to keep the building from freezing in the winter.

Anyway, it was clear that the farmhouse and barn needed a complete new electric service, and this also was done in the "non-restoration" years.[30]

---

[30] Terminology: Electric *service* comprises the main circuit breaker box and its attachments, and *system* is the entire house (and barn) wiring.

The Trench: Power to the Farmhouse

On February 22, 1977, the unheated farmhouse was acquiring a new roof (but not much else was happening there), and architect Bill Miller was drawing plans for bidding on the Nature Center. At that time, I suggested to John Campbell that since we were having new electric and phone lines set up for the park, it would make sense to bury the utility lines to the farmhouse. John said he'd talk to Bill Miller about it.

And, perhaps he did talk to Miller, but nothing came of this for a few months.

In October, while construction was just beginning on the Nature Center, we had another go at this. We learned that the phone company (then New Jersey Bell) would bury their cable for free if the Township dug the trench. But nothing came of this either.

Finally, when the electric service to the Nature Center was connected in June 1978, I began pushing to bury the farmhouse lines in earnest.

I did an unusual thing here, and it is to the reader's good fortune. Because beginning in 1978, this project became one of the most consuming and frustrating projects I have ever done. I was the main coordinator of the work with Parks and Recreation, Public Works, our electrician, the power company, and the phone company. I amassed a pile of papers about one inch thick. There were records of phone calls, intermediate letters sent to a lot of people, and statements of frustration over delays and red tape. And I was so fed up when the whole thing was over that I threw the set of records away.

But I do have a picture, which I've included here. It was taken on March 14, 1979 (two years after I had first suggested burying the lines). And there is a slightly amusing story attached to it; you can read it in the photo caption.

The final tally for this project is that while the phone line was buried for free, the electric line burial cost $8,564.62, paid by the Township. The two cables are buried in the same trench. And with the

March 14, 1979: Digging begins on the trench to bury the utility lines to the farmhouse and remove the poles, wires, and the transformer. But a new transformer will be required on the ground. When planning for this, I met on site with the power company engineer who said that the new transformer, to be installed on a pad provided by the Township, would have to be at the location marked "×" in the photo. I said that this would kill the whole purpose of the project, namely, to get the modern utilities out of sight. Can we put the transformer off of the other corner of the house, toward the woods? "Oh, that can't be done, because the cable would have to go around a bend here." "Are you telling me that electricity can't go around corners?"

(The pad was put near the woods.)

trench came an entirely new electric service in the basement of the old farmhouse, installed by Jean Ruck, and paid for by the PPCC.

In late 1979, months after all the utility lines had been removed from the poles, the phone company came in and removed the poles.

The Historical Society and the Farmhouse

John Campbell, Director of Parks and Recreation, got a lot of things right during his 16-year tenure in Middletown. And, as I have pointed out several times, he played the major role in the design and construction of the Nature Center. This should be evident from the account I have so far presented. The facts speak for themselves.

However, he did take one position that caused us to experience diversions and at times have difficult moments. John felt that the Middletown Township Historical Society (henceforth, "Historical Society") should eventually have their headquarters in the Murray Farmhouse. So, once the PPCC moved into the new Nature Center, we should permanently vacate the farmhouse.

From a parks administrative point of view, this position made sense. John saw Poricy Park as a multi-use facility and separated the functions of environmental education and history-related programs. He felt that there were two organizations with different charters, and the one chartered for history should take charge of the farmhouse. The problem was that this did not take into account the training, interests, resources, and investments of the people in the PPCC.

Gertrude Neidlinger and the Spy House

The "Spy House" is a centuries-old house on the Raritan Bay waterfront. [31] It has a beautiful view of Raritan Bay and the distant New York City. The Township acquired the Spy House in 1972. [32]

---

[31] The Monmouth County Park System acquired this building in June 1998 and renamed it the "Seabrook-Wilson House." Since my account here covers the period of the mid-70s, I will use the term it was known by at that time.

[32] This date was in the *Asbury Park Press* 6/16/2005, Middletown Reporter section p. 3. The reader is referred to a 1986 study by the firm of Short and Ford containing an architectural review of the

The Historical Society had been formed in 1968, and they were charged with administration of the building. This included receiving and managing grants to repair and improve it.

Cathy and I fondly remember Gertrude Neidlinger in the 1970s as a charming woman in her early 60s who managed the Spy House. Her brother Trav (Travers) also helped in this effort.

Gertrude was almost always available to take groups or individuals on a tour of the Spy House, and she told fascinating stories of its history. She also accepted gifts or loans of items to put on display, and told stories behind those items, too. Gertrude was, and remains, an icon in Middletown's history, and one of the most colorful people that lived here. She was a beloved figure by many (but not all) people.

However, there were two problems. The first was that she was, first and above all, an *actress*. She performed on stage in the '50s and '60s in many venues, often as a comedienne. (Herbert Burtis is a fine musician and a friend of mine for nearly 40 years. I even took piano lessons from him, and he is well-known as a voice teacher. He and Gertrude were a team that performed in many places, including at Carnegie Hall in 1965.)

The Spy House was a great place for Gertrude to tell her stories and entertain people. But she was not an historian, and some of her stories had no historical basis. For example, no one has found evidence that the building was used for spying on the British fleet during the Revolutionary War, but Gertrude stated that it was, and further, she named the building the "Spy House."

The second problem was that she was not an administrator, and she did not work well with people on the Board of Directors of the Historical Society. She was on-site almost all the time, called all the shots, and bypassed the Board.

---

building which includes its early history. The Short and Ford study is at the Middletown Library reference desk.

John Feury and the Historical Society

We began our relationship with the Historical Society at the end of 1974, when we asked for their mailing list of 100 names so we could send them our "All is not well" brochure. But as 1975 progressed, it became apparent that we were dealing with two organizations, even though they appeared as one.

The first one was the one run by Gertrude Neidlinger. She put the Murray Farmhouse on a September 1975 tour of Middletown houses built prior to 1700. (Subsequent research showed it was built around 1767, but this is not what matters here.) Some members of the Historical Society went on this tour and were interested in the house, but did not express any interest in doing work to improve its condition.

1975 was the same year that the PPCC ran its first set of summer programs out of the Murray Farmhouse, and also the year that Marcia began to do research on its history, and the same year that, at year's end, we put a roof on the barn with our own funds. That is, we were beginning to build equity in the old buildings.

The "other" Historical Society we dealt with was the one that, in 1975, was run by its Board of Directors, with John Feury as president. I met Feury on a few occasions, but do not remember him well. But he did seem to have a strong influence on John Campbell, and also the Township Administrator George Smith. For example, at the same time we were preparing to put a roof on the barn, we were urging the Township to put one on the house. In October 1975 Smith told me that no roof would go on the house until the board of the Historical Society approved it. In that same month, Marcia met on site with Feury, who agreed to send the necessary approval letter to Smith, but had not done so as of February 1976. (I don't know if he ever did. The roof was put on the house in 1977, as described on page 90.)

Open Warfare: December 16, 1975

The Society's internal dispute came to a head in December 1975 when Feury asked Smith to be put on the agenda of the Township Committee caucus session. The purpose of the meeting was to call Gertrude on the carpet for her alleged mismanagement of the Spy House, and in particular, for ignoring the Board of Directors in things that she did.[33]

The meeting was held on December 16 in the caucus room of capacity maybe 20 people. (I well remember that room when Committeeman Dick Kelly smoked cigars during meetings.) The room was packed. Feury had given Smith a list of people to invite, those that shared his position. And of course, Gertrude had to be invited. When Gertrude got wind of the way the cards would be stacked against her, she invited her own supporters, which included Marcia and me and maybe six other people.

The Township was represented by Mayor Peter Carton, Committeemen Tom Lynch and Allan Mac-Donald, Committeeman-elect Bob Eckert, Administrator George Smith, and Attorney Jerry Massell.

This was an acrimonious meeting from the start. It was, in essence, a cock-and-hen fight between John Feury and Gertrude Neidlinger. Feury didn't stand a chance.

Feury began by stating that this meeting was called to solve the internal problems of the Historical Society. Did the constitution or bylaws of the Society give them jurisdiction over the Spy House? At that point, Jerry Massell began to toss numbers around. Big numbers. They spoke of Housing and Urban Development grants in the tens of thousands of dollars. What happened to them? Where was the money spent?

---

[33] There is no record in Town Hall (in 2005) of this meeting. In 1975, only the regular Township Committee meetings were recorded in the books, not the caucuses. I wrote a brief account of it, but Marcia took more thorough notes, and I have relied primarily on her account here.

After the room was drowning in charges and counishcharges, Carton spoke up: "The museum must stay closed or be operated by Parks and Recreation. The Society could operate the museum on a concession basis, and would have to comply with municipal financial requirements. The present lease has no validity."

Feury stated, "We want to establish our right to administer the museum, and we are willing to keep Gertrude as curator."

At this point, Gertrude burst out, "How can you run a museum? You don't know anything. You've never been there. You've never wiped the faces of children after they've blown their noses, or cleaned the bathrooms after they've left. It's the volunteers that keep the museum running. These people [Board members] are nothing but a social club."

And thus ended the meeting, without result. Except that the Historical Society lost control of the Spy House and was now looking for a new home.

The Historical Society in 1976

John Campbell asked us to keep the Historical Society involved in our work. Marcia had learned of a noted historical architect, Charles Detwiller, whose offices were in Plainfield and we arranged to see him on February 12, 1976. A week prior to the meeting, I invited John Feury to go along with us. On the 12th, Lois Kurz, Marcia, and I waited as long as we could at our car pool site, and we finally had to go without him. We never found out why he didn't show up. (More on the Detwiller meeting later.)

After our summer 1976 programs we had a meeting of the PPCC at Al Oppegard's house on September 9, 1976. There were 15 of us present plus our invited guest, John Campbell.

Things went well until we started to discuss the farmhouse. We were still trying to get a roof put on it, and we also talked of a pending visit to the site by Detwiller to review a design for a possible restoration. At that point, John said, "My position on this matter hasn't changed. The farmhouse will be under the domain of the Historical Society. If you want to get involved with the farmhouse, then join the Historical Society."

Well, this was certainly clearly stated, and was stated to a group of people who had collectively put hundreds of hours of sweat equity into farmhouse repairs over two years, and who had all been involved with running programs there.

How can we help?

We continued to play by the rules. The Historical Society wanted a meeting with us to discuss the history and future of the farmhouse, and we scheduled it at the Middletown Library on November 8. Seven members of the Historical Society were present, including John Feury. Several of us, including Frank Lescinsky, Marcia, Lou, and myself talked for about 45 minutes, going over the history of the site, what we learned of the property ownership over the centuries, the condition of the house, our meetings with Charles Detwiller, etc. Finally we finished and asked if there were any questions.

"Yes," replied Feury, "How can we help?"

"How can we help?"

Marcia's depiction of the Historical Society at our November 8, 1976 presentation at the library.

The remainder of the meeting focused on only one topic, as directed by the Historical Society members: When are you guys going to get into the Nature Center so we can take over the farmhouse?

Nothing was said about how they could help.

I didn't see how we could continue in this manner. I went to see Allan MacDonald (then Mayor) and discussed the difficulties we were having, trying to make improvements in a house that we would have to turn over to the Historical Society, who had already demonstrated their inability to run an historic site with the Spy House. He told me that he understood the situation, knew the players involved, and would take care of it. We didn't hear from the Society again.

The Historical Society in 2005

I am happy to announce that in 2005, I am a proud, card-carrying member of the Middletown Township Historical Society.

After our meeting with them in 1976, they had a change of leadership. I don't know all that transpired, but in the early 1980s the Township acquired Croydon Hall Academy, a former boys' school run by John Carr. The academy became the headquarters of the Department of Parks and Recreation. The academy contained a large building, the MacLeod-Rice House, the first floor of which was given to the Historical Society for their headquarters. The house is shared by other agencies and needs a lot of repair work, but it does have enough space for the Society's library and meetings, and also contains a good exhibit room. Randall Gabrielan, who has helped gather facts for this book, is its current president. The monthly meetings are well attended.

The Spy House after Gertrude

In later years, Middletown Township appointed another agency, the Spy House Corporation, to administer the building. They, too, had difficulty with Gertrude's management practices. By then, Gertrude had started conducting séances, ghost tours, and other programs deemed inappropriate. The corporation dismissed her in 1993. I really liked Gertrude, but realized that she could not continue in that manner.

In 1997, the Monmouth County Park System arranged for a transfer of the Spy House to the county in exchange for work the county would do on Port Monmouth Road. The condition was that the house be emptied of all its contents. Many of the items were returned to their donors or lenders. And for the rest, Walter and Susan Spradley, who administer the Heath Farm on Harmony Road, were willing to take the items and put them on display where they can be seen today. It's a site worth visiting.

Gertrude died in April 1998 at age 87, just two months prior to the county's acquisition of the Spy House. The county has renamed the building the "Seabrook-Wilson House" after Daniel Seabrook, who acquired the property (from Thomas Whitlock) in 1696, also later members of the Seabrook family who lived there, and Rev. William V. Wilson, who married into the Seabrook family in 1842, purchased the house in 1855, and died in 1908. The house is scheduled for a much-needed rehabilitation soon, possibly in 2006.

There is one fact that nobody disputes. During the 1970s and 80s, when there really was no higher level management of the Spy House, Gertrude kept the building maintained and she entertained perhaps thousands of visitors and school children.

The Murray Farmhouse in 1975

Charles Detwiller, Architect

I have no training in architecture, but I do in folk music and early classical music. When I hear a song with certain harmonies, I can tell whether the song is from, say, the 18th century or from a later period. This comes from a lot of listening and performing. But I am way out of my element with architecture.

I can remember, before we went to see our architect, Marcia looking at the farmhouse, whose cause seemed hopeless to most people. Where do you start? "Well," she said, "the first thing that has to go is that dormer on the roof!" And, I thought, okay, I guess, if that's what she wants.

On February 12, 1976, Lois Kurz, Marcia, and I walked into the office of Charles Detwiller, architect, in Plainfield. After the usual introductions, we sat down and Marcia opened her portfolio of pictures and showed the photo above to Detwiller. He looked at it for only a moment, and I swear, the first thing he said was, "Can anything be done about that dormer?"

Charles Detwiller was recommended to us in 1975 by the NJ Historic Sites Division. At the time we met him (1976) he had worked on between 40 and 50 buildings since 1961. He said the first step would be to have him visit the site and write a preliminary report, which would cost around $100 and take one week. Next would be measured drawings for about $500 for one building, around $1,000 for farmhouse and barn, plus travel expenses.

We thanked Detwiller for his time, and there the matter was dropped for several months.

The National Register Rejection

There were grants available for restoration, but government grants required that the property be listed on the National Register of Historic Places, administered by the National Park Service. Even grants managed by the state had this requirement, because they used federal funds as their source.

Here is the outline of our three-year endeavor to get the Murray Farm on the National Register.

- July 21, 1975: Gertrude Neidlinger, in the name of the Middletown Township Historical Society, submitted an application for National Register status for the "John Throckmorton Farm." Such applications were handled by the Historic Sites Division, NJ Department of Environmental Protection. This application was based in part on Gertrude's research.

- December 12, 1975: I called David Poinsett of the Historic Sites Division to see how the application was faring. He said there were problems with the application, and that Gertrude Neidlinger was known to take many liberties with facts, and she claimed that all old houses were built before 1700.[34] She even claimed that the old fossils in the park were 65

million years old. (Which was true! But Gertrude didn't document this properly.)

- December 16, 1975: Jonathan Fricker, from the Historic Sites Division, visited the farmhouse with Marcia and me. In the attic, he misstepped and crashed part way through a bedroom ceiling, fortunately not injuring himself. On return to Trenton, the Division did revise the application for national status.

- July 1976: NJ State Historic Sites Division put the Throckmorton Farm on the State Register of Historic Places.

- January 11, 1977: The National Park Service received the application from the state.

- September 1, 1978. The National Park Service denied the application, thus closing the door on any government restoration grants. (Yes, this was more than 1½ years after they received it.)

Here is the (partial) text of the letter of rejection:

U.S. Department of the Interior
Heritage Conservation and Recreation Service
September, 1978

After careful consideration, we are returning your nomination for the John Throckmorton Farm, as it does not appear to have maintained significant architectural and historical integrity to merit inclusion on the National Register. Extensive alterations have obscured much of the original fabric and design of the house. In its current condition, we do not believe that it depicts or recalls the historical events and persons originally associated with it.

Detwiller termed the grounds for rejection "ridiculous," wherein they stated that there was not enough left of the original structures to be worth saving, despite professional opinion to the contrary, and the indisputable fact that the buildings were on their original foundations.

Marcia put it more strongly: "What the hell is the grant program for, if the only structures they'll put on the register and give restoration grants for are those that don't need to be restored?"

It took two years before Marcia got her revenge.

---

[34] Gertrude was not a professional application writer, and perhaps someone else might have had better luck with this. But, she was the *only* person who gave us help when we asked for it in 1975.

Land Ownership of the Throckmorton-Stillwell-Murray Farm 1667-1973

Compiled by Marcia Rissland, 1983

The original land grant was enormous, comprising southern Middletown, Navesink, Rumson, and "Potoepeck" (now Port au Peck). Every owner sold off large or small tracts as money was needed, or land was divided and sub-divided among heirs. By 1973 the original land had shrunk to the present 90 acres.

Year	Owner	Type
1667	John Throckmorton	Land Grant
1674	John Throckmorton, Jr. (son of above)	Conveyance
1690	Joseph Throckmorton (son of above)	Inheritance
1704	Alice Throckmorton (sister of above)	Inheritance
	Thomas Stillwell (husband of Alice)	By Marriage
1739	Thomas Stillwell, Jr. (son of above)	Inheritance
1767	Joseph Murray	Purchase
1780	Rebecca Morris Murray (wife of Joseph)	Widow's Portion
1806	William C. Murray (son of above)	Inheritance
1815	James Murray (son of William)	Conveyance
	Susan & Maria Murray (granddaughters of above)	Inheritance
1861	Charles Gordon	Purchase
1874	John Headdon (son of above)	Purchase
1879	Jonathan Headdon (son of John)	Inheritance
1899	Lydia Maps	Mortgage Foreclosure
1900	Henry Robinson	Purchase
1930	William Mears	Purchase

The records in the 1930s are confused, with foreclosures, bank failures, vacancy, sheriff's sale, which all went on during the Depression.

Year	Owner	Type
1939	Albert Gebhardt	Purchase
1955	Rose Gebhardt (wife of Albert)	Widow's Inheritance
1971	John Cavanaugh (nephew of Rose)	Inheritance
1973	Middletown Township	Purchase

Walter Willey managed the Whistling Hill (Gebhardt) Farm until its sale in 1973 to Middletown Township. He is shown here in an undated photo, probably in the 1950s, with his daughter Laurace. The photo was undoubtedly taken in the west wing of the barn where the milking stalls were. After the sale of the farm, he became superintendent of Hop Brook Farm in Holmdel until his retirement in 1995. He frequently visited the Murray Farm with his wife, Cecilia, after the buildings were restored. Willey died at age 92 in December 1996.

Laurace married Harlan Hogan, who was a Recreation work crew foreman in Middletown Township, and in that capacity was well known to the Poricy Park staff.

The Architect Back at Work

As 1976 lumbered on with no further progress on the buildings (and by now, it was our own contractor that was stalling on the house roof), we decided to contact Detwiller again. He said he would like to see the site (he had seen only the photographs we showed him in February), and he would then do a preliminary report for $100, followed by measured drawings and a sketch plan for restoration for $1,000.

We saw no problem with the $100 for a report; we would cover it if the Township would not. So, we arranged an on-site visit on October 25, 1976 with Detwiller, attended by John Campbell, Frank Lescinsky, Marcia, and myself.

At that meeting, the "directive" we gave Detwiller was to have the house made into a residence, the main part of the barn restored to a colonial appearance, the south wing demolished, and the west wing (the milking stalls) refurbished into meeting rooms and a workshop. He would write a brief report for his $100, and wait until we told him to proceed with the main plans.

Detwiller wrote a report immediately, the first paragraph of which I already quoted on page 112. I will quote excerpts from the 5-page report. Much of it contains comments on the existing features, and which ones should be retained and which probably thrown out. He did have the benefit of the old drawings from the *History of the New Jersey Coast* (which I will include here). Here is the opening of his statement about the farmhouse:

> The original farmhouse, as it appears in the sketch shown in the *History of the New Jersey Coast*, appears to have had a wing added to the southeast, probably in the early 1800s as much of the materials show signs of that period in use of mouldings and cut nails... It would appear that further changes were made later in the 1800s when the pointed "Gothic Revival" windows were added on the northwest and elevation, and possibly the exterior doorway installed between the fireplaces. It is difficult to

determine the chronology of the many changes that have occurred without making extensive exploratory probes and removal of finished wall surfaces, exploring the basic structure...

After several more paragraphs in this style, he then lists the steps required for restoration:

- Stabilize with new roofs (being done).
- Prepare measured drawings.
- Remove the south barn wing.
- Reclaim the west barn wing, remove cow stalls, install heating system, lavatories [this was not done; the wing was later removed entirely].
- Remove asbestos shingles, install proper siding.
- Rebuild entrances and porches.
- Install a new restroom in "new" wing of house.
- Install a new hot-air heating system in house.
- Restore rooms in house to original appearance.

Detwiller then gave estimates of the costs of these various steps. For the farmhouse and barn, these steps totaled $53,500. This included his fee of $1,000 for measured drawings.

At the Township Committee caucus on November 4, the Committee agreed to the expense of $1,000 for the drawings.

Mrs. Timolat and the Architect

Mrs. Timolat was growing increasingly frustrated with the lack of progress in restoring the buildings. She couldn't understand why, when the Township acquired the farm in late 1973, work crews didn't immediately start on the buildings. That's what would have happened if she had bought the farm.

In January 1976 we had used her funds to put a proper roof on the barn, and we were grinding through the red tape and delays to get a roof put on the house by the Township. Nothing else had happened, save for the cosmetic improvements we had made in the farmhouse for summer programs.

In early November 1976, in one of many conversations Marcia had with Mrs. Timolat, Marcia explained that to obtain grants for restoration, we had to get on the National Register, and that was in progress, and we had already made it onto the State Register. But, we also had to have an architect draw up plans to include with any grant application. We had met briefly with Detwiller, but further work with him was on hold. The Township had agreed to pay Detwiller $100 for his visit in October and also had agreed to the expense of $1,000 for the drawings, but

Marcia pointed out that it could take months, if not a year, for the expense to clear all the petty hurdles and get final approval. It had taken nine months, from October 1975 to July 1976, to get a contract from the Township to put a roof on the farmhouse.

With a cover letter dated November 11, 1976, Mrs. Timolat enclosed her check for $1,100. Now, get going!

Restoring the Barn

Detwiller's drawings were done in early 1977 and included both the farmhouse and barn. But the two buildings were restored two years apart, the barn being first. I will therefore begin with the barn.

The photo at right, taken in late 1976 from the southwest, shows the milking wing at the barn's west side (cupolas on top). The photo below, Feb. 1975, shows the south wing, which nobody wanted to keep. (Please ignore super shed to the right.) Note the boarded up windows and doors, each a point of break-in entry.

Joseph Murray's Barn, as depicted in *New Jersey Coast in Three Centuries: History of the New Jersey Coast, Vol. II*, Lewis Publishing Company, NY, 1902, William Nelson, Editor. The caption reads, "X marks the spot where Joseph Murray was killed [at far left, a crude "x"]. His gun stood against the fence in front of the barn." I think that some 19th-century imagination went into this caption. The original artist and date of drawing are unknown. But, its companion drawing, shown on page 128, shows the farmhouse without its 1830s addition, so this drawing must be not long after the murder in 1780. Note that the entrance to the barn cellar is outdoors, right where we found it in 1973, but which we decided to move indoors.

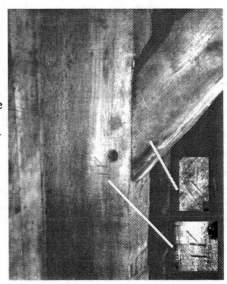

It is a miracle that the barn did not collapse from its own weight. In photo at left, taken April 1978, a support post is so rotted that it doesn't touch the floor. The siding was keeping the barn up!

At right is shown the mortise (cavity) and tenon (tongue) construction. The beams are assembled flat on the ground and then numbered with a chisel, often with Roman numerals (which can be cut with a chisel). Then, the various sections are assembled, held together with wooden pegs, and the frame is swung in place on a great "barn raising" party day.

The drawing Charles Detwiller provided in April 1977. (The drawing is signed "L. Schwin.") He planned to restore the center portion of the barn, tear down the south wing, and reconstruct the west wing (shown at right) for modern usage.

The Decision to Restore the Barn

Our board meeting on May 17, 1977 was our first after the May 2 firebombing of the farmhouse. It was a tough session, with the discussion centered on recovering from the firebombing in time for the summer programs. The Nature Center, out for bids, was a major issue with John Campbell (not present at our meeting). This might not have been the best time to bring up restoration of the barn.

But we did discuss the barn. Despite a new roof, it was in terrible condition. A burglar alarm would be a joke. There were nearly 30 points at which people could break in, and kids were doing so every few weeks. Evidence of smoking, drinking, and even drugs had been found, and the two wings had poor flooring and were dangerous.

Marcia and I argued that we had to do one of two things: restore it or tear it down.

There wasn't much support for restoration. Some people didn't see much value in having it; they saw few uses for programs (especially with a new Nature Center), and they just weren't into old barns. But everybody realized that there wasn't any money to do this. We were in a struggle to build a fund to run our full-year programs starting in 1978, and we had the summer 1977 programs right in our face.

Well, they had good arguments, even if Marcia and I didn't agree with all of them. But, we again argued, that the status quo was unacceptable. We just can't leave it there in its deplorable condition.

The committee did agree that if we could find funding, it would be okay to restore it in 1978, in which case the barn would be finished at the time the Nature Center opened. This way, full-time programs would provide some surveillance for the restored structures.

After the meeting, I wrote a five-page letter to Mrs. Timolat on May 20. In it, I summarized the entire cost of the park to date, $1,121,000, which included land, buildings, and our own expenses of running programs. The barn would cost around $20,000 to restore, including the architect's fee of $1,000. This would be only a small fraction of what had already been spent. If, and this would be highly unlikely, the Township would fund it, it would be a public contract and we would be forced to use the lowest bidder. Also, the Township might do what they did with the Nature Center and replace our architect with one of their choice. We would lose control of the project. It would be so much better if we could do this ourselves. Could she help?

There followed a few months of letters and phone calls in three-way communication between Marcia, Mrs. Timolat, and myself. On August 8, Detwiller, with two associates, visited the site and agreed to prepare plans for just the barn for $1,000.

The Barn Gets Restored

In mid-August Mrs. Timolat agreed to donate $10,000 toward the cost of the barn restoration. Marcia and I would personally come up with the balance.[35] Detwiller made his drawings and in January 1978 we got an estimate from S&W (who had done the two roofs) for $18,250. In March 1978, the PPCC signed the contract to restore the barn.

During restoration, Marcia had to make many decisions when the contractor discovered problems. Two major horizontal beams were seriously rotted,

---

[35] I feel compelled to insert this item, in case someone finds in the board minutes that part of my contribution was a loan to be repaid over a few years by the PPCC. When time for repayments came, I made cash contributions to cover them; hence the loan was negated. No significant amounts from the PPCC treasury went into the barn. Some board members felt that membership funds spent on the farmhouse and barn were a diversion from our charter.

The completed barn was painted in July 1980.

but the rot was not discovered until the siding was removed. L-shaped steel beams were made to support these. The old cellar door wall was filled in with a new section of rock foundation. This was done to reduce chances of intrusion, a major problem in the park. A new trap door entrance to the cellar was constructed in the barn floor.

During construction, the barn was wide open. There was no way the interior could be secured, with one or another wall dismantled. Midway into construction, the contractor, against our advice, installed all the windows in the barn before the barn could be secured. Vandals came in and methodically smashed every pane of every window.

As a result, the contractor was running out of money and needed some help. Marcia managed to get Public Works to spare the contractor from having to remove the debris. Public Works dug a huge hole in the ground just uphill from the barn, and everything was plowed into it.

And, all this time Marcia was managing our move into the new Nature Center.

The barn construction took forever, and the contractor was responsible for many delays. The final payment was not made until November 1978.

Architect's drawing of the proposed Murray Farmhouse restoration, March 1977 (signed "L. Schwin").

Restoring the Farmhouse

The Murray Farmhouse, from *History of the New Jersey Coast*, cited in the previous similar drawing of the barn. The east wing of the house, as shown in the upper drawing to the right of the door, did not exist at this time. Marcia was able to find the hole for the well, at right.

Let's see where we were in fall, 1979. The barn was restored in 1978. The farmhouse had a new roof (1977), and had had a lot of trash removed from it, including the old heating system of radiators and coal furnace. It had a new electric and phone service, with buried cables, and had temporary, barely adequate electric heaters. We had been in the new Nature Center for a year and were busy with our school programs.

But the basic appearance and interior of the farmhouse was unchanged, except for cosmetic repairs. We had been turned down for the National Register in 1978, and we had no money.

Marcia's November 19, 1979 Report

November 19, 1979 marked the tenth anniversary of our first public appearance as the "PPCC" in Town Hall with the Sewerage Authority. Probably without realizing this bit of trivia, Marcia chose this date to write a report on the condition of the farm buildings. The report was just for the file and for Marcia to hand out; it is not addressed to anyone in particular. Here are some highlights:

- Farmhouse foundation. Large gaps where mortar has fallen out, some stones missing.
- Exterior trim. All window sills are rotted. So are some doors, and porch floors.
- Exterior walls. Asbestos shingles broken in many places.
- Interior walls. Increasing damage from water.
- Framework. Construction undermined by termite damage. Several support beams rotted.
- Masonry. Fireplaces dangerously deteriorated.
- Is anything good about it? Yes. Original stonework is strong. Foundation of "new" end is in perfect condition. [The 1830s east wing addition did not originally have a basement. This was added in 1950.] Much of the original framework is still sturdy.

Marcia's report then goes on with a list of patching and repair that could stave off further deterioration and, especially, water damage.

The report contains similar items for the barn, except that the barn had been restored. It had many leaks in the doors and windows fittings, and the lofts, which had not been replaced, had poor flooring.

Al Oppegard, Marcia, and I went to the farmhouse on December 28 to see if we could find a project we could do to provide some element of "restoration." We didn't want to do anything that would be ripped apart with subsequent improvements, should that ever occur. We decided that maybe we could get the fireplaces to work, including the open hearth fireplace in the basement. Such improvements in masonry could remain intact should walls, floors, etc. be redone later.

1980: The Farmhouse is Reborn

When, in 1978, the National Park Service denied National Register of Historic Places status to the Murray Farm, Marcia told Mrs. Timolat about this. Marcia made it clear that we would be ineligible for any federal or state grants for restoration, and for grants from many foundations, which also have this requirement. During 1979, Mrs. Timolat kept making requests to us to get *something* done, and we just didn't have the funds to do anything.

In January 1980, after we made our decision to try to fix up the masonry and fireplaces, Mrs. Timolat did offer to help with modest grants, but she also wanted a nearly day-by-day report on what was happening. That's not always a good idea, because very often, day-by-day, Marcia was just waiting for people to show up for appointments, to return phone calls, and to write letters. So, we entered a period of consulting, waiting, and frustration.

Marcia's Diary

Marcia started to keep a diary. You might think this would be exciting to read, but it is an exercise in tedium if read in its raw form. So, I'm going to use this diary as the prime source of information on what happened, but quote only occasional sections.

There were three major players we dealt with from January through March, 1980. One was a mason, from whom we eventually got estimates for some of the work. Another was a chimney sweep, who would examine the chimneys and try to determine if we could use the fireplaces. The third was Paul Reinhold, Middletown Building Inspector, from whom we would eventually have to get permits to rebuild the fireplaces or have fires in them. He also had the authority to run tests of his own.

On February 14, Mrs. Timolat gave Marcia $500 toward our masonry expenses. Here is a synopsis of Marcia's account of the next day:

Friday, February 15, 1980:

- 10:30 am: Chimney sweep started examination.
- Architect Detwiller arrived on time.
- Mason did not arrive. I reached him at his job in Sea Bright, he had forgotten about it.
- Mason arrived late, and all three consulted together. Chimney man said one upstairs flue and the open hearth flue were not too bad, maybe small fires would be possible.
- Chimney man examined main chimney and found that the roofer in 1977 had put no flashing or tar around the chimney.
- I was in farmhouse from 10:30 to 4:30. Pete, who was working on his day off at the Nature Center, joined us for lunch at the farmhouse.
- At 4:30, I went to the Nature Center and found Pete waiting for Honeywell technician to fix the heating system. [Yeah, for the 128th time. PTB].
- I finally made it home. I was covered with ashes, soot, and plaster dust, and we had dinner reservations for 6:00. No time to wash even my face. Pete and Cathy appeared to pick us up for dinner.
- At that moment the phone rang; it was Mrs. Timolat who wanted a detailed account of the day and of all the estimates I have thus received from all contractors in the past six weeks. She challenged everything. It was a long phone call.
- Went to dinner, came back to our house, and unwound over drinks.

The Smoke Bomb

Marcia was tied up in mid-March, so it was on me to keep contacting the building inspector to get a smoke bomb test. After some delays, we finally got it scheduled for Monday, March 24.

This was something to see. They suspended a smoke bomb on a rope and lowered it into the chimney, then sealed off the chimney to see if any smoke escaped.

The place looked like a smokehouse. We could have cured hams in the parlors, and thick clouds of smoke came pouring out of cracks outdoors from all over the chimney. In fact, leaking chimneys were a major cause of our losing so many old houses over the centuries. We were lucky with this one.

Marcia writes, in her notes, her irritation with the first chimney man. On February 15, without using a smoke bomb, he charged us $135 to tell us that the chimneys were basically okay. Now, the Township has done the proper test for us for free:

To: Marcia Rissland
From: Paul Reinhold, Jr., Construction Official
Re: Fireplaces in Poricy Park Farmhouse
Date: April 1, 1980

As you are aware, I purchased smoke bombs so that a test could be performed on the farmhouse fireplaces. Mr. Fred Beam, fire sub-code official, and Mr. Jack Fowler, chief combustible inspector, made the requested test, and it is their combined opinion that the fireplaces, as they are now constructed, cannot be repaired by just rebuilding the fireplace/firebox areas. Your options are:

A. Rebuild the fireplaces and seal off the chimney and post the fireplaces as decorative and not for use;

B. Rebuild the fireplaces, and rebuild and flue-line the chimney in a manner that would lend itself to the safe usage of the fireplaces in question.

[The letter then goes on to say that when and if we repair the fireplaces, they would be glad to inspect them and issue a permit.]

And then came the call from Mrs. Timolat.

Mrs. Timolat's Offer

On Wednesday, April 9, 1980 Mrs. Timolat called Marcia and said she was totally frustrated with the glacial pace of the project and would pay for the cost of restoring the entire farmhouse, up to $50,000. She had a down payment check for $25,000 for Marcia to come and pick up.

Well, that certainly set a new direction for us. But before we go there, we might take a moment to think about what this grant meant for us.

A true restoration of a home this size, with contractors that are specialists in this work, could have cost up to $500,000 in 1980. We did have an architect who had a fine reputation, and he understood our limitations and that we could not use the contractors he might have wanted.

Mrs. Timolat also understood that we were doing this with limited funds, and would not get the superior results that some other agencies in Monmouth County had obtained with other houses.

But we still had to do it "right," as best as we could. And, with the contractor we were seeking, we had to work under three rules:

- We, that is Marcia, would have to determine what goes and what stays. Was some window or fireplace woodwork really of the period, or could we junk it and replace it with a modern reproduction of something more architecturally correct? How about nails in floorboards? Were they original? How faithfully did we have to stay with the original room arrangements? Should we tear down the 1830s addition (as they would in Williamsburg) and thus deprive ourselves of useful space for meetings, and a modern bathroom? And, Marcia had to be prepared to tell the contractors and also the volunteer demolition crews what to save.

- Volunteers[36] would do almost all the interior demolition work, else the contract would be far too expensive. This meant directing crews that were not professional.

- Volunteers were also going to do all the interior finishing, which mainly meant painting, but also included some caulking and finishing work and maybe even some carpentry.

---

[36] "Volunteers" meant Marcia and anyone she could get to help with the work. Lots of people did help.

Three Concurrent Farmhouse Projects

In the next few months, we had to:

1. Examine the house to try to get down to what was still there from the 1700s and determine whether we could save those features.
2. Find a contractor.
3. And, by the way, the 200th anniversary of Joseph Murray's murder was coming up on June 8, 1980 and the park staff was preparing to honor the occasion with "Joseph Murray Day," complete with tours of the house. So, whatever we did to the house in the next two months had to be relatively inconspicuous.

Picking, Poking, and Prodding

"Prodding" appeared in Marcia's alliterative list of techniques beginning with "p" that you need to make a park. We add "picking" and "poking" to the list. That's what she had to do to figure out what was original to the house. Here are a few excerpts from her diary prior to Joseph Murray Day:

- Sunday April 13, 1980. Joe and Marie Racioppi and I met at 9 am. We took down a small section of basement lath. We found machine-made round-head nails in lath, square machine-cut nails in furring. Furring was run-of-the-mill mass-produced lumber. Whole works no older than 1890. So much for one expert's original opinion that the plaster was over original hand-split lath. We pulled down the whole mess, exposing smoke-stained board & beam ceiling. They cleaned up the mess and left at noon. I continued since I was too dirty to stop…

- Tuesday April 15: Spent whole day (8 hours) going over plans …

- Wednesday April 16: I probed into stone wall of basement next to stairs, having once been told that the plaster was original deer hair plaster and should never be disturbed. Behind the plaster was newspaper stuffing with articles about Eisenhower and the Korean War. All

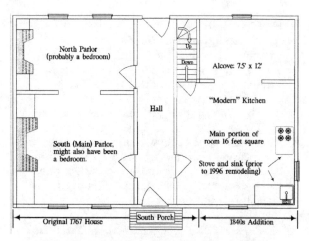

First floor of the farmhouse, after restoration.

This murky photo (sorry about the quality) was taken five years prior to the real restoration. It shows Girl Scouts doing initial clean up of the south parlor on May 10, 1975. Photo was taken from lower left corner of south parlor (see diagram), with the opening toward the north parlor at left. It illustrates three kinds of questions one can face during a restoration: one silly, one trivial, and one serious. (1) The silly one is whether to leave the Christmas tree painted on the wall. For the few people that wanted it to stay, we assured them that Joseph and Rebecca Murray did not put it there. (2) The trivial one is in regard to the one-foot-high sill you have to step over to get to the next room. Is this of historic significance? No – it was put there by one of the Bell Labs engineers that rented the house in 1973 to keep drafts off his harpsichord. (3) The serious one is whether you leave the opening between the rooms, which could not have been present in 1780. This was a small home without the 1830s addition, and, like many Irish one-room houses, all of the main family activity was in the kitchen, that is, in the basement with the hearth. In a one-floor Irish home, the "bedrooms" are simply partitions at the end of the room, but here, they are one floor up and would not have been joined. We left the opening because it was of great practical value in giving tours and running programs.

plaster is so badly deteriorated that it will have to come down...

- [A few days omitted here.] <u>Thursday April 17</u>: Tom McGrath (township maintenance worker assigned to the park) and I lugged out storm windows and other trash. Pulled off sheet rock from parlor closet ceiling, and at first found nothing but 2×4s, dirt, and cobwebs, but then found an old joist with two hand-wrought nails sticking out of the boards.

- <u>Saturday April 19</u>: Went to restoration seminar in Princeton with Cathy and Pete, learned very little but picked up some good publications.

- <u>Friday April 25</u>: Thelma Jelliffe and I met in the farmhouse and agreed that the entire house had been redone around 1830 with original trim removed and replaced with 1830s style trim.

I'm going to skip many entries and jump to:

- <u>Monday June 2</u>: Diane Lehder arrived at 2 pm to photograph all rooms in the house prior to demolition after Joseph Murray Day. [Hundreds of photos were taken by several people at all stages of this project. PTB]

Choosing a Contractor

Marcia had sought advice from many people in her quest for a contractor. Scattered through her notes from February through June are the names of four contractors that seemed promising, and at least said they would come and look at the job. We did not have specs written down; that would come later. What we did have were Detwiller's plans and the farmhouse itself. It was understood that the PPCC would do all the interior demolition, and that the Township would provide a dumpster.

This is how the four contractors ended up.

1. Never showed up.
2. Met with us several times, but was too expensive. His basic cost was going to be around $60,000 plus change orders. And, we would have our own expenses. This far exceeded our limit of $50,000.
3. Would do the job, but without a contract. He was concerned that he couldn't determine what he'd run into in a house of this age, and he wanted a "pay as you go" agreement.
4. The fourth was Creative Craftsmen, in the person of Jim Alverson, whom we met in late May, and who eventually got the job. But, his estimate came in late in June, well past Joseph Murray Day.

So, we plunged into Joseph Murray Day without

At our first Joseph Murray Day, Pat Contreras was our park director. She was a good organizer of festivals. This event included a blacksmith, a group of singers, a reenactment of the murder, and tours of the buildings.

a contract, but with a lot of chutzpah, as you'll see on the next page.

Joseph Murray Day and Marcia's Revenge

Joseph Murray Day in 1980 was one of our earliest "festival events." We certainly could not pass up the chance to commemorate the 200th anniversary of his murder on June 8, 1780. We distributed flyers and invited the world. The whole world didn't come, but 325 people did, and we were pleased with the event.

Joseph Murray Day, June 8, 1980 was held with the house unrestored and the barn still unpainted.

PORICY PARK CITIZENS COMMITTEE
P. O. BOX 36 • MIDDLETOWN, N. J. 07748

May 27, 1980

Mr. William J. Murtaugh
Keeper of the National Register
U.S. Department of the Interior
Washington, D. C.

Dear Mr. Murtaugh,

This is an invitation for you, or any representative, to attend JOSEPH MURRAY DAY in Poricy Park, June 8, 1980.

Joseph Murray was a Revolutionary War patriot – a soldier in the Monmouth Militia – who occupied a house in Middletown, New Jersey. The house, built on land purchased in 1704 by Thomas Stillwell, still stands on its original foundation and in its original farm setting, now known as Poricy Park. The House, and its barn (also still standing), were turned down in 1978 for National Register Status by members of your department.

The grounds of turning down the house were that "it does not appear to have maintained significant architectural and historical integrity." In other words, it was not already restored. This puzzles us, because we thought your agency assisted in <u>restoring</u> buildings, as well as preserving those already restored. I have enclosed the letter signed on your behalf by Mr. Rettig stating this reason. (Perhaps Mr. Rettig would enjoy attending Joseph Murray Day.)

Joseph Murray was killed by Tory sympathizers while planting crops on June 8, 1780. On June 8, 1980, we are going to observe two important events:

1. The 200th anniversary of Joseph Murray's assassination.

2. The 276th anniversary of the Stillwell-Murray farm not being on the National Register of Historic Places.

We will have a gala celebration, and then, when the celebration is over, we – a private citizens group – are going to RESTORE the house, Historic Register or not.

Please plan to attend. We're all going to have a good time.

.... (signed) Marcia S. Rissland, Secretary
.... Poricy Park Citizens Committee

Among the people that received the invitation was William Murtaugh of the National Register. The letter is shown at left and speaks for itself. Marcia enjoyed writing it.

And, we got a reply! They regretted that they could not attend, but in a very cordial (and serious, nearly solemn) tone wished us well with the celebration and good luck and success with our project.

After we did our restoration, Marcia was told by several people over the years how fortunate we were to have received a grant without being put on the National Register. You become bound by many requirements for filing and getting approval to make even the simplest changes. They told her stories of how their own organizations became mired in red tape and were sometimes denied permission to carry out their work.

Well, Mr. Murtaugh missed a nice event. And, it's a good thing he wasn't around for the next few months, because that's when the serious interior demolition began.

Major Probing and Contract Negotiations

With Joseph Murray Day over, there were no restraints on what Marcia could rip down.

- <u>Tuesday, June 10, 1980</u>: Pulled gypsum board off parlor ceilings. AT LAST, FOUND SOMETHING OLD AND <u>GOOD</u>. Beautiful finished beaded beams [on the ceiling] and smooth boards which were meant to be exposed. Also, there <u>was</u> a cabinet next to the fireplace.
- (Skip several entries.) <u>Monday, July 21</u>: Pried off mantle (of recent manufacture) from south parlor fireplace. Original mantle was much lower, as evidenced by large cross timber notched out to hold plaster. The new mantle was 55" above floor, old one was 50" or less. (North parlor was 50", and was original. This design should be copied for south parlor.)

There are many such entries. But a major effort during June and July was with the contracts. On June 21, Al Oppegard, Marcia, and I met with Jim Alverson of Creative Craftsmen to go over the specs. This resulted in our drawing up a proposal which I put into our computer and then gave to Marcia for her revision. It is dated June 26, 1980.

Rather than quote from our document, I will instead quote from the proposal we wrote to present to the Township Committee for requiring permission to have this work done. Here is what will be done:

1. Make the exterior appearance match the drawings of Charles Detwiller, architect.
2. Repair foundation, new brick in basement floor.
3. Put all three fireplaces in working condition.
4. Restore colonial appearance to interior.
5. Remodel the 1830s east wing: cellar to have utilities; 1st floor, a kitchen; 2nd floor, a bathroom.

We pointed out that we had already spent $24,676 on the buildings prior to June 1979, and then gave cost figures for the farmhouse restoration:

Al Oppegard served as treasurer in the 1980s and helped set up the accounting system on the new computer in 1980. Prior to that, he was assisted by Mary Chamberlain who pored over the monthly checks and receipts and generated many yards of tape on our mechanical adding machine. Al helped write the farmhouse contracts. In later years, Judy Berrien became actively involved in business operations.

Proposed Expenses for the Farmhouse, to be presented to the Township Committee August 5, 1980	
Main Alverson contract, includes plumbing	$21,000
Masonry, Enn Onni contractor (includes foundation & fireplaces & chimneys)	12,900
Electrical work (Jean Ruck)	1,350
Lighting fixtures (in cellar)	100
Painting house exterior	1,742
Painting barn exterior	960
Rain gutters, house & barn	450
Special hardware for doors, windows, etc.	500
Architect fees for on-job consulting	500
Change orders and contingencies	2,000
Documentation and photographs	200
Paint and finishes for interior	100
Other consulting costs	250
Already spent since February 1980	745
Total	$42,797

A Change in Handwriting

Lou and Marcia in the Poconos, 1980

Original outside beam has been cut through & removed from south side to basement door area.
Had to leave without cleaning up mess - torrents of rain were washing out the road.

August 4, 1980 Pete Brady pinch hitting for Marcia as Chronicler. Alarm: Another false alarm Thursday nite; on Fri the alarm man came and found the front door magnetic sensor was defective.

In preparing for this book, I assembled all the files I could find from my own collection and from Marcia's and then proceeded to read through them one page at a time, taking notes. Among the last of the files I read were Marcia's handwritten "chronicles" detailing the activity in the 1980s in restoring the farmhouse.

After having read 26 pages of her notes (which took more than one evening to read), I was startled to turn the page and find the notes continued in my own handwriting. I had no memory, 25 years later, of having done that.

And then I remembered why. On July 31, 1980 her daughter Lee, age 24, was riding her bicycle in Minneapolis and turned directly into the path of an oncoming vehicle. She was thrown to the ground and went into a coma. Marcia and Lou went to be with her, and she died one week later. While Marcia was away, the work on the farmhouse went on as scheduled. It was everybody's way of offering their help and condolences to the Risslands.

Cathy and I took a pre-planned two-week vacation in the Poconos, and Marcia and Lou joined us there for two days.

Major Demolition

Saturday August 2, 1980 was demolition day in a big way. To quote from my own chronicles:

The work crew showed up in stages. In all, there were Pat Contreras (Nature Center director), Bernice Trombino, Dick Seeman, Lou Grover, Lou's brother-in-law Gino Guzzi, Paul Hickson, Frank Spang and his son, Al Oppegard, and myself. I had to leave at noon. Work ended at 3 pm. Bernice, Pat, and I arrived early, and Pat and Bernice spent the morning carefully packing kitchenware into boxes, and others loaded it into cars. At 11:30 the heavy plaster smashing began in the kitchen. Paul and Dick stripped to their waists and attacked the walls with sledge hammers. Bernice left the scene, groping her way through the dust. By the end of the day, the crew filled the dumpster a quarter full.

In fact, by mid-September the dumpster, which we had thought ridiculously huge, was two-thirds full and the contractor hadn't started yet.

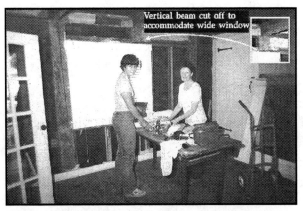

Vertical beam cut off to accommodate wide window

Pat Contreras and Bernice Trombino packing kitchen items. The window behind them is the same double-casement window over the heads of the people in the "dumpster" photo, below left. Somebody cut through a major vertical support beam to install this window. The vertical beam at left is intact, but the next one over has only its upper few inches left above the window (arrow). This window clearly does not belong there, and was not there in the drawing from the early 1800s (on page 128). The two "original" (modern sash) windows on this wall were reinstated in the restoration. Also, a post was reinserted where the original one was cut out.

From the dictionary:
Defenestrate: (Latin, de+fenestra, from a window). To throw a person or thing through a window.

This is the morning work crew on August 2, 1980. Clockwise from the man standing at the dumpster: Lou Grover, Pat Contreras, Paul Hickson, Dick Seeman, Bernice Trombino, and Lou's brother-in-law Gino Guzzi. They did all the work; I took the picture. (Frank Spang, his son, and Al Oppegard arrived later in the day.)

The dumpster was so placed that if you had reasonable aim, you could throw objects from the upstairs window right into it. That saved taking the rubble down the stairs and out the door. One day, Becky Albrecht and I defenestrated an entire wall that way. However, we never did throw a person out.

The Beehive

We had known there was a hive of wild honeybees in the upstairs southeast bedroom wall (the room above the stove in the first-floor plan a few pages back). The upstairs gypsum walls were all coming out, and we first had to get rid of the beehive.

Marcia had arranged for the exterminator to fumigate behind the wall. He assured us that the bees were all dead. *(You think you know where this is going, don't you? Well, read on.)*

One Saturday morning in 1980, Marcia and I began to take out the wallboard to remove the hive. I thought, why not start by removing the baseboard, which was a small strip of wood at the base of the wall? So, I inserted a large screwdriver between the baseboard and the wall and started to pry the baseboard away from the wall.

The baseboard held firm, and the <u>entire east wall moved out a quarter of an inch</u>!

Maybe we should try something else.

We did get the wallboard off, and found a HUGE drippy, gooey mess of honey, combs, dead bees, and insecticide. We spread it all out on a sheet on the lawn and Marcia photographed it for posterity.

A Thanks to All

In our combined notes, there are the names of dozens of people who helped during this phase of restoration. Many did dirty, grunt work. Others offered expertise, ran errands, or took photographs. I could not possibly include all their names here, and if I tried to, I'm certain that many people would still be omitted.

At first, Marcia kept count of the number of volunteer hours people spent here. The total was approaching 500 hours, but after August she stopped keeping track. All I can do, 25 years later, is say Thank You to all, whoever you were.

More Negotiations, We Lose Our Architect

As the contractor kept visiting the house during the summer, we wanted many changes, and on September 22, we prepared a list of change orders. The list contained 20 items, and produced a net increase of $700 to the contract. This was not a large sum, but the number of items on the list illustrated the details that had to be considered. We all signed the change order sheet on October 10, 1980, and the project was ready to proceed.

And, as work was about to start, our architect, Charles Detwiller, had a stroke and was not expected to recover. Marcia was now on her own in the day-to-day decisions.

Marcia and the contractor's crew, November 1980.

The fireplace in the basement kitchen gave a new meaning to the term "open hearth." We couldn't understand why it hadn't collapsed. (We added the supports.) It shared the same chimney flue with the two parlor fireplaces. The entire system had to be taken down, brick-by-brick, and rebuilt from the basement up to the top of the chimney using modern ceramic flue liners but with original bricks where possible.

Marcia with the workers in November 1980, showing exposed beams. The layering of bricks and mud within a wall, as shown above the door, is called *nogging*, and it was found throughout the house, even within interior walls. It is considered ineffective as insulation and was ripped out and replaced with modern insulation, except for a few places left exposed to show people. As the framework became exposed, remains of earlier doorways and window frames became evident, and Marcia had to decide whether to stay with our own plans or modify them for historical correctness.

The opening with the metal frame to the right of the hearth is a beehive oven, whose name is derived from its shape as seen from the rear (at right). It is part of the same flue system. We could not repair this without taking it completely apart, so we sealed it off and left it as an exhibit.

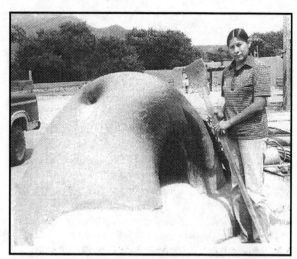

Beehive ovens are used throughout the world. I photographed the one shown here in Taos, New Mexico. You build a fire, then shovel it out, put your bread in it, and cover the front with the large paddle (at the woman's foot). The Richard Waln house, at Monmouth County Park System's Historic Walnford, also has an open hearth and beehive oven dating from the 1700s. There are five beehive ovens from the 18th century still found in Ireland, where Joseph Murray was from. They were fairly common in Colonial America.

The Contractor and the Completion

The contractor started in late October. He told me that this would take between one and two months from start to finish. (Where did I hear that before? Perhaps at the Nature Center?)

As part of the contract, we insisted that the house be completely secured and alarmed every evening. We learned our lesson from the barn. The need to do this was one of the factors that at times delayed the work. And, there were other factors, most too minor to recount here. But the contractor was nowhere near finished after two months.

By the end of January 1981, it was apparent that there was a substantial amount of work left to do.

The basement open hearth smoked heavily at first. A pamphlet from the USDA indicated that a *smoke shelf* was required to block down drafts. Our mason rebuilt the fireplace with a smoke shelf, which then worked fine.

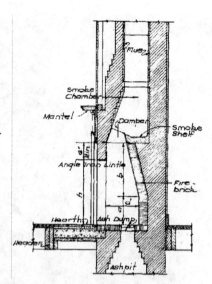

We sent the contractor a long list of unfinished items. Some got done in the next two months, but the work just came to a standstill. Finally, in late March we sent another letter, indicating a cutoff date of April 3. As part of our settlement, we assumed responsibility for some of the masonry, and there were other items that just didn't get done.

The Murray Farmhouse, May 1, 1992

Marcia in the farmhouse basement kitchen, May 1, 1992.

After that, Marcia and a few others spent the summer painting, plastering, and scraping. Many people helped, but one person stands out: Ed Lennon, a man who had some free time, spent day after day painting and otherwise assisting.

Finally, in November 1981 Marcia announced that the restoration was completed.

Marcia prepared a document explaining why she made certain decisions during the restoration. That is included here as Appendix B, <u>Why the Farmhouse and Barn Are the Way They Are</u>.

On October 4, 1994 Marcia gave a talk in the farmhouse on the restoration of the historic buildings. This included some 160 slides, mostly before and after shots of general views, but also of many details, such as framework, windows, etc. I have used several of the photos in this slide show here, and also parts of her text. And, I have added details about the events that led up to the restoration and the interactions of the people involved.

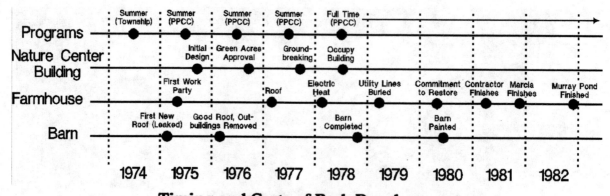

	1974	1975	1976	1977	1978	1979	1980	1981	1982
Programs	Summer (Township)	Summer (PPCC)	Summer (PPCC)	Summer (PPCC)	Full Time (PPCC)				
Nature Center Building		Initial Design	Green Acres Approval	Ground-breaking	Occupy Building				
Farmhouse		First Work Party		Roof	Electric Heat	Utility Lines Buried	Commitment to Restore	Contractor Finishes / Marcia Finishes	Murray Pond Finished
Barn		First New Roof (Leaked)	Good Roof, Out-buildings Removed		Barn Completed		Barn Painted		

Timing and Costs of Park Development

Here is a simplified summary of the park costs. It contains some approximations:

Land purchases: Fossil Beds, $132,000; Farm, $530,000; Boy Scout Tract, $60,000; Cotton Tract (private funds) $7,000; Colts Glen lots, $50,000; Miscellaneous fees $35,000:   Total $814,000
  (Of this total of $814,000, the cost to Middletown Township was approximately $100,000)
Nature Center building and outside improvements, including some cost overruns, approximately $350,000
  (Of this total of $350,000, the Township's share was approximately $190,000)
Farmhouse $60,000 (including power lines and roof), Barn $25,000 $85,000
  (Township's share was approximately $15,000, mainly for buried power lines and farmhouse roof)

The Murray Pond

We did not know if there was a pond on the farm in colonial times, but there was a tiny stream in the ravine next to the farmhouse. In fall 1980, Pat Contreras and Lois Berger said that they would look into the possibility of constructing a pond. Pat contacted the Naval Reserve Construction Battalion, who agreed to dig the hole and build a dam with Township equipment. They began in July 1982 and finished in December. The dam needed reworking, and there were some periods when the water level dropped, but the pond proved to be an asset. This photo was taken in October 1983.

The Full-Time Park: July 1978 Onward

Our First Year: Summer 1978 to Fall 1979

Summer 1978 saw the arrival of Mike Weilbacher as our chief naturalist, a full-time position. He had proved himself in summer 1977 as an innovative and popular creator of programs of many kinds. Also, just for the summer of 1978, we had a second naturalist in the person of April Ward from Rutgers. By now, we were getting used to the idea of summer programs (this was our fourth summer), but we still took many pictures and had a great time.

Our First Board Meeting in the Nature Center

On August 8, 1978, our Board of Directors had its first meeting in the new Nature Center. This was hailed by everyone as a great event. Imagine that – just nine years after we had begun what seemed to be a hopeless cause.

Looking back, however, I believe that this meeting began a slow and subtle process of depersonalizing our organization. For years we had been meeting in people's homes, taking turns at being hosts. My guess is that we had met in at least a dozen homes, and had gotten to know not just each other, but each other's families and life styles. We had become personal friends.

Well, we were still friends in August 1978, and remained so for many years. But new people coming on the board experienced neither the intimacy of meetings in homes nor the bonding experiences of our earlier years. They showed up for board meetings and park events, but they did not share family lives with each other. As time went on and the old board members departed, I believe this changed the character of the board. But, progress is progress.

The First School Year: 1978-79

After April Ward left in August, we had two employees to manage the Nature Center: Mike, and our secretary Barbara Maul (Barbara's picture is on page 85). We took on three entire grades in the Middletown School System, about 100 classes. In addition, we had our public programs, most of which were either conducted or arranged by Mike.

It was too much. Mike was enthusiastic and was a good program leader, but he had an impossible administrative workload. This was partly because we board members naïvely thought the park could operate with just one naturalist and one secretary, and partly because Mike himself helped create a schedule beyond his means. A major lesson we learned is that we either had to get more teachers or cut way back.

To Mike's heavy program load was added the challenge of opening a new facility in the community, and also of having to deal with the problems we were having with the building itself. This all fell on someone that had just graduated from college.

But we had wonderful programs, and many of us felt that this was much more important for our first year than having "proper, professional management." Mike really helped put Poricy Park on the map.

April Ward joined Mike Weilbacher during summer 1978. April was recommended by Professor Richard West of Cook College, Rutgers.

The Poricy Park staff in December 1981 (which had been in place since summer 1980). From left, Rosary Meyer was our full-time teacher. Kathy Whitney was our bookkeeper, helped prepare the calendar, and did some teaching. Pat Contreras was our director, and Albert was the park cat and gets a write-up all his own (page 155). Tom McGrath was our maintenance person, and Joan Hanvey was our secretary. Joan knew precisely how to insult people in a mocking, teasing way and have them love her for it. She remains one of my all-time favorite people in the park, and was also a favorite of the Township workers who came in for coffee and Joan's "abuse."

Mike decided to go on to graduate school, and in early 1979 we hired Patricia Contreras to join Mike in summer 1979 and then take his place as our naturalist in the fall.

That fall, we reduced our Middletown class commitment to two grades, and Pat also began to look for ways to get a second teacher. During that year, we changed her title from "naturalist" to "director," because that is the role she assumed.

The teaching problem was resolved for us, at least temporarily, by the CETA program (the federal Comprehensive Employment Training Act which we already mentioned in Marcia's "Day with Public Works.") We were given a teacher, namely Rosary

Meyer, and also a secretary, Joan Hanvey, who replaced Barbara Maul when Barbara left in May 1980. This, coupled with our own addition of Kathy Whitney as a part-time administrative assistant, and the addition of Tom McGrath as another CETA maintenance worker, provided us with the staff shown at left.[37]

There were many changes to the staff over the next decades, and to recount all of them here would be beyond the scope of providing a history of the "founding" of the park. But I will mention one set of particular significance here.

Pat's knowledge of the community and its artisans was of great benefit to the park in organizing festivals. Our first major event to draw people to the Nature Center was a wine and cheese reception on March 2, 1980, featuring local crafts and wines of New Jersey. This was also the event for which Marcia prepared her poster display of the history of the park, shown on page 61.

---

[37] Tom McGrath died suddenly from a brief illness in May 1983. In July 1983, The Township replaced him with Charles Davis, who provided maintenance services in the park until he retired to Pennsylvania around the year 2003.

Kathy Whitney had moved to Fair Haven from Delaware in 1975 and had become a volunteer in the park, and later a board member. She joined the payroll as a part-time assistant in the early 1980s, primarily as a bookkeeper, and also as "program coordinator" to prepare the public calendar. She left the park in 1984 and her program coordinator duties were taken on by Lethe Lescinsky, who had been a volunteer up to that point. (Lethe's picture is on page 102). When Pat Contreras left the park in 1986, Kathy assumed the role of "administrator," which eventually became the position of *de facto* director.

Kathy remained in her position until her retirement in 1996. Lethe and Frank moved to Lake Placid, NY in August 1999.

The Linder/McGrath Vote

In late 1980 we were in fairly good shape financially, except that CETA was funding three of our employees: Tom McGrath (maintenance), Rosary Meyer (teacher), and Joan Hanvey (secretary). McGrath actually worked for the Township, and the other two, for us.

Also at that time we were restoring the farmhouse, but that was with dedicated funds.

As administrator in 1980, it was my function to go over the budget and see not just how well we were doing at present, but also how well we would be doing for the next several years.

During the fall, we were told that the CETA program was being abruptly discontinued. Maybe Tom McGrath would go on Township payroll, but we'd lose Joan and Rosary.

This was a looming crisis. We might be able to keep Joan, but we could never at that time find the funds to keep Rosary. We'd lose her as our main teacher, and with that, we'd have to cut back or even cancel the Middletown School programs.

Pat and I attempted to get some emergency support from the county, but that failed, and we decided to ask the Middletown Township Committee for a one-time emergency grant of $20,000 to

The board of directors, spring 1980. Up to that time, it never occurred to anybody to have our group pose for a group picture. (In fact, during the initial years we never did this, to our regret years later.) I think Pat Contreras took this photo, but memory is tricky after 25 years! In the back row of five people: Paul Hickson (standing), Marcia Rissland, Becky Albrecht, Diane Lehder, Lois Berger. In front on the floor: Al Oppegard, Pete Brady, Frank Lescinsky, Lois Kurz. Every person in this photo put years of service into the park, almost all at least 10 years, and most more than 20.

carry us through 1981. We hoped to establish a more solid level of local funding, and even possibly obtain some grants. We were put on the agenda for the January 6, 1981 caucus meeting.

Up to that January, the Township Committee had been under Democratic party control, but in the fall, Republicans Joe McGrath and Paul Linder had won two seats, and with Republican Frank Self already there, this put the Republicans in the majority. And, by political protocol, this meant that Frank Self was mayor.

So, our request for $20,000 was to be McGrath's and Linder's maiden vote.

At the caucus meeting, we made our case (I recall that Pat and Marcia were with me, maybe others). We pointed out how much we were annually putting into the Township's facility, how much of our own funds we had spent on the park, how we were currently turning an eyesore into a handsome historic site, and the other benefits that we had brought to the Township.

This fell on deaf ears. McGrath was young and immune to such reasoning, and Linder had moved to Middletown in the late 1970s and did not have the background or appreciation of the public effort that had gone into Poricy Park.

There were several sharp exchanges. McGrath said that we had promised (when we met them at our reception in the Nature Center in December) that the Township would never have to spend any money on Poricy Park. (That was news to us.) Linder said, "We couldn't even afford $15,000 to run the nature center," at which point I asked him, "If we go bankrupt, how much are you prepared to budget to take over and run the entire park?"

Linder's answer: "We'd run the park all right. I'm talking about the nature center."

Great. The Township tried to turn the farm into a leaf dump just one year after acquiring it, and now they're turning the new nature center into some kind of administrative office space. Or whatever.

After several more minutes of this interchange, Dick Kelly said, "I make a motion to give these people their $20,000 request so they can get on with running the park and we can get on with the meeting." A roll call was taken. Kelly, yes. Bob Eckert, yes. Linder, no. McGrath, no.

By protocol, the mayor got the last vote. Mayor Self? After a few moments, "Yes."

It didn't end there. That was just the caucus. The actual deciding vote would have to be taken at the regular Township Committee meeting a week hence. And at that meeting on January 13, one of our "Yes" votes was absent, and the resolution died for lack of a 3/5 majority.

This put us in a month-by-month uncertain position, but we did eventually get the $20,000 put into the recreation budget for 1981, to be distributed to us in dribs and drabs throughout the year. We also obtained a few major grants in the next few years and built up our membership.

Linder and McGrath After the Vote

Remember Tickie Smith, of the *Courier* "Eve Dropper" column? (She's the one that predicted the departure of administrator George Smith.) Here is what she wrote in her column of January 15, 1981:

Congratulations to Joe McGrath, Middletown's new committeeman and soon to be a bridegroom.

He and new committeeman Paul Linder got off to a flying start at the first regular committee meeting this week. Both voted against giving Poricy Park $20,000 until they saw the 1981 budget and made sure the money would be available. And Paul made public the county's plans for a garbage transfer station in the bayshore, promising to keep everyone informed where it would be and when it would start. Thrift and candor. That's what we like to see.

Just to make sure that his constituency heard about his "thrift and candor" vote, Paul Linder spoke at the meeting of the Oak Hill Association on March 11 and took pride in his "No" vote on Poricy Park. He evidently thought it was a good move. He may not have known he was speaking to several long-term supporters of Poricy Park at that meeting.

Paul Linder served on the committee for six years, part of his term as Mayor, and later after as director of Public Works. I do think he later understood what was happening in Poricy Park and was good to work with in his public works position.

With Joe McGrath, there is an interesting twist to the story two decades later.

Joe served his three-year term on the Township Committee and then remained vocal on the sidelines, attending meetings and speaking out. I did not keep track of his whole career (which is not at all over with at this point in 2005), but in 2002 he decided to run for Board of Education. He ran for a one-year unexpired term seat, and was one of five candidates. He came in a distant 4th place. But the election result is not what is of interest here to me.

Tickie Smith, in her *Courier* column, praised him in 1981. Well, Tickie eventually left the *Courier*, and other writers wrote columns, and one of these other writers was Jim Purcell. Here is much of his column just prior to the April 16 Board of Education election:

Candidate Leaves Trail of Bad Decisions
By Jim Purcell (*Courier*, April 11, 2002)

At 22 years old [in 1978], he had a bright future ahead of him.

And then, he lost that future to a string of bad judgments, one after the other, in my opinion.

Joseph E. McGrath was the youngest-ever committee candidate in Middletown history. He lost that 1978 race, but he vowed to be back.

In 1980, he finally found the victory at the polls he had previously found elusive. Subsequently, during his tenure in office, he assumed the role of deputy mayor of the township.

Then, he voted against funding to improve the Poricy Park Nature Center, on January 13, 1981; he urged the committee to consider building a centralized industrial park on January 28, 1981; and on March 19, 1981 he walked out of a committee meeting where restoration of some money to the township's fire department was being discussed....

Now, Mr. McGrath wants to sit on the school board. I do not believe his decision-making processes during his last stint in elected office were very good in key areas.

Storming out of meetings where discussions are not going in a direction where a board member wants them to go is the last thing the school board needs right now... Theater is best saved for the many excellent stage venues in the area, and not for the serious business of government... When he was a deputy mayor, Mr. McGrath voted against educational opportunities for township children in his "no" vote for expanding Poricy Park...

I feel this is an especially inappropriate time for Mr. McGrath to serve [on the board of education].

Our first Blue Grass Concert, June 1, 1979.

The Blue Grass Planning Meeting

We will discuss on page 152 the IMS grant we applied for in 1983 and failed to obtain, but for now, suffice it to say that one of our major weaknesses causing the grant rejection was judged to be in <u>planning</u>. We therefore made a special effort to strengthen our planning process.

But before getting into that, I'll have to tell you about the blue grass concerts.

In 1979, our secretary, Barbara Maul, knew of a group of youths that had formed a band called "Blue Grass Dressing." We thought it would be great to have them come over and give a concert in the barn.

And they did, on Friday evening, June 1, 1979. It was a wonderful evening, and it attracted 400 people, especially families. Some people stood around and listened, some of them danced, others just enjoyed the atmosphere. We had to do it again.

Our second blue grass concert, with the same band, was held on Sunday afternoon October 5, 1980. This time we gave it a lot of publicity, especially in the nearby schools. It was free, because there were so many entrances to the farm it would have been too difficult to set up a gate. So, we hoped to cover the costs by selling food and soda, and we had a grill on which we cooked hot dogs.

- 147 -

The music was fine, but many other things went awry. Kids came and brought their own snacks and drinks, including beer. People were pretty rowdy, and we had discipline problems. Some smoked pot out in the fields. One group set off firecrackers during the afternoon. Almost nobody bought our refreshments, and we lost money on the event. But the final straw for me occurred after everybody left. I was unable to set the alarm in the barn, so I went over all the circuits and found that a pair of wires to one of the sensors had been neatly cut through.

I have been involved in setting up festivals and other public events for more than 40 years. In almost every one, volunteers were required to help run the event. And, when the event is over, the question usually asked is whether to do it again. I have concluded that the primary factor one must consider in answering this question is whether the volunteers *want* to do it again. If they don't, then abandon it.

In the days following our second blue grass concert, there was general agreement: not again.

This, despite the event drawing 600 people.

We return to our planning effort. After our grant rejection, during summer 1984 Pat Contreras and I decided to hold a special long-range planning meeting. And the thing that would make it *very* special is that it would consist of people who were outside experts, not directly involved with the park.

This strategy is a variant of what I (cynically) call the "hotel room solution." (I remain skeptical of its effectiveness.) To solve a problem, assemble a group of people, many of whom have no experience with your site, lock them in a hotel room or somewhere with no outside distractions, and out of this will emerge enlightenment. And there must be consultants from *outside your organization*.[38]

So, we invited six people to help us. Six of "them" would join six of "us" on a panel, twelve in all, and spend an evening suggesting new directions for Poricy Park. We were fortunate to recruit people with really fine credentials. Here are the six:

- John Campbell, our director of Parks & Rec.
- Joseph D. Coffee, Jr., member Board of Trustees, Columbia University.
- Richard Cramer, professional planner.
- Josephine Freyer, manager Volunteer Services, Monmouth County Park System.
- John Karlin, Ph.D. in psychology, specialist in human factors and opinion measurement.
- Tim Nogueira, principal, Deane-Porter elementary school in Rumson, NJ.

We were: Lynn Kough, Pat Contreras, Frank Lescinsky, Lenita Gullman, Diane Lehder, Pete Brady.

Everybody was given written material in advance, including the failed grant application. They were then to come to the park one evening to share their ideas. We would write up a plan and circulate it for comments. We would then describe this process in our next grant application.

The meeting was on Thursday, Sept. 6, 1984. We began with a half-hour overview of the park and its operations, and then turned the meeting over to the guests, who enthusiastically set to their task.

One word can be used to encompass their advice: _more_. Do *more* of everything you are doing. Get *more* people into the park. Raise *more* money. Get *more* publicity. Have *more* programs, with *more* variety. When they found out we were not open on Saturdays, they were amazed. Why not? Most museums are open Saturdays. If you were open on Saturdays, you'd attract *more* people.

They did make some suggestions that were innovative, but they concentrated mainly on doing more of what we were already doing.

And then we made our big mistake. We brought up the blue grass concert as an example of an event that brought in 600 people the last time we did it but we didn't want to do it again. There were other considerations besides just increasing attendance.

---

[38] A variant of this idea is the saying, "An expert is someone that lives more than 20 miles away."

Our decision went entirely against the grain of a few participants. They couldn't understand why anyone would ever refuse to run an event that would bring in 600 people. So, we went through our blue grass history. OK, they said, maybe you had a few tough breaks, but maybe you could have help from the police department in maintaining order. For heavens sake – *it drew 600 people* – do it again!

The meeting continued, but the blue grass concert just kept coming up again and again. For a few of us, the meeting was henceforth known as the "blue grass planning meeting."

The report that came from this meeting contained some good ideas such as:

- Increase community involvement.
- Improve land management.
- Offer consistently high-quality programs.
- Serve as an educational resource center.
- Enhance the visit of non-program visitors.
- Develop better measures of quality.

These are fine goals, but most could have been written without having an evening's meeting. A few specific ideas were suggested and later implemented, including sponsoring a high-school biology club and building a boardwalk through the marsh.

It is of interest to note some things that were done in the next few years that were never thought of at our meeting. They included: (1) forming a quilt guild (page 157), transforming the annual reception into a concert/fundraiser presenting ballads of Colonial America (page 164), acquiring the use of the ranch house ("Annex") for programs (page 158), and, in 1985, reconstructing the east classroom wall with one-way glass to observe birds from the classroom. Each of these actions was the result of an inspiration of the moment or an idea that evolved over the years rather than from a scheduled planning session.

The meeting did indeed help land us the grant. However, in my opinion, the success was not so much a result of the *plan* the meeting produced, but rather, because we impressed the grant application reviewers by going through the *process* of having the meeting, especially with outside consultants present.

Founding Continues in the Background

By the end of 1981, all the land was acquired, the Nature Center was built, and the historic buildings restored. In later years, some remodeling was done to the buildings, and the Annex was acquired (the Annex gets separate treatment on page 158). But there was still work to do in establishing the organization as a business.

Some of these activities have already been covered here, but here is a partial list:

- Telephone system: extending it into the farmhouse and later the Annex, doing much of the cable work ourselves.
- Heating system. A long saga, already covered.
- Insurance. Are volunteers covered? What kind of liability should we have? Various agents kept giving us conflicting advice.
- Managing funds and building an endowment.
- Hiring, managing, and replacing employees.
- Vandalism, which is tied in with the alarm system, which was a constant headache.
- Funding of school programs, which became difficult when the Board of Education withdrew their funding for two years.
- Public program policy, including setting fees, cancellations, refunds, and so on.
- Managing sales of items and keeping track of inventory.
- Working with printing shops for various needs.
- Membership management and growth.
- Establishing our computer system, adding and revising software.

The list could be extended, and these items could be considered as "founding" efforts, even though the results were not visible to the public and in general are not of great interest here. But there is one item that deserves a special place in this account: programs.

The Programs

It was an inspiring and overwhelming experience to read through every program calendar published by Poricy Park, beginning in 1978 (with full-year operation) and continuing onward.

I think that had that pile of calendars been available to the small group assembled at the first meeting of the PPCC in 1969, we probably would have given up right on the spot, believing that we could never be capable of starting a project that could produce such ambitious programs. More to the point, we would have realized how much work would have been required to get there and most of us would have backed away from that.

The founders did preserve the land, build a nature center, and save historic buildings from demolition. But the founders were mainly *facilitators* in the process of establishing programs.

I mentioned the influence of Professor Richard Fischer at Cornell, in providing someone to first tell us how to provide school programs (Peter Brooks) and then providing people who designed and carried out the school and public programs (Woody Bousquet, Mike Weilbacher). And then, in the early 1980s, came Pat Contreras with the experience she had gained in the Monmouth County Park System.

So, the programs were designed and scheduled by people trained in education, environmental studies, and recreation. But, there was another factor that set Poricy Park apart from other sites, namely, the involvement of volunteers and the community in the program design and execution.

I'm not talking about volunteers who participate in mailouts, or who serve refreshments at events, or do other such "interchangeable" tasks. These kinds of volunteers are essential to every site and are growing scarcer as years go by and families need two incomes. But I'm talking about volunteers that actually designed the programs, such as Lenita Gullman, and Frank and Lethe Lescinsky who were excellent presenters of programs on Colonial life.

I have selected the Fall 1983 Calendar to illustrate this point. We begin with programs conducted by our own professional staff:

Not even listed on the calendar were the programs for three school grades coming for a full day. Middletown, with 68,185 people in 2004,[39] has one of New Jersey's largest school systems, with about 33 classes in each grade. So, these programs alone accounted for 100 days per year. Other school systems also participated, but to a lesser extent.

Second were the afternoon programs for children in early grades, in three series: kindergarten (four programs talking mainly about animals preparing for winter), grades 1&2 (winter preparation in more detail, such as a program on insects and egg cases), and grades 3&4 (a field trip involving reptiles, a study of the new Murray Pond, making a pumpkin pie from scratch, starting with a whole pumpkin).

Third, there was a set of adult programs coordinated with Brookdale College, in which the registration was through the college but the events were held in Poricy Park.

All of the above programs were conducted by our professional staff.

There were three art exhibits scheduled, in which local artisans had a chance to show their works. Some artists were amateurs who would not get such a chance in an art museum.

And now we come to programs for families and adults, the ones often conceived by volunteers. Here is what was on the calendar in just the fall of 1983:

- **Paper making by Lorraine Niemela, a woman that had a personal love for crafts.**
- **Field trip to Hawk Mountain, Pennsylvania. This was organized by Kathy Whitney, a staff member, but was done on a volunteer basis.**
- **Natural foods, presented by Gayle Richardson, an early founder of the park.**

---

[39] *Asbury Park Press*, June 30, 2005.

- Old South Jersey Decoys. The collection of Grove Conrad, with his descriptions.
- Brunch at the farmhouse, a popular program put on by volunteers the day after Thanksgiving.
- Smocking for Christmas, put on by Kathy Hodecker, daughter of board member Ruth Hodecker.
- Hobo hike. This was my program, and consisted of a walk along the railroad tracks in a flat area that was a miniature marsh ecosystem.
- Dog training demonstration, put on by the Bayshore Companion Dog Club.
- A is for Apple. Conducted by Lethe Lescinsky, then a volunteer (she later became a staff member). This was all you need to know about preserving apples, with some to be cooked on the open hearth.
- Waterbirds on Film. Conducted by Bob Henschel, of the Monmouth County Park System. (The park system often provided people to conduct programs.)
- Ghost Hunt. 1983 was our first ghost hunt. Frank Lescinsky has told me that this was originally the idea of Pat Contreras, but as the years went on, Frank became its major director. His premise was that you have a richer experience if you hike through the fields at night without a flashlight, since that would allow you to better hear the sounds and even see the sights of night. There were several "stations" at which various actors performed their skits. We had a witch, a mad magician, an underwater pond creature, and many other players. Students from the high school gave a special horror show in the barn. Refreshments were served, and then, at around 9 pm, we closed the Nature Center and went off for pizza. It's one of my fondest memories of the park.
- An afternoon of films. Short films with nature themes, mainly for children and parents.
- Bringing in the harvest. A demonstration of what you do with crops in the late fall and how to store them in the barn.

All of the above were on just one three-month calendar. And this went on year after year.

My wife Cathy and I made several trips to the British Isles, and gave at least three talks at the park on our experiences, focusing on (1) the Celtic culture of Great Britain (i.e., Wales and Scotland), (2) linen manufacturing in Ireland, and (3) Irish music, featuring our week at the Willie Clancy Festival. Bill Bryant has traveled all over the world several times, and gave talks on many of the places he had been.

One of my favorites was a program given by Cindy Gagnon, a friend of mine who had biked solo from the west coast to the east coast. She didn't give just a travelogue of America (which you can get in a rented video), but rather, told of her personal experiences on the trip.

You might think, "What's so remarkable about people giving talks about trips?" Well, what was remarkable is that it was done under the umbrella of a local center for environmental, cultural, and historic education, which gave people from the whole community a chance to exhibit their own skills and share their experiences. It gave their programs publicity, and provided an intimate atmosphere, often in winter with a fire in the fireplace.

Lethe Lescinsky was the program coordinator in the late 1980s through the 1990s and was responsible for preparing the public calendar. She and Frank moved to Lake Placid, NY in 1999, and we corresponded in preparation for this book. Here is an excerpt from a letter Frank sent me in January 2005 (the parenthetical remark is Frank's):

Under a bed in our guest room is a box with all Lethe's records of the programs she arranged or did. (Lethe's records at the Nature Center were discarded when she retired.) We have had rare occasions to refer to back program information, but basically we never look at that old stuff, which we cannot bring ourselves to part with.

The one thing I feel really made Poricy Park is the advantage we took of the talents that were around in the community. For example, I once went through all of Lethe's quarterly program schedules looking for programs on 18th-century life. When I listed them all, the coverage was as good as Colonial Williamsburg. Of course, we did most programs only once, not continuously like Williamsburg, but it was impressive.

The Twilight of the Founders

Are founders pariahs?

Some professionals think so. J. Kevin Graffagnino has been director of the Kentucky Historical Society and the Vermont Historical Society. He wrote an article giving advice to aspiring CEOs of nonprofit agencies.[40] In the article he gives two caveats that are relevant to founders and volunteers:

1. **Be wary of becoming the first professional to head an organization that has always been staffed and run by amateurs and volunteers.**
2. **Do not take the top job at an institution where the founder[s] ... are still deeply involved.**

Before proceeding with my account, I wish to announce to all managers that it is now safe to work at Poricy Park. The founders are all gone.

Obviously, founders can't last forever, because they will all eventually expire. But before that happens, founders can leave for other reasons:

- Poor health of themselves or family members.
- They move out of the area.
- They get frustrated or burned out and cannot carry on in such a confining atmosphere.
- Either the project takes on a new direction or they themselves develop other life interests, and the project no longer matches their goals.
- They are deliberately forced out, such as by a vote of the board of directors.

At Poricy Park, there has been at least one example of each kind of departure listed above.

And, one more clarification. A founder can still be involved without being on the board of directors. By *departure*, I mean that the founder severs almost all ties to the organization, even as a volunteer.

Jim Gold and His Assessment Report

The founders of Poricy Park did not leave all at once. They did not line up and walk the plank accompanied by a drum roll. Their departures were one at a time over a 15-year period.

However, there is a precise date that marks the beginning of the process that caused them to depart: March 6, 1985. That is the date of the visit of Jim Gold, an expert called in to make an assessment.

We had applied to the Institute of Museum Services (IMS) in 1983 for a General Operating Support (GOS) grant.[41] The GOS grant is the holy grail of government grants, because you can use it for current, ongoing expenses rather than a special project.

We were turned down for this grant, and ranked 1140 from the top out of 1240 applicants. We were nearly at the bottom. The reviewing process involved the IMS sending the application to three independent, anonymous reviewers, two of whom apparently only skimmed it and then made significant errors in their reviews, as pointed out to us by a member of the IMS staff. And, subsequent readers thought the application was well done and should have been ranked higher. NEVERTHELESS, it failed.

We went through a tortuous process of writing a second application,[42] determined to overcome the problems with the first one, and we mailed it off on January 11, 1985. We were notified on June 21, 1985 that this one was successful, and we received $19,695. But that is not what is relevant here.

While we were still smarting from the rejection of the first grant, our director, Pat Contreras, and I attended a workshop sponsored by the IMS at the University of Delaware on July 9, 1984. They give advice on how to improve your chances for grant

---

[40] "Do You Really Want to be a CEO?", J. Kevin Graffagnino, *History News*, magazine of the Am. Assn. for State and Local History, Autumn 2003, pp. 7-11.

[41] The IMS is now the Institute of Museum and Library Services. Readers should consult their web site for current information about their grants.
[42] See the <u>Blue Grass Planning Meeting</u>, page 147.

approval. At that workshop, we were told about the Museum Assessment Program (MAP) grant. Just ask for the grant of $1,000 and you'll get it. The money is to be used to have an expert come and assess your museum (or nature center, etc) and write a report. So, we applied for the MAP grant and James P. Gold came to Poricy Park on March 6, 1985. (This was just after we submitted our second application, but in that application we made it clear that we were in the process of having a MAP evaluation.)

Mr. Gold had excellent credentials, and produced a thorough, carefully constructed report. He was Director, Bureau of Historic Sites, New York State Office of Parks, Recreation, and Historic Preservation. Pat had sent him our failed IMS application and our pending one, plus supporting material, and it was obvious that Mr. Gold had carefully read everything she sent him.

The format of his visit was to arrive in mid-afternoon, tour the site, have dinner with us, stay overnight in commercial accommodations (this was specified in the grant: nobody could put him up for the night in their home), return to the site the next morning, and leave after lunch. A 24-hour visit.

After Mr. Gold's initial tour, he came to my house for dinner. Present were my wife Cathy, Pat Contreras, Marcia and Lou Rissland, and myself. I well remember Marcia was there because of an observation she made which I will now share with you.

After we had made introductions and possibly served drinks, Mr. Gold turned to us and said, "How much funding do you get annually from contributions from individuals on your board of directors?"

In other words, as Marcia put it many, many times in later years, *Board members are expected to keep their checkbooks open and their mouths shut.*

Mr. Gold finished his tour the next day and later sent us his report. The report covers many aspects of the park and its operations. But it's the third page that stands out in my mind. Because it is the philosophy expressed on that page that started the founders on the path toward departure.

While he was here, Mr. Gold made clear in many ways that he believed that an organization such as ours should be run by professional managers. Period. Volunteers should stay in the background and help when asked. Period. And, in his section titled "Governance and Board," he singled me out:

The PPCC is governed by a board of directors numbering eleven members who serve two-year terms. A number of the directors have been associated with the PPCC since its formative years and have maintained an active role in the development and leadership of the organization throughout its history...

While the board contains many individuals who contribute a great deal of time, it does not include major financial contributors. [See Marcia's remark, above.]

The PPCC employs a full-time professional director [Pat Contreras] who oversees all day-to-day operations and reports to the board at its monthly meetings. The park also has a founding board member [Pete Brady] who serves, in a volunteer capacity, as administrator, handling fiscal, legal, and procedural matters. Although the relationships of the board and the director and the administrator seem to be quite positive at present, the significant involvement of this board member [Brady] in the institution's day-to-day business has the potential for real conflict between staff and management and management and board. The success of the present arrangement appears to have more to do with the personality and dedication of the present administrator than to a formalized structure which would define relationships...

Well! The gloves were off. At that time, I wrote an "administrator's report" prior to each board meeting, and this is what I wrote for the meeting to be held on May 20, 1985. I quoted the same above paragraph in Mr. Gold's report, and then wrote:

[Quoting myself]: With Mr. Gold's ambivalent opinion of myself, I feel like the man who has one hand frozen in a block of ice and the other in boiling water, and on average is supposed to be comfortable. I was not comfortable with Mr. Gold's analysis, and therefore I read on to see what he recommends. Alas, in his role of expert he has no recommendation about my position but instead continues his paragraph with this interesting comment on the board members:

[Quoting Mr. Gold]: No limit is placed on the number of terms a board member may serve nor does there appear to be much rotation. Some consideration might be given to limiting the number of terms one serves, although there is no indication that the present board has any dead wood.

I don't know if Mr. Gold was provided with complete information about the board, but of the eleven members at the time of his visit (1985), six had joined since the beginning of 1981. However, he was correct in that no limit was placed on terms, and four of the board members had been there forever and called many of the shots. Evidently we called too many of the shots, in Mr. Gold's eyes. And perhaps, in the eyes of others who spoke with him.

So, what happened next?

I had decided to end this account at the year 1985, because that is the year that marked the end of the founding effort, save for some odds and ends (which are covered in the next chapter). But I will give a brief summary of the next many years, just so as not to leave the reader completely in the dark.

Pat Contreras left the park in May 1986, and Kathy Whitney became the "administrator." This was really the position of "director," although we did not call it that. I became business manager.

Then, we did establish term limits for board members: four years and out, but you could come back after a year's absence, as did only a few people. This was effective in removing some founders from the board and in some cases, from the park.

Board members came and went, and a few years later, the board decided to establish committees that would control the various aspects of the park. For example, a "building and grounds" committee oversaw all projects and all expenses, even minor ones, involving the farmhouse and barn. Some of its members, new to the park, had no experience and even little interest in management of historic sites but they insisted on controlling what Marcia did.

Marcia was able to work with this for only 18 months, at which time (May 1994) she resigned, in frustration, as curator. For similar reasons, I resigned earlier as business manager in March 1993.

Other founders just drifted away when they had to leave the board. The last founders that remained active in the park were Frank and Lethe Lescinsky, who moved away from Middletown in 1999.

Some people feel that the "four-years-and-out" rule did considerable damage to the park. But I return to my opening statement of this section, that founders can't last forever, and no matter what happened in the mid-1980s we all would have left anyway. However, I am grateful that Mr. Gold did not visit us earlier than he did, because the founders made many contributions right up through 1985.

———————————

During the course of this project, many of the founders became burned out. I regret that I am one of those people. You've just plain had it. It may be because it's no longer "fun," or that you are frustrated, or you feel that you have lost control of the project and all you are doing is fighting with people.

Nevertheless, we can now look at the park and realize that had we not done what we did, it would be a housing development bordered by a silted marsh with its banks destroyed, with the historic buildings torn down. Instead, it is a 250-nature preserve, with its historic buildings restored, and with more than 10,000 program visitors every year. That's not bad for a bunch of inexperienced people who had no idea what we were getting into.

At the end of Marcia's talk she gave at the farmhouse in 1994, a member of the audience asked, "With all your experience, I expect you're ready to take on another old house." Marcia's reply was, "I will never feel sorry for another old house for whatever is left of the rest of my life."

Nobody has asked me a similar question about establishing a nature preserve, but if they do, I will give the same answer.

Finis.

Coda: Diversions and Later Projects

"Coda" is a musical term for a short theme that is tacked onto the real end of a piece. There are a few items that post-date my intended end of this book, namely 1985, and also a few others that just don't fit into the outline I used here, but which I could not fail to include. Here is the potpourri.

Albert, and Marlene Harper

Marjorie Sullivan, a former quilter at the park, is a friend of my wife Cathy. She said that I could not write a history of the park without including Albert.

However, before we introduce Albert, we must first introduce Marlene Harper. Marlene was a volunteer at the park in the early 1980s and, for a while, served on the board of directors. She was, among other attributes, a fine cook, especially at the

Tavern Party (more on the Tavern Party later). She rented a house on the remnants of a nearby farm.

On that farm, Albert was born in early 1980, as Marlene puts it "a pedigreed farm cat." She brought him to the park in fall 1980, and he soon became Middletown's most famous cat. He loved children and routinely attended classes with them. He was an outdoor cat, and would come up to anybody entering the park in off-hours. It was a miracle that nothing happened to him, especially getting stolen.

My own delight with Albert was feeding him turkey gizzards which I occasionally brought from home. He clearly thought these were a special treat.

In the early 1990s Albert developed stiff joints and began to snap at children who got too rough with him. Marcia took him into her home, where he lived in splendid retirement until he died in 1996.

Marlene Harper and Al Oppegard at the March 1985 Tavern Party. Marlene eventually bought a print shop, "Harper's Copy Center Plus," in Red Bank. Al was our treasurer, and a description of his involvement can be found on page 135.

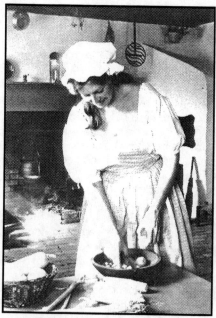

Joseph Murray: Lost History

Well, now you know exactly what Rebecca and Joseph Murray looked like. (Photo of Lou: Chuck Steiner)

Actually, Rebecca might not have been as pretty as Evelyn Lewis, and Joseph not as handsome as Lou Rissland. These two reenacted the murder of Joseph Murray on our second Joseph Murray Day on June 4, 1983. The papers printed the gory photos of Joseph lying on the ground in his blood-stained shirt while Rebecca knelt next to him wailing mightily.

Evelyn was our farmhouse interpreter in the interval from fall 1982 through June 1983. She had a talent for caring for artifacts, but our limited funds could not support the position. Evelyn later became curator of the Neptune museum for several years.

Marcia had to rediscover the Murrays and their history. But it was known on November 14, 1895 in an unsigned article published in the *Monmouth Democrat*, a weekly paper in Freehold:

Soon after the first quarter of the 18th century, Joseph Murray purchased from Thomas Stillwell about 50 acres of land upon the east bank of Porocy [sic] Brook. About 100 yards from the brook, Joseph built a house and barn. Both buildings were small but the foundations were of massive stone masonry and the frames were of heavy rough-hewn oak timbers… These buildings are still in a good state of preservation and are now owned by Mr. Jonathan Hedden… Murray lived in this house with his mother, Elizabeth Murray… About 1770 Murray was married to Rebecca Morris by the Rev. Abel Morgan.

It is too bad that Ernest Mandeville didn't have this article when he put Murray's house on Kings Highway (see end of Appendix A).

I am indebted to Glenn Cashion of Middletown who found this article and passed it on to Randy Gabrielan, who then gave it to me.

Lynn Kough and the Quilt Guild

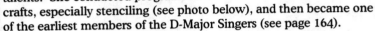

I met Lynn Garrison in the late 1960s when we both sang in the Shrewsbury Chorale. That was before Poricy Park.

There followed a gap of some ten years. Lynn married Al Kough and was attracted to the park because it gave her an opportunity to exercise her many fine talents. She conducted programs in crafts, especially stenciling (see photo below), and then became one of the earliest members of the D-Major Singers (see page 164).

Perhaps Lynn's outstanding skill was in fabrics, especially quilting. She organized the park's first quilt show in May 1985, two days with attendance of 172. The following January, she announced the formation of a quilt guild, which early on adopted the name "Rebecca's Reel Quilters" (a play on words for those not into quilting). The logo was based on a traditional spinning wheel block pattern, and Barbara Harwood did the drafting of the design shown here. In Lynn's own words,

RRQ was formed as an adjunct to the history programs already extant at Poricy Park. It is an educational and service program, with its members being members of the park. Its purpose is to provide opportunities to learn and share the history and craft of quilt making as well as to support the park through volunteering and fundraising. It has a unique place among quilt guilds.

Lynn Kough, October 1986. Below: In the early 1980s, Lynn and Patty Rambert applied the decorative pineapple stencils in the farmhouse kitchen.

The guild first met in the farmhouse, but soon overwhelmed it with a membership of 120 by August 1986, eventually growing to more than 200. They then met in the Nature Center and in the Annex (see next page). The quilt show is held every two years and is a continuing success.

Lynn moved to Arizona in 1996, but we keep in touch and she visits the park, often in a professional capacity as an expert on quilts.

The Annex

The Annex, May 1, 1992

When we first saw the Gebhardt Farm, the ranch house was the only structure on the farm other than the farm buildings at the base of the hill. The house was built in the 1950s, and in 1969 was the home of Rose Gebhardt, widow of Albert Gebhardt, who had died circa 1955. Marcia met Mrs. Gebhardt, but we had no real dealings with her.

Rose Gebhardt died August 7, 1970 and the farm passed to her nephew, Jack Cavanaugh, who had his own home in Red Bank. I do not recall who, if anyone, lived in this house in the next few years, during which time the cows were sold and farming was discontinued. The ranch house was included in the Township purchase of the farm in November 1973.

In 1974, George Smith became Township Administrator and lived in the house until his departure in early 1977. It was then rented in succession to Officer McClellan, Patrolman John Estock, Administrator James O'Neill, and Township Planner Richard Cramer. I hope I didn't miss anyone.

There were some problems. The tenants were varied in their care of the building. Some were model tenants and some were not, but none took a great interest in long-term maintenance. One of the tenants had a large, harmless, but in appearance aggressive dog which bounded over the lawn and barked at and frightened children visiting the park. One or two took little care of the grounds and the place looked decrepit. We had hoped that whoever lived there would watch over the farm and keep vandalism and other items under control, but this did not happen. None of the tenants was willing to be put on the burglar alarm list, so a few of us, myself included, often drove to the farm in the middle of the night to meet the police, while the ranch house occupant slept soundly.

By 1985, our programs had expanded such that we needed more space, and the ranch house was a likely candidate. So, we decided that when Richard Cramer moved out, we would ask for the use of the building.

Cramer resigned his position in 1986, and in my role as business administrator of the park, I wrote a letter dated December 11, 1986 to Bud Bradshaw, Township Administrator, asking that we be allowed to use the ranch house. As a result, on January 5, 1987, Lynn Kough and I attended the Township Committee caucus and made our case for the use of the ranch house. We were actually solving a problem for the Township, because they were told that they could no longer rent the house to someone of their choice, but it would instead have to go out for public bidding. And, we pointed out, we've already had one or two difficult tenants, and with bidding we would have no control over who lived there.

Accordingly, after some minor negotiations, the Township agreed to let the PPCC use the house. At the caucus meeting we stressed that it would be used for public functions, available for general programs, but the quilt guild would have one or two rooms for their use in storing items.

There followed in summer 1987 several work parties in which extensive gardening was done, removing two decades of overgrowth. We put in wall-to-wall carpet, track lighting, extended the phone system into the building from the Nature Center, and made many other renovations. The house has since served Poricy Park well.

There remained the question of what to call the building. Our wonderful cat, Albert, liked to visit the house, and someone (perhaps someone on the staff, perhaps a quilter) suggested "Albert's Annex." The name was adopted with enthusiasm, except that it has usually just been called "The Annex."

But the full name, "Albert's Annex," did get a

life of its own. In 1994 the park received a letter from a solicitation mailing list, which address on the envelope is reproduced here.

Cathy Johnston and Virginia Carmichael

Cathy Johnston

Cathy was a neighbor of mine when we both lived on Marcshire Drive. At the park, we needed clerical assistance to fill in the off-days when Joan Hanvey, then a part-time worker, would not be there. So, in the early 1980s, I asked Cathy if she could work at Poricy Park for a few hours a week.

In June 1983, Kathy Whitney left her part-time position as bookkeeper and Cathy Johnston took on that position, which she held for many years. But Cathy did more at the park, especially as a volunteer for programs. She was a wonderful scarecrow in the fields for our Ghost Hunt.

Virginia Carmichael

In 1985 we had to find someone to replace Gayle Richardson as a membership data entry person. Board member Lynn Kough suggested Virginia Carmichael, whom she knew as a quilter. This set Virginia on a long career at the park, partly as a volunteer and also as a part-time employee.

Virginia's grandfather was a cousin of Hoagy Carmichael. Virginia may not have had Hoagy's musical talents, but she had plenty of other talents of her own. She was adept with fabric and she also painted. She was meticulous in data entry of more than 1,000 transactions each year. She was for a time the Sunday receptionist. Her crowning achievement was making outstanding onion soup, from scratch, for the annual Tavern Party.

- 159 -

The Logo

We wanted a logo to put on our stationery, flyers, and other documents. Marcia had many times demonstrated her skill as an artist, and so, in late 1976, she drew a scarlet tanager. She had seen the bird in the park on several occasions, and it was her daughter Lee's favorite bird.

But then came the problem: how do you convert it into a logo? You need to embed it in a circle and supply lettering that follows the circle.

Any kid today with a computer can toss this out in five minutes, but not in 1976. It turned out, however, that Marcia's husband Lou worked for the Avery Label Company, which had a graphic art department, and they produced the logo shown here.

At the board meeting in January 1977 this logo was formally adopted as the PPCC logo.

But the story doesn't end there. These were the days before we had a nature center and a staff, and twice, in later years, two different directors decided to replace the logo with a design of their own, perhaps without knowledge that there was a prior board decision to adopt the bird logo.

In the first case, the staff was told that "there are no scarlet tanagers in the park," and therefore the logo should be replaced. This first replacement was an undistinguished mass of silhouetted trees. This new logo lasted a few years, but somehow the original logo found its way back into use. The Monmouth County Audubon Society, in their 2002 Check List, puts the scarlet tanager in the "common" category, second only to "abundant" in a 5-catetory rating. Perhaps someone looked out the window and saw one of the tanagers that lived in the park.

The second logo was a tiny, crude sketch of the farmhouse and lasted only a month or two.

I played no role in the substitutions or the restorations of the original logo, and at the time did not even comment on either. However, nothing lasts forever, and the logo may be replaced again, perhaps this time permanently. But, while it lasts, it's a nice reminder to me of Marcia and Lou.

The North Star Horizon Computer

In autumn 1979 we became one of the first small nonprofit agencies anywhere to acquire a desktop

computer. We chose the North Star Horizon S-100 computer. It came only with Basic. No windows. No text editor. (And that's because such programs simply weren't available.) So, I went to work and wrote a lot of software for it. Eventually the computer was phased out in the 1990s. It had 65k (not megs) memory, a Z-80 processor at 4 megahertz, and two 5¼" floppy disk drives at 360k each.

I wrote an article for *Byte* magazine on how little commercial software was available and that it was up to the user to bridge the gap. Titled "Bridging the 10-Percent Gap," it appeared in the October 1981 issue (pp. 264-274) and included the photo shown here. From left are our secretary Joan Hanvey, director Patricia Contreras, and bookkeeper Kathy Whitney. The computer is on top of the cabinet at right, with Perkin-Elmer peripherals.

June 27, 1979, 26 Federal Plaza, Manhattan. John Campbell, Pete Brady, and Conrad Simon, Director, Water Division of the U.S. Environmental Protection Agency at the award ceremony.

The EPA Award

In early 1979, unknown to me, several of my friends applied for an award to be presented to me by the EPA. I felt at the time, and still do, that the award should have been given to the PPCC as a whole rather than to one person, but that's what they wanted, and further, they would want the award mentioned in this book. So, we all made our way to the EPA offices on the morning of June 27, 1979. There were one or two others also receiving the award, but not from New Jersey that year.

After the award, John had to get back to Middletown, but Marcia, Cathy, Diane Lehder, and I had lunch in nearby Chinatown. This was a nice gesture, and I do appreciate it.

The text of the citation is as follows:

Paul T. Brady, Administrator, Poricy Park Citizens Committee, Middletown Township, NJ, has been the dynamic force behind this organization, giving generously of his time, talents, and money to help preserve a principle in which he strongly believes.

Mr. Brady's outstanding leadership and dedication have helped to implement extensive environmental education activities in the school system, as well as programs and courses for the general public. He has demonstrated an ability to rally citizens' support which has led to the creation of the Poricy Park Nature Center. Through his leadership, an outstanding natural resource has been protected and made available to the citizens of Middletown Township.

We appreciate Mr. Brady's untiring dedication and we join his nominators in wishing him continued success.

Jean Markowitz and the Holiday Shop

Jean Markowitz lived in Little Silver and was attracted to Poricy Park primarily by the formation of the Quilt Guild in 1986. She got on the park's board of directors, and in 1988 volunteered to organize the Holiday Shop.

The Holiday Shop was successful and proved to be an enduring tradition. It was set up in the Annex, began the day after Thanksgiving, and was open for ten days. It specialized in home made crafts and foods, and to sell your items there you had to become a member of Poricy Park.

Some people incorrectly believed that the Shop was run by the Quilt Guild. There were many guild members helping out, but in fact, the Shop was run by the park members in general.

Jean briefly left the board, but rejoined in 1993 and remained there until she moved to Kent, Ohio in mid-1996. She has kept in touch with our family and with her friends in the Quilt Guild.

A Lesson in Politics, Learned Late

Gene Farrell and Richard Van Wagner

For obvious reasons I could not have met Oscar Wilde (1854-1900), but I did know his reincarnation in the person of Eugene (Gene) Farrell.

Gene was first of all, and above everything else, a member of the local Democratic Party. He found out about us when we first started in 1969, probably from his keen sense of detecting a chance to join an organization that was at odds with the current government, which was at that time the local Republican Party. So, Gene was one of the founders of Poricy Park. But, despite his political leanings, he was a fine team player, coming to meetings, collating printed material, stuffing envelopes, and performing all the other mundane tasks of the project.

Gene had a brilliant, sarcastic wit, and wielded his sharp comments about local politicians with surgical, stiletto-like precision. He was entertaining and often accurate. Most of his comments were deliciously wicked but, unfortunately, unprintable. He was with us for a few years, but after we had achieved a measure of success and, especially, after the Democratic Party took control of the Township Committee, he drifted away, but still remained in touch.

For someone not given an Ivy League liberal education, he had an impressive grasp of history and was wonderful with words. In early 1973, at the start of the second year of Democratic Party control, he was dismayed at what he felt was needless excessive new spending by our government. So, he wrote a letter to the *Daily Register*. The details of the spending are not relevant here, but I have quoted the first paragraph of the letter to show Gene's style.

Richard Van Wagner was an acquaintance of Marcia and Lou, and at our request, joined us at the Risslands' home on January 15, 1976 for a discussion about possible state funding of Poricy Park's educational programs. Richard was a State Assemblyman

---

The *Daily Register* (Red Bank), Feb. 28, 1973

Civic Fantasies

To the Editor:

Since January 1971, five new members have taken seats on the Middletown Township Committee. Each in his turn has campaigned under the meritorious banners of fiscal responsibility and austerity in government spending. Today these courageous standards lay as deserted as the Roman maniples at Cannae... (letter continues)

[And, to spare the reader a trip to the encyclopedia, I will rewrite the last sentence: Today, these courageous standards lay as deserted as the Roman troops after their crushing defeat in 216 B.C. by the Carthaginian general Hannibal at Cannae, in S.E. Italy.]

---

at that time (Assembly 1974-84, State Senate 1984-91). Richard was informative and helpful, and gave us names of several people to contact. Unfortunately, these particular ones did not pan out, but we kept in touch with Richard over the years.

We now fast forward to November 1987. We were trying to find ways to fund the teaching staff at Poricy Park, and we read several times about state grants that had been given to other local organizations. Why not to Poricy Park?

Well, it turned out that our good friend Gene Farrell was now working directly for Senator Van Wagner as his special administrative assistant. I called Gene and asked if we could discuss a state grant with Richard. "Of course. Come on over."

At that time, Kathy Whitney was Administrator of Poricy Park. On November 30, 1987 Kathy and I went over to Van Wagner's office on Route 35 in Middletown and met with him and Gene. Gene ushered us into Richard's office. I especially remember the photographs – the walls were covered with well over 100 photos of Richard posing with the ordinary folks as well as with the famous. Richard was very good at publicizing his efforts, as any good politician should be.

The meeting went very well, far better than we had thought possible. We began by telling Richard of our very severe budget crisis, and mentioning that other agencies received state grants, why not Poricy Park? So, Richard went over some of the in-place state programs to fund nonprofit agencies, but in each case indicated why we didn't quite qualify. He said that this might lead nowhere. Then he said,

"Why not just apply directly for a state grant?"

"What does that entail?"

"I will sponsor a bill in the Senate for a grant for Poricy Park, and if it passes, it will go on to the House for approval and then go to the Governor for signature."

"How much should we ask for?"

"How much do you need?"

There followed some agonizing thought. If we ask for too much, we could be considered greedy and might fail to get anything. If too little, we would be foolish and would blow away this unique chance.

"Is, err, $50,000 too much?"

"That is not a problem. I'll sponsor the bill. Here is what I'll need from you ..." And then he told us what forms we needed to fill out, what documents to give him such as budget statements, and so on. Kathy and I departed in a state of elation.

For a while, we heard nothing, so in February 1988 I called Gene, who assured me that the bill was in the mill. And, on May 16, 1988, the Senate passed bill #S-2306 for a grant of $50,000 for Poricy Park.

Wow!

Van Wagner immediately issued a press release:

Gene Farrell called me and gave me names of people to contact in the Assembly to lobby for passage there, and I did make those calls.

Well, a funny thing then happened. Nothing. I was told that the House Appropriations Committee would meet next year, possibly, and decide on this, but it never happened. No bill. No vote. No dough.

A little later, I told this story to a friend who was much more politically savvy than I was. He just laughed. "This is done all the time. Favors are traded back and forth in the legislature, and when Van Wagner introduced this bill, its passage was almost automatic. The senators knew it didn't matter whether it passed the Senate or not, because it would just fall into the cracks in the House. Or, maybe it would pass in the House, and that would be even better. So, the sponsor, in this case Van Wagner, got a gift from you guys. He got that wonderful press release to add to his collection, and it all happened because you initiated it. He behaved faultlessly. Just chalk it up to experience."

The Tavern Party & The D-Major Singers

To celebrate the restoration of the farmhouse we had a dinner party on February 22, 1982. The party began with wine and cheese at the farmhouse, where there were musicians performing baroque music, and then proceeded to a sit-down dinner at the Nature Center with venison stew. We charged $17, which wasn't enough, and it was too much work, but it was well attended.

The following year, on March 6, 1983 we held a "reception" at the farmhouse. It was sponsored in part by the Laird's company of Scobeyville and we had Marjorie Mollenauer play Irish tunes on an Irish harp. We didn't call this a "tavern party" at that time, but it was actually our first one.

In fall 1983 we decided to do it again in 1984, but this time with vocal music. One of our board members knew a woman that accompanied herself on the guitar as she sang folk songs. We thought this would work well, but I wanted to hear her first.[43] I scheduled a meeting with her the day after Thanksgiving, 1983.

She called that morning to cancel because of illness in the family, and then she called the board member that she knew, and was furious that she had to audition. "I don't do auditions. I perform." And, she backed out.

We were in a bind. I played the harpsichord but knew nothing of folk music. I had a good friend, Peggy Noecker, a fine singer, who agreed to take the role. So, Peggy and I rummaged around in the library and in our own collections and cobbled together a program which we performed to the people that were wandering through the house during the Tavern Party on March 4, 1984. We

The D-Major Singers at the Seabrook-Wilson House in 1998. Pete Brady and Irene Hauge (at left) and Jim Cusick and Lois Lyons (at right) are joined by Lou & Marcia Rissland.

didn't call ourselves anything, but this was in reality the birth of the "D-Major Singers."

In 1985, we still did not regard this as an ongoing tradition, but Lynn Kough (page 157) had been active in the park, was a good singer, and offered to perform. Lynn and I were joined by Rand Hix, music minister of the Freehold Presbyterian Church.

We kept at it. Jim Cusick joined us at the Tavern Party in 1987, Lois Lyons (Berger) in 1990, and Irene Hauge in 1997, after Lynn moved to Arizona. We are pictured above, with Lou and Marcia.

The D-Major Singers gave our last performance in Poricy Park in March 1997, and were replaced by a professional group, "Spiced Punch." The D-Major Singers now perform annually for the Monmouth County Park System, as well as for other organizations, and as of 2005 we have given nearly 100 performances at 18 historic sites in five states. We have distributed our tapes and CDs throughout North America and the British Isles.

---

[43] I will not mention her name here, except to say emphatically that it was not Adaya Henis, who is a friend of mine, a wonderful performer especially of children's songs, and has appeared at Poricy Park many times.

Appendix A: A Notoriously Violent Rebel

By Marcia Rissland

Poricy Park History Series, June 1986, Revised March 1996

Shortly before 1767, a young stone mason from the Province of Ulster in Ireland took a ship from Derry bound for America. He was probably typical of others who had been migrating in great numbers from the northern part of Ireland: of Scottish descent, mostly Protestant, physically tough, plain-living, and independent. The increasing population and high land rents in Ireland had driven him and thousands of others to seek a better life in the North American British colonies. He did not find it for long.

His name was Joseph Murray, and his farm is now part of Poricy Park. His purchase was a 40-acre tract from the large holdings of Thomas Stillwell, Jr. Stillwell's ancestors had owned the land for over 100 years; English settlement in Middletown dates from 1664. Murray built the present house and barn in 1767. At about the same time he married an American-born woman, Rebecca Morris. Their first child, William, was born in 1771, followed by two more sons, James and Joseph, and then by a daughter whose name is not known today.

At the outbreak of the Revolution, Murray enlisted as a private in the First Regiment, Monmouth County Militia. The residents of Middletown were bitterly divided, the majority at first remaining loyal to the Crown and regarding those who favored independence as rebels and traitors. The war set neighbor against neighbor, split families, and fragmented communities. It was, in actuality, our first civil war.

Hemmed in by British strongholds in New York, Staten Island, Sandy Hook, and Raritan Bay, Middletown suffered constant depredations. Thousand-man raids by British regulars swept the area clean of livestock and crops to supply their troops, and there was no possible opposition to such forces. Prior to 1778, there was some attempt to pay Loyalists for these requisitions; up to then it was a war with some rules. But after the Battle of Monmouth in June, 1778, it became a war without rules. The total breakdown of order and discipline in General Clinton's army and its camp followers as they withdrew from Monmouth Battlefield to Sandy Hook resulted in plunder, destruction of property, and atrocities against civilians. Loyalists as well as Rebels suffered, and local sentiment swung towards the cause of independence. From then until the end, it was a war without scruples of any kind, and the level of brutality in Monmouth County was worse than anywhere else in the North.

In addition, Middletown suffered the constant ordeal of guerrilla warfare, local feuds, and raids by vicious gangs of thugs known as "refugees." At the British garrison on Sandy Hook, around the old lighthouse, there collected a motley assortment in a tent city known as "Refugees Town." Some of these were sincere Loyalists whose property had been confiscated (without due process of law) by the Rebels. Most were the sort of flotsam that surfaces in any period of anarchy — loving violence, but lacking the courage for open combat. Their aim was robbery, aimless destruction, and terrorism. They were used by the British to spy and inform, steal supplies, capture rebel prisoners, and keep things stirred up generally.

Isolated farms such as Murray's were always in danger, especially those that adjoined inlets from major waterways. The usual procedure was to slip in at night by boat and attack before the inhabitants could organize resistance. Any man known or suspected as a rebel was taken prisoner, the women abused, and the children terrorized. The house was ransacked for valuables, and anything not wanted was smashed with musket butts or torn apart with bayonets. Clothing, bedding, and papers were piled up and set afire. Sometimes the house burned down, and sometimes it did not. The fear and apprehension, the disruption of normal life, and the need for constant vigilance tested the endurance and wore down the nerves far more than open combat against a visible enemy.

After a raid, the loot and prisoners were taken to Sandy Hook. The men were then conveyed to the prisoner-of-war "facilities" in New York — windowless warehouses, or hulks of ships anchored in the Hudson. For enlisted men, conditions in both British and American war prisons were so bad that three-fourths of the men sent to them never came out alive. Murray was one that did come out alive. He was taken in a raid in 1779 when his house was attacked and looted, and his personal property destroyed, including the unrecorded deed to his farm. How long he survived in prison, and how he made his escape is not known, but in January of 1780 he reappeared in Middletown and rejoined his militia regiment. He was doubtless emaciated, but still full of fight.

The Monmouth Militia did not differ much from other militia units throughout the colonies — poorly paid, poorly trained, poorly armed, poorly led, and often poorly motivated. George Washington could never depend on local militias anywhere to augment his regular 35,000-man Continental Army, even though the militia rolls had ten times that number. When called up, many men failed to show, and if engaged in combat, then would often disappear as soon as their own homes were out of danger.

A notable exception to this lackluster record was the regiment commanded by Col. Asher Holmes, in which Murray served. Holmes was a brave and able officer who commanded an effective fighting unit. Murray was known as "the boldest and most active of the Monmouth County patriots."[1] His activities made him well-hated by those local loyalists that still remained in town. He had been charged with assault and trespass by an unnamed complainant, and had caused the arrest of some leading Tories. He also had military orders to commandeer horses for the use of the militia. In executing this last maneuver, he probably made himself the number-one target for reprisal. Edward Taylor (of Marlpit Hall) was the most influential Loyalist in the county. He had been disarmed and placed under house arrest in 1777. Family lore relates that Murray appeared one day at Taylor's stable, entered, and reappeared riding a fine young horse. Taylor, having no weapon, ran out and threw his hat in the horse's face, hoping to spook it into throwing the rider. Murray dismounted, picked up the hat (which was no doubt better than his own), placed it on top of his own hat, and rode away with both hat and horse.

On the night of June 7, 1780, Murray and 250 others in his regiment were on duty reconnoitering on the bay shore to prevent the smuggling of goods to the British fleet, and to intercept raiders. The following morning he was given leave by his commanding officer, Lt. Garret Hendrickson (of the Holmes-Hendrickson House) to go home and tend his crops "for he had a family and had to work for their support as he could find the time."[2] The soldier who accompanied him, Thomas Hill, was anxious to be about some business of his own, so Murray told him to go on; that he would work alone. So dangerous were the times that it was customary for one man to stand guard while the other had to go unarmed about his farm chores.

Murray leaned his musket against the nearest fence, hitched up his horse, and proceeded to harrow his corn field from the barn to the woods above Poricy Brook. When he turned around towards the barn an armed man emerged from the foliage and fired a shot into his back. Despite his wound he turned on his attacker and had almost succeeded in wresting the musket away from him when two more men came at him with bayonets. Murray was stabbed repeatedly, fighting furiously all the while, and was then shot a second time at point-blank range.

Thomas Hill heard the shots, as did others, and hastened back. According to Hill's deposition at a hearing which followed, "...aforesaid Murray lay dead with his wound bleeding and had been shot and bayoneted in several places."[3] The attackers fled down Poricy Brook to the Navesink River, pursued by men who had heard the shots. Mathias Conover killed one whom he found hiding in the bushes; the others escaped. There was a persistent rumor at the time that one of the escaped killers was a former slave of Edward Taylor — he of the commandeered horse. A letter from General Foreman to Governor Livingston, discovered in 1980, lends some credence to this (see endnote).

Joseph Murray was buried on his farm, the Rev. Abel Morgan of the Middletown Baptist Church officiating at his funeral. He quoted from Matthew, 24:43: "If the good man of the house had known at what watch the thief would come, he would not have suffered his house to be broken up. Therefore, be ye also ready, for ye know neither the day nor the hour..."

Rebecca Murray was left to run the farm, raise four small children (the oldest was nine), and cope with the evil times as best she could. The children survived to carry on the name, and the musket with which Mathias Conover shot a killer is still in the possession of a Murray descendant.

In 1855, Joseph's grandson, William W. Murray, had Joseph's remains moved from the farm to the Baptist Church cemetery on King's Highway. His stone is in the Murray plot bearing the inscription, "Sacred the Memory of Joseph Murray. Departed this life June 8, 1780 while in the service of his country."

Murray's comrades in the militia described him as a "plain, strong, fearless patriot, earnest and true."[4] The Tories called him "an obnoxious persecutor of Loyalist subjects," and "a notoriously violent rebel."[5] Which of these estimates best describes him? Probably both, depending on one's point of view during "the times that tried men's souls."

REFERENCES

[1]. Ellis, Franklin. *History of Monmouth County, New Jersey.*

[2]. Salter and Beekman, *Old Times in Old Monmouth.*

[3]. *History of the New Jersey Coast, Vol. II,* Ellis Historical Publishing Co.

[4]. Ibid.

[5]. Ibid.

GENERAL SOURCES

1. Leyburn, James G., *The Scotch-Irish,* Univ. of North Carolina Press, 1962.

2. Mandeville, Ernest, *The Story of Middletown.*

3. Stryker, Adgt. Gen. William, *Register of Officers and Men of the American Revolution.*

4. Ellis, Franklin, *History of Monmouth County, New Jersey.*

5. Salter and Beekman, *Old Times in Old Monmouth.*

6. Ellis Historical Publishing Company, *History of the New Jersey Coast.*

7. Monmouth County Hall of Records, Freehold, New Jersey.

8. Foreman, General, letter to Governor Livingston, in Monmouth County Historical Association library, Freehold, N.J.
9. Adelberg, Michael, lecture series on Monmouth County in the Revolution, presented at the Monmouth County Historical Assn.

SETTING THE RECORD STRAIGHT

Ernest Mandeville's book, *The Story of Middletown*, places Joseph Murray's house on King's Highway. This is an error. The King's Highway property was bought by Joseph's son, William C. Murray, in 1815 from John Smock of Woodbridge. The deed is recorded in Freehold. The Bicentennial Map of Middletown perpetuates Mandeville's error, and also lists the Poricy Brook farm as belonging to a Van Dorn in 1700. In fact, the land belonged to the Throckmorton family from 1667 to 1704 when Thomas Stillwell acquired it through his marriage to Alice Throckmorton. It then passed to the Stillwell name, and 40 acres of it was sold in 1767 to Joseph Murray by Thomas Stillwell, Jr. This is made clear in a quit-claim deed, recorded in Freehold. As a result of the raid on Murray's house in 1779, his deed was destroyed along with other property. In 1804 the heirs (three granddaughters) of Thomas Stillwell, Jr. gave a quit-claim on the property to Joseph Murray's son William C. Murray.

Prepared by Marcia S. Rissland, Curator of the Murray Farmhouse 1975 – 1994.

Endnote: Letter from General Foreman to Governor Livingston

Monmouth Court House 9th June 80 [1780]
10 o'clock at Night

Sir

I am desired to inform your Excly that we have this minute an Express that a party of Negroes about 30 in number did this afternoon attack and take Capt. Barnes Smock and a small party that was Collected at his house for there Material Defence — this was done Sun an Hour High 12 Miles from one of the Landings 15 miles from the other.

The Day before yesterday Joseph Murray was Murdered by a party of those Refugees while he was at His Harrow in his Corn field — this we doubt not when taken into the acct. of our other numerous distresses will induce your Excly to exert your self in Establishing sutch a guard and will tend to restore in some measure the Security of this country — I am in behalf of the Inhabitants of the Town.

Your Excely's Obd. Humble Serv.
David Foreman

Note: We are this Minute to March from this Village & shall not have a Single man for its defence.

[Marcia's notes to the endnote: (i) Spelling, punctuation are as in the original. (ii) "The day before yesterday" is a mistake by the writer, since family records firmly establish June 8 as the day of Murray's murder. (iii) "Corn" in those times referred to any grain crop, including corn, wheat, etc. What we call "corn" today was called "maize" or, sometimes, "Indian corn" in Colonial times.]

Appendix B: Why the Farmhouse and Barn Are the Way They Are

Prepared in 1993 by Marcia Rissland
Curator, Murray Farmhouse, Poricy Park [1975-1994]

The Poricy Park Citizens Committee operated a summer nature center in the present farmhouse from 1975 to 1978. The area was then known as the Gebhardt Farm, formerly Whistling Hill Farm. There were many buildings, all in very poor condition. The original barn was almost obscured by 20th-century additions, and most of its roof was gone. The house had a decidedly un-colonial appearance. Careful examination of the original components of the house and barn revealed sturdy, skilled 18th-century workmanship. Thorough research of the history proved that this was indeed the home of the Revolutionary War patriot, Joseph Murray. A vision of restoring the farm was born, with a determination to realize that vision. The vision was shared by Mrs. Louis Timolat, whose generosity made it possible.

So much volunteer work has gone into research and manual labor that we sometimes forget the professional expertise that enabled us to proceed. The buildings were inspected by several architects from the State Historic Sites Division in Trenton. They implemented placement on the State Register of Historic Sites, and they applied for placement on the National Register.[44] Among other agencies that were consulted for advice were the Middletown Historical Society, the Middletown Landmarks Commission, the Monmouth County Historical Association, and the National Trust for Historic Preservation. We also read every book on the subject that was recommended to us.

The State recommended Charles H. Detwiller, Jr., a noted historical architect, who drew up the plans for the barn, and then the house. He visited the site many times, met with the contractors, and inspected their work. All work on the house had to be coordinated with the Middletown Building Inspector, the Fire Inspector, the Plumbing Inspector, the Electrical Inspector, and the Department of Parks and Recreation.

We have occasionally been chided for not having a "pure" restoration. The sensibilities of some knowledgeable visitors have been jarred by such anachronisms as electric baseboard heat, aluminum rain gutters, asphalt roof shingles, carpet in the hall and rugs in other rooms, track and spot lighting in the barn, and mercury vapor lights on both buildings. From 1975 to 1978 we had ample time to contemplate the future possibilities of both buildings. We visited many other meticulous restorations. They looked beautiful and had authentic furnishings, but for the most part they were unusable for six or seven months of the year because of lack of heat. Their fireplaces did not work because the original bricks were no longer safe; there was no plumbing, and wells and outhouses were not tenable in a sanitation-conscious and vandal-ridden modern world. There was little for visitors to do but go on a please-don't-touch tour and then leave. Children were strictly warned to keep their hands off. Any social events were restricted to standing up with plate and glass in hand at all times because the furniture was too valuable to be used for its original purpose.

We did not want such a restoration, nor could we afford the antiques that would have made such an undertaking worthwhile. There were some 19th and 20th-century changes that made the house livable without detracting from its 18th-century charm. Chief among these was the circa 1830 addition which now houses the modern kitchen, the

---

[44] The National Register rejected the application because of the (then) unrestored appearance of the house. This turned out to be a blessing in disguise. [Marcia's footnote.]

office, the bathroom, the spinning room, and the utility end of the basement. A pure restoration to the 18th century (which would have been required by the National Register) would have consigned all this useful space to the dumpster. By moving the bathroom and the electric panel to the "new" end, we were able to restore the old end and still have a useable house.

By taking down all the chimneys and lining them with fire brick in conformity with the Middletown building code, we are able to use all three fireplaces. We believe that cheerful fires add more to an 18th-century atmosphere than cold, dead fireplaces with the original brickwork.

Electric heat is obvious to look at and expensive to operate, but it does no damage to install. There had already been a great deal of careless structural damage done by previous owners, first with stove pipes in the 19th century, and then with steam pipes and radiators in the 20th century. We did no further damage.

When the newly-restored basement kitchen filled up with ten inches of water after heavy rains, we went for aluminum gutters. Wooden gutters would have been historically correct, unbelievably expensive, and totally impractical because of frequent rot. The same held for the barn; the root cellar flooded until gutters were installed.

The asphalt roofs were dictated by financial constraints. We would love to have cedar shingle roofs on both buildings, and we invite anyone who feels strongly about this to begin the necessary fund raising for such an undertaking before the present roofs have lived out their life span.[45]

Carpet in the hall was necessary for noise reduction and safety. The floorboards were partially eaten out by termites and had to be covered, and the small runners which we had been using were a nuisance to clean and a menace to footing. The rugs

in other rooms protect the floors from grit and the impact of high heels, and muffle the noise and footsteps of school groups. 18th-century farm houses of modest means were bare of floor coverings and curtains; they were also cold, drafty, smoke-filled, and echoingly noisy. In summer they were hot, smelly, full of flies, and noisy. There are some aspects of 18th-century life that we do not want to duplicate.

The track and flood lighting in the barn is standard museum practice. It has been determined that it is better to have frankly modern electric fixtures where good illumination is necessary than attempt to fake it, and fail both in illumination and authenticity. As for the mercury vapor lamps: enough ugly experience with vandalism has dictated safety first, aesthetics second.

Another practical consideration that governed the restoration/rehabilitation of the house was the possible dissolution of the Poricy Park Citizens Committee. With a view to that eventuality, the house was made compatible with the Middletown building code for a residence. A certificate of occupancy could be granted to enable someone to live in the house full-time to ensure the survival of both buildings.

Above all, we wanted buildings that would be welcoming to visitors, especially children, with an absolute minimum of don't-touch items. Working fireplaces, useable furniture, paintable walls, and cooking utensils that could be handled were a priority.

Certain standards were also set. Neither building was to be a catch-all for cast-offs. We have consistently declined donations of items that are unsuitable. Neither was it ever intended that buildings friendly to children should be child-centered buildings.

We have studied what is available already to the public in our area of Monmouth County with a view to not duplicating any other resource. We believe that we have succeeded in this. These

---

[45] [A wooden roof was installed on the barn in 1995 and on the farmhouse in 2001. PTB]

buildings are important to both Middletown and New Jersey history. The barn is one of only two survivors from the Revolutionary War era in our area that are publicly owned. (The other barn is adjacent to the Craig House, Monmouth Battlefield State Park.) All the others have succumbed to everything from Tory raids to tract housing developments, 19th-century fires to 20th-century vandalism or neglect. Joseph Murray's excellent stonework and framing timbers are intact. We hope that future stewards of this park will familiarize themselves with these buildings, their history, and the philosophy of their restoration with a view to maintaining standards suitable to such a unique facility.

Editor's note: It is fortunate that Marcia wrote this account, because it shows her insight into the way she wanted the house to be designed for people to get involved in 18th-century life. But it is a little sad that a major reason she wrote it was to address the criticism she received from several historical architects over the "unprofessional" and "improper" way she went about this project. Some of these experts have done some fine work of their own in restoring buildings, but I have many times visited and even given musical performances in houses in which the fireplaces were non-working, candles were not allowed, food and drink were prohibited, rooms were roped off, and you could not sit on any of the furniture. Yes, you do have to be extraordinarily careful of the way you let people treat Thomas Jefferson's home at Monticello, but here in Middletown you can be a comfortable guest in Joseph Murray's home. Bravo. PTB

Appendix C: Pronunciation of Unusual Names, Name Changes

Pronunciation

Bousquet, Woody. Baahs-KAY
Cotton, E. Leigh. Leigh is pronounced "Lee"
Deotte, Pat. DEE-ott (final "e" silent)
Detwiller, Charles. "willer" rhymes with "miller"
Finan, Bernie. FYE-nan
Fricke, George. Fricke rhymes with "mickey"
Kough, Lynn. "kuff"
Kurz, Lois. Kurz rhymes with "hers"
Lagan, Larry. LAY-gan
Lehder, Diane. As in "follow the leader."
Leistner, Mrs. "leis" rhymes with "rice"
Lescinsky, Lethe. LEE-thee, "thee" as in "Theodore"
Malavet, Joe. MAL-a-vay. MAL rhymes with "pal"
Neidlinger, Gertrude. "linger" as in "lingering"
Noecker, Peggy. Noecker rhymes with "decker"
Poricy. Accent first syllable, POR-ih-see
Rissland, Marcia. "Riss" rhymes with "miss"
Roneo (mimeograph) ROE-nee-oh
Schuylkill (river in Philadelphia). SKOOL-kill
Timolat, Lou. TIM-o-lat, "lat" rhymes with "cat"
Trefriw Mills, Wales (page 39) I haven't a clue.

Name Changes

Lois Berger is now Lois Lyons.
Patricia Contreras is now Patricia Held.
Denise King is now Denise Stovall.
Diane Walton is now Diane Walton Wood.
Kathy Whitney is now Kathy Gahn.

The Recreation Commission is now the Recreation Advisory Committee.
The Conservation Commission is now the Environmental Commission.
The Poricy Park Citizens Committee is now the Poricy Park Conservancy.
The Spy House is now the Seabrook-Wilson House and is owned by the Monmouth County Park System.
The Gebhardt Farm is now simply "Poricy Park," and the area encompassing the farmhouse and barn is the "Murray Farm." We requested that "Gebhardt Farm" be discontinued in early 1982.

Appendix D: The Fossils of Poricy Brook

The following text is excerpted from a brochure, "The Fossils of Poricy Brook," by Frank Lescinsky. It was issued originally in 1973 and revised a few times. This is the 1986 version.

The Poricy Brook fossil beds are well known to fossil collectors in the Northeast. The fossils date back to the Cretaceous period of the Mesozoic era. The Cretaceous period lasted from 135 to 65 million years ago and was the summit of the age of reptiles. Dinosaurs dominated the earth, but mammals were beginning to evolve. At the beginning of the Cretaceous period, a warm tropical climate prevailed and oceans covered much of the earth. Gradually, over the 70 million year period, the climate became cooler and drier, new mountains emerged, and the oceans receded. The flora changed from nonflowering plants such as giant ferns, cycads, and ginkgos to hardwood trees and flowering shrubs pollinated by bees. Among the plants that developed then are many that are familiar today: oak, maple, willow, dogwood, laurel, magnolia, ivy fan palms, and palmetto.

During the Cretaceous period, the area of Poricy Brook and the rest of the Atlantic coastal plain was shallow ocean. When the ocean animals died they sank to the bottom. Their soft parts decayed but gradually the hard parts such as bones, teeth, and shells were buried. Over the millions of years the level of the ocean rose and fell; forming different layers of deposits with remains of different animals. The particular layer that is exposed by the cutting action of Poricy Brook is called the Navesink Formation and is estimated to be approximately 72 million years old.

The Navesink marl is colored by green glauconite, an iron material, and is rich in lime from the sea shells. In the 1800s the marl was mined locally for use as fertilizer because of the high lime content. Glauconite is currently used in water softeners.

THE FOSSILS.

Fossils are any recognizable remains of things that lived in geologically ancient times. The most popular concept of fossils is that of things turned to stone. However, that is only one of many ways fossils may be preserved. Most of the fossils of Poricy Brook are 72 million-year-old seashells, sharks' teeth, etc., that have been preserved in the greensand and clay of the Navesink marl. Some of the more delicate shells have been dissolved and all that remains are internal casts that filled the insides of the shells before they were dissolved. Those delicate shells, which remained whole while buried, quickly break when exposed; however, they leave impressions in the clay which may be collected.

Vertebrate fossils are rare. They may be either teeth or bone fragments. The bone fragments look much like waterlogged wood but have a distinctive grain pattern.

COLLECTING

Some fossils may be found lying loose along the stream. However, the best way to find fossils is by sifting the sand and gravel of the stream bed. The sifting is done by digging in the stream bed, dumping the sand and gravel on a screen of ¼-inch hardware mesh fastened to a wooden frame, and shaking the screen in the water to wash away the sand.

The most commonly found fossils are *Exogyra, Pycnodonte, Agerostrea*, brachiopods, belemnites, and sponge borings. Complete, unbroken specimens are rare except for the brachiopods and *Agerostrea*.

Examine shell fragments for fossils that may be attached to them. These may be worm tubes, bryozoans, or other shells.

The stream continues to expose new fossils, so feel free to take home a few of your best samples. Limit yourself to a handful so the next collector can also have the pleasure of discovering the remains of creatures that lived at the time of the great dinosaurs, more than 70 million years before the earliest man.

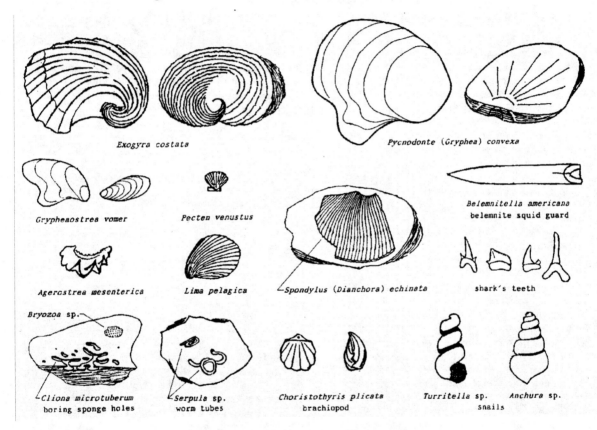

Exogyra costata

Pycnodonte (Gryphea) convexa

Grypheaostrea vomer

Pecten venustus

Belemnitella americana
belemnite squid guard

Agerostrea mesenterica

Lima pelagica

Spondylus (Dianchora) echinata

shark's teeth

Bryozoa sp.

Cliona microtuberum
boring sponge holes

Serpula sp.
worm tubes

Choristothyris plicata
brachiopod

Turritella sp.   Anchura sp.
snails

SOME FOSSILS OF PORICY BROOK
Sketches by Frank Lescinsky, 1986

Appendix E: Essays: 1981-1990

In the period from 1981 through spring 1990, I wrote an essay for every calendar, at first six times a year, later four times. They weren't signed (perhaps that's why I didn't receive a Pulitzer Prize). Here are two of them that are perhaps among the better ones. The first, "Beauty and the Beasts," was highly regarded by people in the High School print shop, and the second (and final one) was Lou Rissland's favorite. PTB

Beauty and the Beasts (Spring 1988)

The following letter appeared in a recent issue of Audubon, the magazine of the National Audubon Society: "The picture of the leopard devouring the antelope in your July issue was repulsive and gave my five-year-old son nightmares... I prefer to emphasize the beauty in nature. That's why I subscribed to Audubon."

That letter represents a difficult problem for people who teach others about nature. The problem lies not in the writer's desire to avoid unpleasant things, but rather, in the application of the concept of beauty.

"Beauty" is a human perception, or to quote the time-honored phrase, "Beauty is in the eye of the beholder." The bald eagle, our national bird, may be perceived by people as beautiful as it soars overhead. But in reality, the eagle is a predator, and is probably looking for a meal – which means an animal it can kill and eat. A field mouse or rabbit, on seeing the eagle, see not beauty but rather, a threat to its life.

On the other hand, we could also err if we decided that nature is "harsh" or "cruel," which are also terms of human perception. Nature has its own rules and does not ask for our judgment.

For countless years, people have enjoyed applying human emotions and behavior to animals. Beatrix Potter (an excellent scientist in her own right) dressed up Peter Rabbit and Benjamin Bunny and had them raid Mr. McGregor's garden. Smokey the Bear, Ranger Rick, and Mother Goose's characters have much to say to us. At Poricy Park, we enjoy telling stories and singing songs about animals that live in a make-believe world created by humans.

But there is also the real world of nature, a world that is unfiltered by human perception. On occasion it may be worthwhile to examine this world on its own terms.

Colonial Baloney (Spring 1990)

A recent issue of People magazine tells us of a couple who, in 1986, bought an old house in New England and turned it into an inn where they serve "delectable fare cooked the old-fashioned way." Their American colonial specialties include "scallops, roast pheasant with wild rice stuffing, capons, geese, and spider bread."

Yum, yum! And, along with their 18th-century food, the guests receive a generous dose of 20th-century baloney. Because it just wasn't like that except in elegant homes or very unusual inns.

Historian James Trunslow Adams writes that "Many inns in the early 1700s were atrociously bad. Travelers often reported the food to be uneatable, the beds and houses dirty, and the landlords insolent."

In 1704, a Madam Knight made a seven-day overland journey from Boston to New York, and kept a journal. Some of her entries read, "We reached an inn where dinner was so poor it was impossible to eat it," and at another inn, "The food was so bad that no one could eat it after having paid for it."

In 1796-7, Louis-Philippe, later King of France from 1830 to 1848, traveled through the United States and kept a fine diary: "The food in the inns is nothing much; generally it amounts to no more than fried fatback and cornbread. Eggs have disappeared and the potatoes are finished [it was April]. In better places they make us wheat cakes that are rather good. There is coffee everywhere, but bad, very weak." Other authors have noted that breakfast often consisted of what people wouldn't eat the prior night, served cold.

At the Murray Farmhouse at Poricy Park, we serve food at some programs. We may not serve scallops and roast pheasant, but our food is hearty and cooked in colonial style. We, too, enjoy a pleasant excursion into the past. But when we take a close look at colonial life, we realize that the 20th century does have its advantages.

Index